THE BOUNDARIES OF THE FIRM

Also by Neil M. Kay

* THE INNOVATING FIRM: A Behavioural Theory of Corporate R&D

* THE EVOLVING FIRM: Strategy and Structure in Industrial Organisation

* THE EMERGENT FIRM: Knowledge, Ignorance and Surprise in Economic Organisation

PATTERN IN CORPORATE EVOLUTION

* *from the same publishers*

The Boundaries of the Firm

Critiques, Strategies and Policies

Neil M. Kay
Professor of Business Economics
University of Strathclyde

First published in Great Britain 1999 by
MACMILLAN PRESS LTD
Houndmills, Basingstoke, Hampshire RG21 6XS and London
Companies and representatives throughout the world

A catalogue record for this book is available from the British Library.

ISBN 0–333–71901–8

 First published in the United States of America 1999 by
ST. MARTIN'S PRESS, INC.,
Scholarly and Reference Division,
175 Fifth Avenue, New York, N.Y. 10010

ISBN 0–312–22043–X

Library of Congress Cataloging-in-Publication Data
Kay, Neil M.
The boundaries of the firm : critiques, strategies and policies /
Neil M. Kay.
p. cm.
Includes bibliographical references and index.
ISBN 0–312–22043–X
1. Industrial organization (Economic theory)   2. Corporations.
I. Title.
HD2326.K38   1999
338.5—dc21   98–31056
                                                                  CIP

© Neil M. Kay 1999

This book is printed on paper suitable for recycling and made from fully managed and sustained forest sources.

10   9   8   7   6   5   4   3   2   1
08   07   06   05   04   03   02   01   00   99

Printed and bound in Great Britain by
Antony Rowe Ltd, Chippenham, Wiltshire

To James G. McGilvray
A great colleague and friend

Contents

List of Figures and Tables

FIGURES

TABLES

xi

Preface

This is the fourth book I have produced for Macmillan. It differs in that the others were specially written as books while this one is based around papers I wrote over the period 1985–96. However, it does represent a natural development of the work of the first three books. My first book in this series was my PhD thesis published as *The Innovating Firm* (1979), the second was *The Evolving Firm* (1982) and the third was *The Emergent Firm* (1984). The similarity in the titles was intended to communicate kinship relations between the three books; essentially all were concerned with attempts to look at problems in the theory of the firm from a systems perspective (and the present book continues this emphasis). With the wisdom of hindsight, there was also a downside in the similarity in the titles. Some accused me of trying to corner the market in adjectival firms, while strangers would ask me conferences, 'Didn't you write *The Something Firm?*' Replying that I had written three Something Firms always seemed a bit weak.

Consequently I have tried to differentiate the title of this book from those that have gone before, though no doubt there are those who will think that I have simply run out of adjectives. The major theme running though the book is the setting of the boundaries of the firm and this is perhaps most clearly illustrated in the Strategies section (Part II) and the Policies section (Part III). These sections are concerned with problems of where the boundaries are set (e.g., corporate diversification and multinational enterprise), how they are set (e.g., merger and joint venture) and factors influencing the setting of these boundaries (most especially, technological change). The Critiques section helps sets the context by looking at how certain writers have contributed to analysis of the nature of the firm and the relevance of certain concepts and approaches to this enterprise.

The articles were carefully selected for the book and were judged both on their own merits and how they contributed to the overall balance of the book. The older ones were of a vintage that certainly warranted attention being given to whether or not they were displaying signs of obsolescence, or at least as to whether or not they needed an overhaul. Perhaps there is a halo effect in returning to pieces you have not been working directly on for a while, but, rightly or wrongly,

I decided for the most part that the pieces could be reproduced with only minor tinkering, corrections and updating. An exception is Chapter 9, where I dropped a section on the completion of the European internal market since I looked at these issues in more detail in the subsequent chapter.

I thought it would be helpful to set out detailed acknowledgements in a separate section, but I would also like to make some personal acknowledgements here. Firstly, to my wife Lorna Ahlquist for the creation and maintenance of a zone of tranquillity around the production of this book. Thanks, Lorna. Secondly, to Katerina and Kieran for bursting through the zone of tranquillity at regular intervals and reminding me of the real priorities in life. Thanks, Katerina and Kieran.

Lastly, there is Jim McGilvray, to whom this book is dedicated. Jim was a colleague and friend who I first met when he taught in my department at the University of Stirling when I was a student. We finished up in the same department when I joined the Economics Department at the University of Strathclyde where he was Professor and Head of Department in the early nineties. It is no exaggeration to say that I owe my present position to Jim and his Headship of that period. My colleagues and I also owe him many happy hours in his company outside work. His sudden death in 1995 was a terrible blow that took away a great colleague and friend. He is very badly missed. I am grateful to Alison, Caitriona and Daniel for letting me dedicate this book to Jim.

Acknowledgements

Fuller details and acknowledgements are given at the start of the relevant chapter.

Chapter 2 'Industrial structure, rivalry and innovation: theory and evidence,' in, P. E. Earl (ed.) *Management, Marketing and the Competitive Process*, Cheltenham: Edward Elgar, 1996, pp. 47–77.

Chapter 3 (with Peter Earl) 'How economists can accept Shackle's critique of economic doctrines without arguing themselves out of their jobs', *Journal of Economic Studies*, 12, 1985, pp. 34–48.

Chapter 4 'Markets, false hierarchies, and the evolution of the modern corporation', *Journal of Economic Behavior and Organization*, 17, 1992, pp. 315–33.

Chapter 5 'The economics of trust', in *International Journal of the Economics of Business*, 3, 1996, pp. 249–60.

Chapter 6 'The R&D function: corporate strategy and structure', in G. Dosi, C. Freeman, R. L. Nelson, G. Silverberg and L. Soete (eds.) *Technical Change and Economic Theory*, London: Frances Pinter, 1988, pp. 282–94.

Chapter 8 (with C. S. Galbraith) 'Towards a theory of multinational enterprise', *Journal of Economic Behavior and Organization*, 7, 1988, pp. 3–19.

Chapter 9 'Collaborative strategies of firms: theory and evidence,' in A. Del Monte (ed.) *Recent Developments in the Theory of Industrial Organization*, London: Macmillan, 1992, pp. 201–31.

Chapter 10 'Industrial collaborative activity and the evolution of the modern corporation', *Journal of Economic Behavior and Organization*, 17, 1992, pp. 315–33.

Chapter 11 'Mergers, acquisitions and the completion of the internal market', in K. Hughes (ed.) *European Competitiveness*, Cambridge: Cambridge University Press, 1994, pp. 242–61.

Chapter 12 (with H. Ramsay and J-F. Hennart) 'Industrial collaborative activity and the European internal market,' *Journal of Common Market Studies*, 34, 1996, pp. 465 -7 5.

In addition, many colleagues gave valuable advice and criticism on the various papers over the years. It is a daunting task to make a comprehensive catalogue of these contributions and I know some will be omitted, for which I apologise in advance. However, particular mention should be made of Peter Earl, Felix Fitzroy, Martin Fransman, Christopher Freeman, Craig Galbraith, Jean-François Hennart, Kirsty Hughes, Brian Loasby, Jim Love, Eleanor Morgan, Alfredo Del Monte, Richard Nelson, Harvie Ramsay, Andrew Scott, John Scoullar, Frank Stephen, Douglas Strachan, Steve Thompson, and a number of anonymous referees of journals which published a number of the chapters. Also, four of the papers were first presented at conferences: Chapter 2 to a conference on the Firm and Technical Change, Centre for European Policy Studies, Brussels; Chapter 5 to a conference on Technical Change and Economic Theory, Merit, University of Limburg, Maastricht; Chapter 9 to a conference on New Directions in Industrial Economics, University of Naples; and Chapter 11 to a conference on European Competitiveness, Wissenschaftzentrum, Berlin. A number of participants made valuable contributions at these conferences, and this is gratefully acknowledged. In addition, I would like to thank the organisers and sponsors of the respective conferences for making my contributions possible in the first place. Of course, none of those who have assisted me in these various pieces of work are to be implicated in any errors of omission or commission that remain. Last but not least, my thanks are also due to Moira Devaney, Morag Pryce, Jean Roberts, Joyce Russell and Sharleen Toland for cheerfully and efficiently typing the various pieces in their different manifestations.

1 Overview

The eleven chapters that make up the body of this book complement and overlap each other in a variety of ways. Each piece first of all falls naturally into one of three categories; critiques, strategies and policies. In the critique section, four major bodies of work are reviewed and conclusions drawn that help set the context for analysis of strategy in Part II. In Part II, four major strategic issues are analysed; R&D strategy, diversification, multinational enterprise and collaborative activity. The third part builds on points that emerge from analysis of strategies in Part II and help provide a framework for analysis of the policy implications for corporate strategy in markets that are moving towards completion or liberalisation. While the discussion focuses on market completion in the European context, it has implications that are of relevance to other blocs that are liberalising their internal trade. In general, the chapters that make up the three parts are ordered in a temporal as well as a logical sequence, with the Schumpeter and Shackle critiques being written before the strategies chapters, and the three policy pieces following from, and stimulated by, the earlier strategy chapters. The later critiques of Williamson and Casson in Chapters 4 and 5 respectively break with this pattern.

Chapters 2, 3, 4, 5, 6, 9 and 10 were demand-led with the topic being influenced or dictated to greater or lesser extent by the respective editors or the nature of the respective symposia and their organisers. In general, the selection of a target by someone else had a stimulating and challenging effect, and the existence of symposium or publication deadlines also served to concentrate the mind. Chapters 7, 8, 11 and 12 were supply push, with the determinants of a particular strategy or policy being considered in each case. Four of the pieces were written with collaborators: Chapter 3 was written with Peter Earl, then at the University of Tasmania; Chapter 7 with Peter Clarke, Heriot-Watt University, Edinburgh; Chapter 8 with Craig Galbraith, then of the University of California, Irvine. The last chapter was written with Professors Harvie Ramsay (Department of Human Resource Management, University of Strathclyde) and Jean-François Hennart (University of Illinois).

The various chapters have been published in refereed journals or edited volumes with one exception, the Boeing paper (Chapter 7). We did submit this to one journal, and while the referees comments were complimentary and encouraging, the editorial request to shorten it was predictable and understandable. We decided not to do so and did not resubmit or seek publication elsewhere. Readers must make their own judgment on this, but it was felt that to shorten the papers to normal journal length would be to compromise the material and arguments presented in the respective cases adversely. If we are wrong, I apologise in advance both on my own and Peter's account. However, samizdat distribution has resulted in valuable comments from colleagues and encouraged us to retain the paper in the form published here.

As is appropriate in a book which focuses on the notion of linkages between resources, the various chapters are strongly interlinked. To begin with, Chapter 2 serves both as a piece of analysis in its own right and as an introduction to topics discussed in more depth in later chapters, especially the strategy Chapters – 6, 7, 8 and 9. The invitation to review the status of the Schumpeterian paradigm of technological competition for a symposium at the Centre for European Policy Studies in Brussels in the mid-eighties provided the crucial stimulus for this paper. It encouraged a focus on the twin issues of the extent to which Schumpeterian's contribution could still be regarded as relevant today, and possible modifications or extensions to the paradigm in the light of contemporary developments.

Having to actually read much of the considerable theoretical and empirical literature that has been generated by Schumpeter's approach was itself an extremely valuable exercise. The imminence of the deadline for the Brussels symposium concentrated the mind in a way that might not have been possible with a more leisurely schedule. As paper followed paper in the process of reviewing the studies stimulated by Schumpeter's path-breaking work, some questions began to appear and some possible conclusions reached. One early puzzle that the abundance of studies raised was the question of why Schumpeter's arguments had been so influential to the extent that they had been effectively assimilated into the conventional wisdom of the economics profession – a profession dominated by the neoclassical paradigm that he set out to attack.

It must be made clear that to raise this question is in no way to belittle Schumpeter's contribution. Indeed it might be suggested that the quality of individual ideas has never been either a necessary or sufficient condition for recognition by the mainstream in economics.[1] Nor is this entirely undesirable. By its very nature, mainstream scholarship tends to have its own momentum and be resistant to change[2] reflecting the need to maintain structure, coherence and direction in research programmes. It was in the light of acknowledgement of these points that the widespread recognition of Schumpeter's contribution appeared especially impressive.

An obvious explanation is that the power and elegance of Schumpeter's arguments won over a critical mass of the profession. There has to be some weight given to this explanation, and indeed failure to accord such recognition would be unjustified and demeaning to one of the twentieth century's great economists. However, while this was persuasive up to a point, it did not seem to tell the whole story for reasons discussed above.

A further influence suggested in the paper was that Schumpeter's argument were highly radical at certain levels, yet could appear remarkably conventional at others. The foci of competition and the nature of the competitive process identified by Schumpeter were quite different from those associated with the neoclassical paradigm. However, when Schumpeter discussed the structural variables that underlay and influenced technological competition there was little, if anything, that was unfamiliar to a conventionally trained industrial economist. Size of firm, economies of scale, product-market structure, industrial concentration, monopoly profits – all of these were discussed or implied by Schumpeter's analysis. It was only the dependent variable (innovation) that represented a real departure from the typical dependent variable of price in neoclassical theory and its applied offshoot, the structure-conduct-performance approach.

In these circumstances the Schumpeterian paradigm would be meat and drink to orthodox applied economists. True, the measurement of 'innovativeness' was more problematic than measurement of price in structure-conduct-performance. However, this merely served to add another dimension to empirical measurement. True also, Schumpeter's emphasis on dynamic competitive processes usually got lost in the wash of empirical investigations. However, when this was recognised, it could simply be discounted as the price of abstracting from a work constructed in an era that pre-dated the heavy mathematisation of present-day micro-economics. Further, when anti-Schumpeterian arguments were framed, they also could draw on the same basic stock of concepts and methods inherited from structure-conduct-performance in conventional industrial organisation.

The paper goes on to argue that some of the features that facilitated the assimilation of the Schumpeterian paradigm are also features that require modification today. Schumpeter wrote at a time when it was reasonable to treat the firm as synonymous with a given product-market and technology. In this respect it is quite consistent with the neoclassical theory of the firm. However, major features of contemporary industry include single firms operating multiple products (diversification), as well as single products produced by multiple firms (collaboration). The Schumpeterian paradigm (and its antitheses) tend to focus on the influence of product-market structure to the neglect of other considerations that include diversification and collaboration. In particular, the potential existence of internal and external markets in finance and technology means that the Schumpeterian emphasis on product-market structure has to be qualified and extended to include other considerations such as bounded rationality, transaction costs and corporate capabilities. This paper also had samizdat distribution, and I did not seek to publish it for similar reasons that led to the stalling of the Boeing paper. However, Peter Earl thought it would fit in with the tenor of a volume he was editing for Edward Elgar, which led to its eventual publication some years after it was written.

In looking over the paper for this volume I was concerned that it would be somewhat dated and superseded by subsequent empirical work. However, this turned out not to be the case; in a survey article Cohen and Levin (1989: 1096) point out there has been some dwindling of empirical work on strategic interaction in the field of technological change in recent years. In Kay (1997: 26–7) I suggested that the development of game theories of technological competition could be at least partly responsible for the crowding out of empirical work in this field; if, as some game theorists claim, virtually any strategic action could be modelled in game theory then it removes clear signposts for empirical analysis. At least the traditional Schumpeterian approach discussed in this paper gave clear signposts and helped to both stimulate and focus the empirical work that is discussed here.

Chapter 3 was also an invited contribution, in this case for a Festschrift in honour of George Shackle. It was a privilege to be to invited to contribute not only because Shackle was one of the great economists referred to above that the mainstream unjustifiably ignored, but also because Shackle's stature was matched by his genuine modesty and humanity. It was thought that Peter Earl and I had overlapping approaches that might lead to an interesting contribution in this context.

The task that Peter and I set ourselves is captured by the title. If Shacklean 'surprises' are endemic and indeed intrinsic features of economic activity, how can anything constructive and sensible be said about economic behaviour and institutions? If the unexpected is the norm, what does this mean for the evolution and identification of patterns?

Working with Peter on the paper was a highly enjoyable and stimulating experience, although collaborating with an resident antipodean did throw up its own logistical problems and surprises (in 1987, before fax and e-mail). Having raised the question of whether or not Shackle's thesis meant that economists were redundant, it was comforting to answer in the negative. We argued that there was no necessary contradiction and that it was possible to reconcile the co-existence of surprise and pattern. The key lay in recognising that surprise and pattern could have impact and be observed at different levels. For example, environments might be characterised as 'surprise-rich' or 'surprise-poor' (e.g., high technology vs. low technology environments), a characterisation which itself involves identification of a basic pattern at a level above that of individual surprises. Such discrimination helps contribute to analysis of a variety of issues including modularity, decoupling, mechanistic vs. organic systems, search replacing planning, and diversification.

The paper may be read as providing systemic or holistic arguments against the reductionist perspective of neoclassical economics. Since the neoclassical perspective treats higher-level systems as the simple aggregate of lower level systems, the idea of novel patterns emerging at higher levels simply cannot be accommodated in this framework. As with the Schumpeter critique, arguments developed here have application later in the book, especially in the strategy chapters. For example, Chapter 6 depends critically on distinguishing stable patterns at the level of the R&D *function* even when these may not be observable at the level of the R&D *project*, while Chapter 7 looks at patterns in Boeing's strategy at *corporate* level and how these may have evolved in part as a response to the propensity for the environment to throw up specific surprises. Also, the influence of environmental surprise on multinational strategy is a feature of Chapter 8.

Chapter 4 was stimulated by a conviction that Williamson's restatement of transaction cost economics (1985) did not provide a satisfactory basis for explaining the boundaries of the firm, despite claims to the contrary. A fundamental problem is Williamson's claim that asset specificity (assets specialised by use or users) is a fundamental driving force behind the creation of transaction costs of market exchange and the consequent replacement of markets with corporate organisation.

The debate is complicated by Williamson's representation of such arguments as consistent with transaction cost economics when in fact it is perfectly possible to recognise the importance of transaction costs while disagreeing with Williamson's particular version.

Of all the chapters in this volume, this one is the most negative in tone and content. However, it was felt necessary to make the arguments in the chapter both to point out critical flaws in the transaction cost framework and to suggest how it may be redirected, and in that respect the conclusion is entirely positive. The chapter points out that the only type of internalised market that the transaction cost argument as developed by Williamson might explain is the special case of vertical integration.[3] The diversified firm typically exploits economies of scope, which by definition depend on assets being *non*-specific in terms of application (see Chapter 7 here), while the empirical literature suggests that a recurring reason for the evolution of the multinational is to protect property rights in intangible assets including leaky technology – again dependent on assets being potentially *non*-specific in use or to user (see Chapter 8 here). Williamson does explain the existence of a special case of diversification (the conglomerate) in terms of the advantages that internalisation and divisionalisation may give the conglomerate over a collection of individual firms dealing with the external capital market. However, this does not explain why the conglomerate evolves. A specialised firm or one diversified along market and technological links could exploit the same advantages of internalisation and divisionalisation that the conglomerate exploits as well as the bonus benefits of economies of scale or scope.

The transaction cost framework suffers from other deficiencies that reflect its static nature, but these are potentially remedial. There is a great deal at stake in the debate outlined in this chapter. Williamson has provided an immensely valuable service in getting institutional consideration onto the mainstream agenda. However, in the process a price has been paid that threatens to limit the applicability of this new approach to industrial organisation. The focus on asset specificity and vertical integration in transaction cost economics echoes the product-market orientation of the conventional theory of the firm and likewise neglects other considerations relevant to the determination of firm boundaries. There is an interesting parallel between the assimilation of the Schumpeterian paradigm and transaction cost economics' rapid recognition in the profession. The retention of neoclassical elements such as product-market focus in both approaches facilitated their elevation to new orthodoxy, a major difference between Schumpeter's and Williamson's approaches being the extent to which the limitations are self-consciously imposed in the case of transaction cost economics.

It will be interesting to see the extent to which the current limitations of the transaction cost approach documented here will be recognised, accepted and attended to in the near future by Williamson and other transaction cost theorists. The view taken in this chapter is that failure to respond will limit the potential applicability of the transaction cost approach to the special case of the economics of the make-or-buy decision in vertical integration – undoubtedly an important topic in its own right, but rather a cul-de-sac when set against the ambitious claims and targets of this new research programme. More recently, I have built on the arguments of this paper in Kay (1997) to present an alternative analysis of the costs of co-ordinating economic activity associated with alternative forms of organisation.

Part II (Chapters 6 to 9) looks at particular topics in corporate strategy that draw upon arguments in Part I, as well as earlier analyses in Kay (1979, 1982 and 1984). Chapter 6 was first presented at a conference in Maastricht and was to become part of the volume edited by the conference organisers on technical change and economic theory. I had been asked to look at the implications of R&D for corporate strategy and structure and I concluded that there were four features of R&D – non-specificities, lags, uncertainty and cost – that were particularly relevant in this context. Issues influenced by these characteristics include internal financing of R&D, optimistic biases in R&D estimation, time-cost trade-offs, public funding of basic research, first mover vs. second in advantages, and how shortening lags to commercialisation may contribute to compromise of scientific norms of open and free disclosure and dissemination of information. The advantage of such a rapid overview and audit of issues is that it helps demonstrate how a variety of apparently unrelated issues are joined together at a deeper level by the influence and interaction of four elementary characteristics of R&D activity.

The chapter shows that uncertainty and unpredictability at project level may be consistent with stable characteristics and patterns at the higher level of the R&D function. One point that emerges from the analysis of R&D characteristics is that three of the basic features – non-specificities, lags and uncertainty – all militate against effective handling of it within divisional profit centres where narrow product focus, short time horizons and risk-averse management may all conspire to discriminate against it. However, while strategy formulating levels in the firm may provide a more compatible home for R&D in view of its particular characteristics, simply shoving R&D upstairs may separate it from complementary functions such as production and marketing and impede the treatment of divisions as independent profit centres. The conclusion is that issues of centralisation vs. decentralisation of R&D involve efficiency trade-offs, and examples are given of systems and procedures that have been developed to attempt to deal with the particular problems posed by R&D for internal organisation.

Chapter 7, with Peter Clarke, pursues a line that was signposted in Kay (1982). Peter and I explored the possibility that analysis of resource linkages at the level of corporate strategy could provide a systemic framework for business policy that was otherwise lacking. In strategic management, conventional SWOT analysis (Strengths-Weaknesses-Opportunities-Threats) helps provide insights in particular cases, but carries with it the danger of *ad hoc* application and interpretation. The 1982 work had shown how resource linkages lay at the heart of diversification and helped provide the key to analysing corporate strategy. One central concept that transferred from the earlier work and was applied to corporate strategy was the double-edged sword effect of resource linkages. Resource commonalities could help provide internal strengths, opportunities and competitive advantage through the scale and scope economies they helped generate, but they could also create vulnerability to external threats by exposing the firm to vulnerability to external attack along particular linkages. The chapter is based on the idea that the fundamental building blocks of the firm are its constituent resources, and that analysis in this area that carries over the product-market orientation of neoclassical theory runs a real danger of mis-specifying and obscuring issues. Parallels can be drawn here with the views of those that analyse the firm in terms of its capabilities, as well as the value chain analysis of Michael Porter (1985).[4]

The subsequent analysis can be read at one level as an account of how one firm's strategy developed over time, and the associated strategic management issues. At another, more explicitly economic level, it can be read as analysis of how one firm drew upon Penrose-type resource capabilities to grow and survive in a world characterised by Schumpeterian creative destruction and Shacklean surprises. If there is a further set of issues that could be emphasised, it is that with the benefit of hindsight it provides evidence of path-dependent historical processes in institutional development along the lines suggested by David (1985) and Arthur (1989). Unless historical processes

are recognised and explicitly incorporated in analysis of firm development, certain events may simply remain puzzling or incompletely dealt
with. For example, Boeing's success in entering the guided missile
market is at first sight surprising in view of the fact that the leading
edge and key technologies in this context were possessed by the electronics companies. It might reasonably have been expected that competitive advantage would have gone hand in hand with possession of
key technological knowledge. In fact, Boeing's competitive advantage
in this arena reflected the totality of competencies developed in other
fields, not the least of which was the extent to which the new business
could draw upon marketing skills and linkages built up over years of
experience of selling to the government and the military.

In Chapter 8, with Craig Galbraith, we explored the issue of how a
transaction cost explanation of multinational enterprise should be
framed. It is argued that multinationalism has to be explained in terms
of why it should be preferred to a variety of other strategies for corporate expansion that include diversification, exporting and licensing.
One point that emerges from a resource based analysis of the multinational is that it only provides weak linkages and associated economies
compared to some alternative strategies, yet can incur a high degree
of exposure to environmental surprises such as technological change.
The circumstances conducive to the emergence of multinationalism
turn out less obvious than might be first thought. The conclusion that
multinationalism depends on transferred know-how being composed
of both specific and non-specific elements suggests that multinationalism may depend on balance being struck between product-
specificity and non-specificity of R&D; low specificity and domestic
diversification may exploit most of the know-how economies of multinationalism and add more besides – high specificity and a licensee
would have few opportunities for opportunistic behaviour, raising the
attractiveness of this alternative method of market entry. As with the
previous chapter, the analysis revolves around analysing the bundle of
resources exploited by the firm and how they interact to influence and
direct corporate strategy.

The analysis of diversification and multinationalism looked at particular problems in corporate strategies, and our analyses suggested
how a resource based approach could contribute to analysis in this
area. However, one issue had been neglected in both of these pieces
and was difficult to ignore in terms of its growing importance. This
was the development of collaborative activity such as joint ventures in
many industries, especially the high-technology sectors. In our paper

on Boeing, Peter and I had noted the growing importance of this phenomenon but left it on one side as being beyond the scope of our
analysis. The analysis of the multinational with Craig had certainly
made it difficult to ignore the importance of this issue, but again it
was difficult to attend to it in the context of an analysis focusing on the
single firm.

Chapter 10 began to explore this issue and was written for a symposium in Naples in response to a particular puzzle; if joint ventures are
the organisational and contractual disaster areas that the managerial
literature suggest they are, why does any firm indulge in them? The
answer appears to be that they are high cost devices of last resort that
are only adopted when blocks or constraints exist with respect to all
other alternatives. One of these blocks is corporate diversification. It
was concluded that diversification is not just a *substitute* for joint ventures, but may be the *cause* of joint ventures.

The argument is relatively straightforward. In earlier days when
small specialised firms (by today's standards) perceived significant
potential complementarities between their respective businesses that
could be co-ordinated and exploited by instituting a common decision-
making apparatus, there was usually a simple and obvious option –
merger. Over time the growth and development of such firms through
internal expansion and merger created complex diversified systems
from the original simple and specialised starting points. Business units
(now divisions within the expanded firm) still encounter opportunities
to co-ordinate common opportunities with other firms. However, if
the opportunities involve divisions between two large diversified firms
(e.g., Daimler-Benz and Mitsubishi), merger would be a sledgehammer to crack a nut. Setting up decision-making apparatus through
joint venture may be the most expensive option over the restricted
domain of the joint venture itself, but it avoids the even more costly
alternative of combining two large and diversified systems.

Why could one firm not simply sell its co-operating business unit to
the partner firm? The general answer is that most firms diversify along
related market or technological links and so selling a constituent unit
is likely to cut across and threaten links that the co-operating unit is
currently exploiting with other units in its present home. These links
might continue to be exploited by making collaborative arrangements
with the unit after its sale to the other firm – but it is to *substitute* such
collaborative arrangements that such an asset sale would be proposed
in the first place and so such asset sales and swaps would not solve
these problems.

It has to be said that there was a predisposition here to see such patterns by virtue of the previous work discussed above and which we had discussed. Once firms such as Boeing are seen and analysed as richly linked systems that have evolved from simple specialised routes, the later evolution of joint venture as strategy of last resort appears natural and indeed obvious. An economy of complex molecules such as Boeing suggests an economy conducive to joint ventures, just as an economy of simple specialised atoms suggests an economy more conducive to merger activity. However, this does have important implications for the relationship of strategies such as joint venture and diversification to each other, and it suggests a stages interpretation of corporate evolution with joint venture typically being associated with later stages in the development of firms and industries. It also has to be said that it was not a picture of joint venture activity that more conventional industrial organisation approaches to joint venture activity were predisposed to recognise; in a review of collaborative activity later contributed to a Naples symposium (published as Kay 1992b), it was noted that the most striking aspect of conventional economic approaches to collaborative activity was the extent to which such points were *not* recognised. In retrospect, the reason is quite simple and again relates to the product-market focus of conventional microeconomics. If conventional industrial organisation concentrates on individual product-markets and associated business units to the exclusion of the implications of corporate strategy and linkages across business units, then there is nothing in such a product-market orientation that would allow the type of relationships discussed in the Naples paper to be recognised in the first place.

In turn, the arguments developed in the Naples paper led to the policy-orientated paper reproduced here as Chapter 10. The completion or liberalisation of markets is one of the most important current policy areas in global economics, but the implications for corporate strategy are curiously neglected or underdeveloped in many policy analyses. The programme to complete the European Community (EC) internal market in the early 1990s has been one of the most ambitious and is already arguably one of the most successful.

However, it was in the area of corporate strategy that official arguments and analyses seemed most inconsistent and just plain wrong. As Chapter 10 discusses, the view taken by the European Commission that liberalising markets *within* the EC would lead to an increase in joint ventures over the same domain is unsustainable. As Chapter 9 shows, firms tend to turn to joint ventures when they have run out of choices – as, for example, when it is the only option for market access. Open up markets and you open up options and reduce the propensity to opt for the joint venture route in the process. Yet despite evidence along those lines from their own consultants' research, the official version remained that market completion would directly stimulate joint venture activity. Chapter 10 shows how this official view is mistaken.

However, the policy programme set out in the White Paper on the completion of the internal market (Commission of the European Communities 1985) also identified mergers as a corporate strategy that would complement and assist the process of market completion in tandem with joint ventures. In view of the flaws in the analysis of joint venture activity, it was thought worthwhile looking at the Commission's policy analyses in these areas also. The resulting paper is reproduced here as Chapter 11. It was first presented as an invited contribution to a conference on European Competitiveness at the Wissenschaftzentrum, Berlin, and later published in the book of the conference. The analysis published by the Commission found that there was a prima-facie case for encouraging mergers in many cases, especially the high-technology sectors. A review of the same empirical analyses cited in the analysis published by the Commission, and a critical appraisal of research methods, suggested that no such conclusion was warranted. On the contrary, no reason was found to challenge the consensus in the empirical literature that, if anything, mergers tend to lead to efficiency losses.

An obvious question is why economic analyses published by the Commission should have stuck to flawed policy prescriptions in the face of evidence that flatly contradicted them. One answer may be that, as Chapters 10 and 11 show, many of the relevant analytical and policy conclusions were already set out in the White Paper and pre-dated the later economic studies designed to explore the implications of the completion of the internal market. If a mental set has been created in which mergers and joint ventures are a 'good thing' that go hand-in-hand with market completion, then it may be difficult to easily switch perspectives. Such a perspective would be reinforced by a commonly stated belief among European policy makers in the late 1980s that consolidation of European industry was needed to achieve the critical mass required to compete effectively against the American and Japanese. Add the fact that the Treaty of Rome made no provision for an EC-level industrial policy, and there is the temptation to graft *ad hoc* industrial policies on to a programme of market liberalisation not explicitly designed for such purposes.

After the publication of the paper on European collaborative activity (Chapter 10) in 1991, I planned to publish a subsequent analysis using the Commission's own data series to review what had happened in this area at European level in the subsequent five years. I brought this plan forward for two main reasons; firstly, Harvie Ramsay (University of Strathclyde) and Jean-François Hennart (University of Illinois) both started using the notion of aversion ratios published in the 1991 paper and it seemed sensible to combine our resources in an update. Secondly, the Commission changed the data series which precluded further meaningful collaboration of domains of collaboration after the early 1990s. However, there was enough to give us the basis of an interesting short note, and this is included here as Chapter 12.

The points made in Chapters 10, 11 and 12 are quite simple, but they do have important implications. A considerable amount of European public money is being devoted to subsidise and encourage collaboration between European firms, especially in the high-technology sectors, and it is clearly a matter of more than just academic interest as to whether successful market completion is likely to facilitate or impede such collaboration. Decisions to let through individual European mergers and subsidise particular joint ventures may still be justifiable in individual cases, but what the analysis here does suggest is that such strategies collectively may be much less efficient and much more expensive than the European Commission acknowledges.

Thus, the book as a whole develops analyses of corporate strategies and public policies from a basic foundation that grows out of earlier work in the industrial organisation literature. If there is one recurring theme, it is that the firm is a linked system that typically does not decompose into separable, individual product-markets. Instead, the firm should be seen as a complex system with its constituent elements bonded together by various types of resource linkages. Analysing the firm in systems terms opens up a new perspective on firm behaviour compared to that provided by more conventional product-market-based approaches. The critical issue is the extent to which such an approach helps generate explanations and insights that warrant its serious consideration as an alternative approach to industrial organisation; it is hoped that the analyses that follow help make such a case.

NOTES

1. An example of this is the continuing neglect of Herbert Simon's in mainstream economics despite his receipt of the Nobel Prize for Economics.
2. For 'mainstream scholarship' could be read 'normal science' (following Kuhn 1970).
3. But see Kay (1997) for discussion of problems for transaction cost economics in this area also.
4. In view of the arguments being put forward here, it is worth noting that Porter's 1980 text has a strong product-market focus, while the 1985 work places much more emphasis on the nature and influence of resources in corporate strategy.

Part I Critiques

INTRODUCTION

Part 1 looks at four quite different approaches to economics. Each chapter focuses on the work of one economist (Schumpeter, Shackle, Williamson and Casson respectively). In this context at least, each writer is also particularly associated with one particular concept and the opportunity is taken to look at some implications of the respective concepts in this section. Thus, Chapter 2 looks at Schumpeter and technological change, Chapter 3 at Shackle and surprise, Chapter 4 at Williamson and transaction costs, and Chapter 5 at Casson and trust.

There is a great deal of potential complementarity between the respective chapters; for example technological change (Chapter 2) may be one of the most important sources of surprise for decision makers (Chapter 3), while surprise itself can lead to problems of potential opportunism (Chapter 4) and the need for trust (Chapter 5).

Each chapter was written independently from the others; with the exception of Chapter 4, each also is the consequence of an invited contribution.

2 Industrial Structure, Rivalry and Innovation

Theory and Evidence[1]

2.1 INTRODUCTION

Innovation has long been recognised as a vital ingredient in fuelling economic growth and raising economic standards of living. However, despite its acknowledged importance, it has not been a central occupation of economic analysis until relatively recently. Its very nature made accommodation with the prevailing economic conventions difficult. Its tendency to involve long time horizons, uncertainty, novelty and heterogeneity fitted uncomfortably with the deterministic, static, perfect competition framework of conventional theory. Joseph Schumpeter's major contribution was to develop a systematic and coherent analysis of the effect of market structure on innovative activity. In doing so he had to break with the straitjacket imposed by traditional micro-economic theory:

> The first thing to go is the traditional conception of the *modus operandi* of competition. Economists are at long last emerging from the stage in which price competition was all they saw.... But in capitalist reality as distinguished from its textbook picture, it is not that kind of competition which counts but the competition from the new commodity, the new technology, the new source of supply, the new type of organisation ... competition which commands a decisive cost or quality advantage and which strikes not at the margins of the profits and the outputs of the existing firms but at their foundations and their very lives.
>
> (Schumpeter 1950: 84)

Perhaps disappointingly, despite Schumpeter's arguments the picture in most economic textbooks is still dominated by price competition. The essence of Schumpeter's contribution was that an industry composed of a few large firms was the most appropriate industrial structure as far as stimulating technological progress is concerned. Their competitive

17

interactions were characterised by the process of 'creative destruction' described in the quote above by Schumpeter. We shall explore the foundations of Schumpeter's arguments more fully in the next section. Galbraith (1972) was a leading advocate of the Schumpeterian perspective, but has failed to have a major impact on mainstream economics. However there has been considerable testing of the Schumpeterian hypothesis, and in this chapter we shall consider the results of these investigations, and also discuss to what extent it is possible to develop the theoretical framework and associated empirical analysis.

In Sections 2.2 to 2.6 inclusive, it will be argued that the traditional Schumpeterian perspective on product-market structure has to be extended to include the effects of internal and external markets in finance and technology. Section 2.7 reports empirical investigations of the Schumpeterian hypothesis and the early findings of what may be promising research avenues in inter-firm co-operative agreements are analysed. Consideration of the possible relevance of game-theoretic formulations of the concept of rivalry is also given as a precursor to further discussion of rivalry in Section 2.8. In this section, new theories in industrial organisation and business policy are discussed, and the implications for reformulating the strands of technological change considered.

The distinction made by Schumpeter between invention (the origination of a new idea) and innovation (commercial application of a new idea) is recognised and respected throughout this chapter. However, as a convenient shorthand, innovative activity is also interpreted as an umbrella term describing the whole process itself from idea generation to implementation.

2.2 THE SCHUMPETERIAN TRADITION

Schumpeter's heirs have spent much time and energy arguing over the meaning and relevance of a number of clauses in the various testaments left by him. Kamien and Schwartz (1982) provide a useful representation of the consensual view as to what Schumpeter actually meant:

1 Innovation is greater in monopolistic industries than in competitive ones because
   (a) A firm with monopoly power can prevent imitation and thereby can capture more profit from an innovation.
   (b) A firm with monopoly profits is better able to finance research and development.

2   Large firms are more innovative than small firms because
   (a) A large firm can finance a larger research and development
      staff. There are other economies of scale in this activity also.
   (b) A large diversified firm is better able to exploit unforeseen
      innovations.
   (c) Indivisibility in cost reducing innovations makes them more
      profitable for large firms.
3   Innovation is spurred by technological opportunity.
4   Innovation is spurred by market opportunity (demand-pull).

(1982: 47)

In support of the first hypothesis, Kamien and Schwartz argue that monopoly power in the form of a patent, trade-mark or copyright is necessary to provide a profit incentive to innovate. If there are appropriability problems in intellectual property rights, the potential benefits of innovation may be diffused throughout the economy in the form of externalities. If the firm fails to internalise a sufficiently high level of these potential gains, innovation would be discouraged. A firm with monopoly power may also be able to generate excess internal funds that can be used to fund research and development; firms in atomistic, competitive markets may not be able to afford the cash fees required to compete in R&D, especially if there are barriers in the form of threshold effects.

As well as monopoly power stimulating innovativeness by generating incentive and enabling effects in a particular market, Kamien and Schwartz develop a second strand in Schumpeter's analysis relating to the possible scale effects of firm size on innovativeness. Major points made by them in this connection include the possibility that a large research effort may be needed to create a critical mass in teamwork, to exploit specialisation and division of scientific and engineering labour, to exploit indivisibilities in specialised equipment, and (in the case of the diversified firm) to exploit serendipity in research findings.

Kamien and Schwartz also identify two hypotheses of more recent origin which may be regarded as falling within the Schumpeterian tradition. The 'technology-push' or technological opportunity hypothesis suggests that the underlying scientific base will determine the pace of innovation in particular sectors; a particularly fertile and rapidly changing scientific base will facilitate a high level of commercial innovativeness, while a relatively sterile or slow-changing scientific base will inhibit innovation activity in sectors with which it is associated. Kamien and Schwartz see the laser and its applications as a classic

example of technology-push in innovation. The firm which can finance
a large R&D team that can exploit the existing scientific base will have
a competitive advantage in this perspective. The 'demand-pull' or
market opportunity hypothesis is particularly associated with
Schmookler (1966), and essentially is based on the premise that innovative activity is stimulated by perceived need. The perception of profit
opportunities feeds back into R&D activity, which may draw upon any
scientific base in an attempt to develop innovations that will satisfy
the latent demand. In this case, diversity in firms' products and R&D
activity is important as well as sheer scale of activity. Diversity would
facilitate generation and recognition of new profit opportunities, as
well as a greater ability to respond quickly to such opportunities.

These constitute the major elements in the Schumpeterian or neo-
Schumpeterian tradition. There have been counter-arguments against
the supposed advantages of monopoly power and firm size. These may
be characterised as the anti-Schumpeterian position; the absence of
competitive pressure could encourage inertia and laziness on the part
of the monopolist;[2] the monopolist could prefer to let someone else do
the hard work of innovating and then use its considerable resources to
adopt a 'fast second' imitative strategy; or the monopolist might be
deterred by the prospect of attacking and cannibalising its existing
product line if it innovated (Kamien and Schwartz 1982: 29–30).
Collectively, these hypotheses represent a wide-ranging set of perspectives on the alleged merits or demerits of large monopolies. Before
we look at the empirical evidence, however, there are some points that
should be made regarding considerations that are often not made
explicit in studies of the effect of product-market structure on innovative activity or are missed altogether; these relate particularly to capital
market implications, and the role of strategic alternatives for the
modern corporation.

2.3   PRODUCT-MARKET STRUCTURE, CAPITAL-MARKET
EFFICIENCY AND CO-OPERATIVE AGREEMENTS

The role of the capital market is often relegated to the side of the
stage in analysis of the effects of product-market structure on innovative activity. This is unfortunate, because the functioning of capital
markets is critical in determining product-market efficiency both in
theory and in practice. In fact, if capital markets are operating
efficiently, then the various problems associated with competitive

market structures (in the Schumpeterian tradition) and monopolistic firms (in the anti-Schumpeterian perspective) should be eliminated. Product-market structure would not matter. We can briefly consider why this should be.

Firstly, it would be helpful to define efficiency in capital markets. Fama (1970) gives three interpretations of capital-market efficiency; the weak form, the semi-strong form and the strong form. The weak form states that a portfolio holder cannot use past and present information on share prices to achieve a higher level of performance than an investor who randomly selects a portfolio with the same level of risk. The semi-strong form states that shares' prices will reflect all publicly available information, while the strong form states that shares' prices reflect all relevant information, whether public or not. In the strong case investors outside the firm suffer no informational disadvantage with respect to managers, scientists and engineers inside the firm. Misrepresentation, incompetence or laziness on the part of the internal management would be reflected in the capital market's valuation of the company's shares, just as would trustworthiness, competence, commitment and creativity. It is the strong version which provides the yardstick by which efficiency issues can be judged; the weak and semi-strong forms are consistent with efficiency problems resulting from separation of ownership and control.

If the strong version of efficiency in external capital markets holds, and there are sound mechanisms for establishing and policing appropriability in intellectual property rights, product-market structure should not be a drag on dynamic efficiency or innovativeness. Firms with innovative potential in atomistic market structures would be able to signal their profit opportunities to potential investors who then conduct mutually advantageous trades with these firms, marrying technology with finance. The presumption here is that there are no transaction costs in the capital market; bargaining and exchanges can be agreed and policed without cost to either party.[3]

As far as scale effects of specialisation and equipment indivisibilities in R&D activity is concerned, large firm size may not be necessary for the exploitation of these scale effects. Williamson (1975) points out that technological indivisibilities do not necessarily imply economic indivisibility.[4] Joint ventures such as R&D consortia could pool the limited R&D resources available to small firms, exploiting physical indivisibilities and specialisation and division of qualified scientists and engineers. Similarly, if a small firm has a narrow specific technological skill that requires augmentation with other firms' technological, marketing and/or financial resources, joint ventures or licensing may provide a basis for mutually advantageous agreements. In principle, if a firm has innovative potential, even if this is narrow, selective and partial as far as an entire innovative package is concerned, inter-firm co-operative agreements provide mechanisms whereby the necessary critical mass of innovative activity can be reached. In such circumstances, small firm size is no barrier to creating and exploiting innovativeness. A similar argument holds for the supposed advantages a diversified firm provides as far as the exploitation of unexpected innovation is concerned; as long as firms *in toto* are sufficiently diversified in their collective output, licensing or joint ventures should exploit profit opportunities.

The caveat is the same as for capital-market efficiency; the inter-firm co-operative agreements may exploit profit opportunities as long as specification and protection of property rights are not problematic and there are no transaction costs in forming and policing such agreements.

As far as the anti-Schumpeterian thesis that monopolistic control contributes to innovative inefficiency is concerned, this also depends on implicit assumptions regarding capital-market inefficiency. If capital markets are strongly efficient, then X-inefficiency, dynamic inefficiency, and pursuit of non-profit goals by managers should be signalled to the capital market. Since capital-market efficiency in these terms should facilitate the joining of ownership and control of the firm, renegade management who fail to maximise profits could be penalised or replaced. Even if an innovation promises to cannibalise a firm's own products, as long as any net gain from expanding demand or reducing cost exists, there is an incentive to innovate under efficient capital market conditions. While the incentive may be less than for competitive firms, or firms entering the market for whom cannibalisation is not an issue, efficient capital markets would still stimulate innovation as long as there is the prospect of supernormal profits.[5]

In short, when the possibility of efficient capital markets is combined with the possibility of efficiency in the creation and maintenance of inter-firm co-operative agreements, the foundations of both the Schumpeterian and anti-Schumpeterian positions are removed. In those conditions, product-market structure ceases to exert the distorting influences mooted in both these traditions. This does not mean that these perspectives and their associated hypotheses are invalidated; there are likely to be substantial transaction costs involved in capital markets and the market for inter-firms' co-operative agreements, as we shall see in the next section.[6] However, it does mean that an adequate analysis of the determinants of innovative activity must go beyond analysis of product-market structure effects to include effects in both the capital market and the market for co-operative agreements. With this in mind we consider the possibility of imperfections in both these latter markets in the next section.

2.4   INNOVATION, TRANSACTION COST AND PROPERTY-RIGHT PROBLEMS

Innovation does in fact pose severe efficiency problems both in the capital market and the market for co-operative agreements. Transactors in both sets of markets typically face severe information problems in searching out potential partners, establishing mutually agreeable contracts, and policing actual agreements (Dahlman 1979). Coase (1937) pointed out that there may be substantial information problems in market transactions encouraging substitution of the market by in-house organisation in order to economise on these costs. A particular difficulty with market agreements involving technological innovation is the severity and form of information problems in this area. The supplier of innovative inputs into any market agreement is often the best placed to judge its real potential; in such cases there is an informational asymmetry between innovator and partner in favour of the innovator.[7] On the other hand, those firms or institutions co-operating with the innovator may also be the best placed to judge whether they themselves will respect the innovator's intellectual property rights (to the extent these can be established) and deal honestly and responsibly according to the letter or spirit of the market agreement; in this respect there is an information asymmetry in favour of the institution cooperating with the innovator. The presence of genuine uncertainty[8] and bounded rationality[9] on the part of transactors contributes to the creation and maintenance of these information asymmetries.

As long as transactors can trust and respect the actions, assurances and intentions of their potential partners, information asymmetries do not necessarily pose severe information problems; relevant information may be revealed to potential partners, raising and equalising the level of knowledge possessed by both or all parties. The real problem in efficiency terms arises when Adam Smith's ideal of pursuit of self-interest is combined with information asymmetries. Deceit, cheating and misrepresentation may be possible consequences of such market situations, especially if it is too difficult or costly to invoke sanctions against such behaviour. Williamson (1975) describes opportunism (self-interest seeking with guile) as a potentially severe transaction cost in conditions of high uncertainty. In such circumstances, actual transactions may be impeded by transaction costs associated with bounded rationality, information asymmetries, uncertainty and opportunism. Agreements that could have been mutually advantageous to both parties in the absence of these transaction costs may be abandoned or not taken up, especially if potential opportunism is perceived to be a serious issue. Both capital markets and the markets for inter-firm co-operative agreements may be impaired by such issues.

Arrow (1962) provided an early analysis of one set of implications arising from these problems, the possibility of 'moral hazard'. Moral hazard can arise in conditions of uncertainty in so far as the actual award of a contract (such as to conduct specific R&D search) can adversely affect the incentive structure for resource allocation.[10] Providing dishonest or negligent behaviour cannot be discerned and penalised, and the implications for obtaining future R&D contracts can be ignored, it does not matter to the R&D contracting firm whether search is successful or not; all the risk and uncertainty is now borne by the provider of funds.[11]

The moral hazard problem may or may not involve opportunistic behaviour.[12] However, the concept of opportunism itself, as developed by Williamson (1975), helps illuminate considerable difficulties in contractual situations involving technological change. Parties to any capital market or inter-firm agreement may be regarded as providing particular resources or skills (for example, R&D, finance, production or marketing) in exchange for access to resources possessed by the other party and in which they are deficient. Innovators may misrepresent the true potential of their technology to get access to finance, venture capitalists may misrepresent their intended contribution to secure control of the firm, established firms in joint ventures with innovators may misrepresent their true intention to appropriate the technology of their partner. Patenting, copyrighting and litigation may be imperfect devices for policing contracts because of expense and problems in specifying property rights, responsibilities or obligations.

One response to the obvious existence of severe informational problems in these markets is to restrict attention to the implications of product-market structure as in the more traditional Schumpeterian and anti-Schumpeterian theses discussed earlier. This would be legitimate if the information problems prevent these markets forming, or break them up once formed. A second response is to recognise that active markets do exist in these areas and that there is therefore a need to extend the traditional Schumpeterian analysis; government funding of R&D, venture capital, joint ventures and licensing all provide examples of active trades in high technology.

In fact, the second response does not go far enough. A third response is to recognise that severe transaction costs may exist in external capital markets and the market for inter-firm co-operative agreements, but that the evolution of the large modern diversified corporation may provide substitute *internal* markets to transaction-cost-ridden external markets. In the next section we discuss how these possibilities necessitate further modification of the traditional market structure hypothesis.

2.5 INNOVATION, INTERNAL MARKETS AND THE M-FORM

Although Kamien and Schwartz treat diversification as a sub-clause in the Schumpeterian thesis regarding the advantages of large corporations, they recognise it as a relatively recent addition to this tradition, dating from the work of Nelson.[13] More recently, work by Williamson (1979) on the role of internal organisation or hierarchy in inhibiting or facilitating the creation of internal markets within the firm has helped to provide a basis for relating corporate strategy to efficiency considerations. This is of particular relevance in the case of the diversified firm, as we shall see below.

One theme of Williamson's analysis is that internalisation of markets may eliminate or at least mitigate the transaction costs associated with external markets discussed in the previous section.[14] Senior management may be in better positions than external markets to evaluate both subordinate management and their associated proposals, whether innovative or not; they may be more familiar and experienced in dealing with the subordinate managers and the technology than external agencies, and also are likely to have access to better-quality information than would be disclosed to outside institutions. Further, rewards and penalties (such as bonus, promotion, redundancy) can be more direct and immediate than the blunt and cumbersome control options available in external markets (such as expensive and time-consuming litigation).

Thus, internalisation *per se* may help provide devices to inhibit opportunistic behaviour on the part of managers, scientists and engineers in innovative corporations and reduce associated transaction costs. However, there is a second theme in Williamson's analysis which suggests that a particular type of internal organisation, the M-form or multidivisional structure, may further reduce the bargaining costs associated with external transactions. The M-form is based on the concept of divisionalising around natural decision centres.[15] Divisions are often granted profit-centre status and given responsibility for operating and minor strategic problems. Major strategic decisions (merger, takeover, major innovation and investment, divestment) are the responsibility of senior management at headquarters level.

Divisionalisation, especially if it is combined with profit measurement at this level, can contribute to the creation of internal markets within the firm. Adopting the profit criterion as the universal yardstick at divisional level helps to audit, measure and compare divisional management performance. An internal capital market may be created with allocation of funds to high-yield areas being facilitated through profit-centre competition and the control advantages of internalisation. Thus, in Williamson's view, internalisation and divisionalisation reinforce each other to provide attractive transaction cost-reducing and profit-orientated advantages in the M-form corporation. To the extent that these advantages are realised, internal capital markets may substitute external capital markets in funding innovative activity. At this point we should add a word of caution: the *internalisation* aspect of Williamson's thesis should in general facilitate innovative activity, very much in the Schumpeterian and Galbraithian tradition. To the extent that *divisionalisation* and the internal capital market is expected to contribute, it is most likely to generate short-term minor innovation or imitative developments. The incentive structure at divisional level revolves around short-term operating decisions. However, if the internal control apparatus can compensate for the short-run orientation of profit-centre operation, internalisation may still uncover and support areas of real innovative potential within the firm.

A second possibility implied, but not developed, in Williamson's analysis is that the creation of internal markets in the diversified firm may provide mechanisms that allow the circumvention of external markets such as inter-firm joint ventures and licensing agreements. To the extent that opportunism and other transaction costs are suppressed or reduced in the M-form, there may be potential for mutually advantageous interdivisional exchanges in the diversified M-form in the area of technological innovation.[16] In a sufficiently diversified firm, breadth of knowledge and resources in a wide variety of markets and technologies may create opportunities for intra-firm divisional co-operation, marrying necessary marketing and production resources to innovative ideas. The existence of an effective control apparatus would prevent or reduce the transaction costs associated with external joint ventures or licensing, while the availability of an internal capital market may contribute financial resources.

If efficient internal markets exist, this has profound implications for the traditional market-structure-orientated Schumpeterian tradition. In such circumstances, if innovative possibilities arise anywhere in the M-form structure, product-market structure is irrelevant as far as the exploitation of profit opportunities is concerned. If a product division operates in competitive markets, cross-subsidisation through the internal capital market can provide the requisite financial support to search for innovation, or fund it. If a product division operates in monopolistic markets, the internal control apparatus would monitor and penalise divisional management failing to maximise profit. Product-market structure simply does not matter.[17]

Williamson perhaps pushes the advantages of the M-form structure further than is legitimate. Bounded rationality, opportunism and uncertainty do not disappear in internal markets, though the internal control apparatus and internal capital markets may mitigate their effects. The M-form structure is also expensive in managerial terms; a new level of experienced and able general managers is required at middle or divisional level, while divisionalisation may cut across similarities in markets and technologies, resulting in wasteful duplication of functional activities in R&D, marketing and production. Nevertheless, internalisation of major markets in large, diversified corporations may have important efficiency implications for innovative activity.

2.6 WHAT IS LEFT OF THE SCHUMPETERIAN HYPOTHESIS?

Expressed in its original form, there is not much left of the Schumpeterian hypothesis, or even early anti-Schumpeterian attempts to legitimate and rescue the competitive model as the welfare ideal. If there exist adequate external *or* internal markets, product-market structure ceases to exert the dominant influence posited by Schumpeter. A corollary is that product-market structure re-emerges as central to considerations of dynamic efficiency only when there exist significant impediments to the smooth functioning of internal or external markets.

An adequate research programme should now recognise three strands in the determination of innovative activity: product-market structure, external markets and internal markets. The simple observation that joint ventures, licence agreements and internal markets do exist in the area of technological innovation is sufficient to require the modification of the traditional Schumpeterian hypothesis in this fashion. It is unlikely that each strand should be unattended by efficiency problems, and for that reason it would be desirable to express the programme in comparative institutional terms. The pattern and method of support for innovative activity in different sectors is likely to reflect the relative efficiency advantages or disadvantages of alternative firm and market devices in respective cases. Schumpeterianism appears as only one strand in this expanded agenda.

The difficulties involved in this kind of three-strand research programme are considerable and are likely to contrast with the experience of the Schumpeterian paradigm. The Schumpeterian paradigm was assimilated remarkably easily by the economics establishment; in some senses this is surprising because the spirit and content of Schumpeter's analysis is fundamentally different from that of neoclassical theory and its applied wing in industrial economics, the structure-conduct-performance approach. One feature which may have lowered the barriers to entry into economic orthodoxy was the emphasis on independent variables on the market structure side which paralleled those in neoclassical theory; scale economies, market concentration and demand elasticity are the structural components of neoclassical theory as much as they are of Schumpeter's analysis. These similarities on the structural side eased the theoretical absorption and empirical investigations of Schumpeter's analysis; the theoretical apparatus and empirical techniques for measuring them were already in place and established. One consequence was a fairly mechanistic interpretation of the Schumpeterian position, with structure-performance connections being emphasised, and intervening behavioural processes downplayed.

A research programme of the type implied here would not face such accommodating features. Firstly, the agenda revolves around three major elements and their inter-relationships; the Schumpeterian paradigm restricted its focus to product-market structure, extending consideration to internal and external markets adds substantially to the complexity of the analysis. Secondly, the structure variables associated with the Schumpeterian approach are, in principle, readily measurable,[18] though the measurement of innovative output is as problematic in this framework as in any other. However, the efficiency problems of internal and external markets are attributable to such issues as bounded rationality, opportunism, uncertainty, and appropriability in property rights. By their very nature, these phenomena are characterised by difficulties as far as observability and measurability are concerned. Thirdly, it is likely that there will be difficulties in generalising results beyond individual sectors. The transaction costs and property-right problems may differ substantially from one technological regime to another. However, this may only be making explicit features that were often unjustifiably ignored in empirical tests of the Schumpeterian hypothesis; measurable and comparable variables like size and concentration are emphasised at the expense of potentially significant issues relating to the conduct and behaviour of the firms and industries studied.

Extending the analysis in this fashion is difficult but necessary. If product-market structure is the only item allowed onto the innovation agenda, associated empirical analysis would be myopic and distorted. To the extent that much of the empirical analysis has been limited in this fashion, there must be reservations as to the relevance of some of the findings. However, it would be useful to review the empirical literature at this point, both to examine the contribution of more traditional Schumpeterian analysis, and to examine useful signals for further redrawing the research programme. In particular, it will be argued that the role of rivalry and technological opportunity may help provide guidelines as to how to add detail and direction to this programme.

2.7 EMPIRICAL ANALYSIS, MARKET STRUCTURE AND INNOVATIVE ACTIVITY

There have been many empirical studies of various aspects of the Schumpeterian paradigm. In addition to studies of the traditional hypotheses that market structure and size of firm directly affect innovative effort, there have been variants that may be taken as falling within the Schumpeterian tradition. We shall examine each in turn below. However, it is important first to recognise the problems of empirical estimation faced by researchers in the area, and in their classic survey Kamien and Schwartz (1982: 49–52) list a variety of difficulties in this respect. For example, although patent statistics are frequently used as an indicator of innovative activity, they are an imperfect measure; they do not discriminate between major and minor innovation, many patents are never commercialised and many innovations are never patented. Also, operationalising the structural variables is often problematic; the level of abstraction at which the Schumpeterian debate was conducted leaves unresolved such issues as to whether R&D activity is best measured by qualified scientists and engineers employed or R&D expenditure, whether size is best measured in terms of sales, assets or employees, and which of many indices of monopoly power should be utilised. Further, Kamien and Schwartz point out that causality may not be simply unidirectional, but that innovative activity may feed back and affect the Schumpeterian structural variables – for example, if an innovation encourages concentration (Kamien and Schwartz 1982: 50–2). One of the basic features of the innovative process itself is heterogeneity and difficulties in standardisation and comparison; it is perhaps appropriate and inevitable that these characteristics should be reflected in empirical studies of the process. Culbertson (1985) has also pointed out difficulties in disentangling the various strands of the Schumpeterian hypothesis in econometrics tests.

The 'technology-push' and 'demand-pull' sub-hypotheses have also provided their own particular problems. It is true that a consistent finding in empirical analyses is that industrial technological opportunity is a critical determinant of innovativeness. However, if technological opportunity is exogenous to economic analysis as assumed in many studies, it abrogates the possibility that innovativeness is an economic phenomenon. Schmookler's 'demand-pull' hypothesis offers greater possibilities for the incorporation of innovation within economic analysis. But Scherer (1980b) found Schmookler's initial finding of a strong relationship between demand factors and innovativeness was weakened if analysis was extended beyond Schmookler's original narrow base into all manufacturing. Also, Mowery and Rosenberg (1979) queried the legitimacy of the concept of market demand used in many of the empirical studies, and found their findings were, in general, inconsistent and heterogenous.

As if these problems were not sufficient, there has been considerable debate recently in the literature as to what Schumpeter actually meant, and whether empirical tests actually test the relationship he hypothesised (see, for example, Fisher and Temin 1973, 1979; Rodriguez 1979; Lunn 1982; Kohn and Scott 1982 and 1985). We recognise this debate but sidestep it here since there may be more important issues at stake, such as those discussed in the previous sections. Instead we shall look at the empirical studies for clues as to how the Schumpeterian paradigm may be modified or extended.

Because of the sheer volume of empirical analysis in the Schumpeterian tradition, we shall not attempt to discuss individually all relevant studies. Instead we shall base discussion on Kamien and Schwartz's summaries and update their conclusions with reference to more recent empirical analyses where appropriate.

2.7.1 Market power and innovative activity

One group of empirical studies has explored possible relationships between market structure and innovation. Kamien and Schwartz (1982) identified two major types of investigation in this area: firstly, studies of possible effects of concentration on research activity; and, secondly, studies into the relationship between concentration and output.

Kamien and Schwartz concluded that there was little consensus as to the nature of the relationship, if any, in the ten studies which had investigated the effect of concentration on research activity. However, a number of these studies did indicate that there appeared to be strong industry effects in so far as the degree of technological opportunity[19] associated with respective industries often appeared to influence R&D activity significantly and positively.

There have also been a number of studies investigating possible relationships between concentration and innovation output, the latter usually measured by productivity changes, patenting activity, or subjective estimation of important industry innovation. The nine studies reviewed by Kamien and Schwartz tended to produce a mixed and inconclusive picture, reinforcing the unclear signals received from the input studies. Angelmar (1985) has also attempted to look more deeply at possible concentration effects in high-technological opportunity. The study of 160 firms from the 1978 PIMS database first of all confirmed that concentration appeared to have a negligible effect on research spending. However, when industries were classified by type of R&D activity, concentration appeared to have a significant part to play. Industries with low-cost R&D, low R&D uncertainty and strong barriers against imitation appeared to generate sufficient incentive for innovation even in the absence of high concentration. In those cases, concentration tended to reduce research spending. By way of contrast, industries in which R&D activity tended to be associated with high cost and uncertainty and in which there were low barriers to imitation tended to link concentration with research spending. In those cases, concentration appeared to be necessary to encourage research activity.

Therefore, as far as the market power aspect is concerned, a simple or naive Schumpeterian approach does not seem to have shed much light on the innovative process. To the extent that this area should be included in any research programme, Angelmar's approach is suggestive of possible directions for refinement. Industry-specific effects, uncertainty, appropriability and strategic considerations may all augment the effects, if any, of market concentration.

2.7.2 Firm size and innovative activity

Studies of the effect of firm size on innovative activity have also tended to fall into either input or output characterisations of innovative activities. The 24 input-orientated studies surveyed by Kamien and Schwartz tended to use sales, employment or assets as a measure of firm size, and expenditure or employment as a measure of R&D activity. To the extent that any pattern was discernible, it appeared that R&D activity tended to increase more than proportionately with firm size up to a certain point, after which R&D intensity tended to level off or decline in most industries. Reinforcing the points made in the previous section regarding the implications of Angelmar's study, Kamien and Schwartz (1982: 81) point out that most studies do not control for factors other than size, and imply that the next generation of studies should perhaps include factors that may augment any possible size effects. They also emphasise strong inter-industry difference in the relationship.

The eight output-orientated studies in this area surveyed by Kamien and Schwartz used either patents or subjective estimation of significant innovation as their output measure of innovative activity. The findings here tended to reinforce those of the input-orientated studies, just as in the market-power groups of studies. Typically, after a certain point, size did not appear to contribute to innovative activity in most industries. The precise relationship tended to be industry specific.

Rothwell and Zegveld (1982) also found evidence that smaller or medium-sized firms were frequently more innovative than larger firms, for a number of sectors and countries. Kaplinsky (1983) also provided an interesting analysis of how the effect of firm size on innovative activity may vary over time for particular industries. In an analysis of the computer-aided-design industry, he argued that larger firms tended to take the lead in innovative activity in the 1950s, new small firms played an important role in the 1960s and early 1980s, while medium-sized firms were relatively important in the mid-1970s. Another study of relevance here is that of Mansfield *et al.* (1979) who looked at the effect of internationalisation of activity on R&D activity. The authors found evidence that the greater the level of a firm's overseas activities (including exports), the greater is the level of R&D and the share of basic research within the R&D function. There were strong indications that internationalisation in general, and multinationalism/licensing in particular, stimulated innovative activity. The global nature of the multinational helped spread R&D costs over an extended market.

If size does have a role to play in determining R&D activity as Kamien and Schwartz suggest, it is likely that past studies may have had difficulties separating out the effects because of the significance of omitted variables. Corporate strategy (such as multinationalism) and industry-specific relationships are likely to be important. Kaplinsky's study also serves as a useful indicator that any effects may be transitory, depending on prevailing industry circumstances.

2.7.3   Taking stock: where should analysis go from here?

At this point it would be useful to break up an analysis of the empirical studies to consider how theoretical and empirical investigations should proceed in the light of the discussion so far. We are faced with a number of options. One option against which there is a clear consensus is further testing of the simple unmodified Schumpeterian hypotheses. The end result of a large number of empirical investigations has not been impressive. There are tantalising hints in many of the studies that, if concentration and scale are important, then their significance depends on interaction with other variables which are likely to be specific to firm, industry and even time-period.

This brings us to the second option, which is to extend explicitly the research programme in the manner discussed earlier. We shall argue later that there already exist theoretical tools that may be of help in the pursuit of this option. If the extended programme captures relevant variables neglected in the analysis following the Schumpeterian tradition, we would expect performance improvements in empirical analysis.

However, there exists a third option to which consideration must be given. It is one which has received some impetus from the empirical studies discussed above. If there is any conclusion to be drawn from these studies, it is that extreme pro- or anti-Schumpeterian stances are not justified; Scherer (1980a), in a review of the empirical investigations, concludes that a little bit of monopoly power may be helpful as an enabling factor, but that high levels of concentration are more likely than not to repress innovative activity. He argues, 'What is needed for rapid technical progress is a subtle blend of competition and monopoly' (1980a: 438). There is some support for Scherer's position, at least from the firm size studies reviewed above. It is certainly the case that innovative activity typically takes place in oligopolistic market structures characterised by relatively few firms, and it is these sectors which we would expect to reflect the 'subtle blend' of competition and monopoly mentioned by Scherer.

Such considerations have helped fuel the development of game-theoretic oligopolistic rivalry models. These models are reviewed by Kamien and Schwartz (1982: 105–215) and are generally characterised as a race to be first amongst potential innovators.[20] A central question is the optimal market structure for innovative activity. While Kamien and Schwartz (1982) provide a comprehensive review of this literature, including their own work, there have already been a considerable number of subsequent studies.[21] Reinganum (1984) also provides a useful review of this literature.

In fact, the oligopolistic rivalry literature lies closer to the neoclassical literature that Schumpeter was revolting against, than it does to the Schumpeterian tradition itself. It is characterised by an abundance of theoretical models but a dearth of empirical analyses. Typical assumptions include homogenous firms, homogenous innovation targets for all competitors, profit maximisation, deterministic or probabilistic description of possible outcomes, and equilibrium. Some studies (Scherer 1965; Grabowski and Baxter 1973) have conducted empirical analyses and suggested that apparent matching behaviour in R&D spending in certain industries may be accounted for by an oligopolistic rivalry model. However, in Kay (1979: 187–205) it was argued that a non-rivalry explanation for apparent R&D matching was both superior and simpler than the rivalry alternatives.

It is a methodologically suspect tactic to criticise a theory in terms of the alleged unreality of its underlying assumptions (Blaug 1980). On the other hand, a legitimate criticism is that the oligopolistic rivalry literature is primarily concerned with formal modelling and optimising techniques. It is just conceivable that it may provide useful insights into a process which is characterised by firm heterogeneity, competitors differentiating their products, true uncertainty (not quantifiable probability), disequilibrium behaviour, bounded rationality, novelty and serendipity. Nevertheless, it is fair to say that reservations are quite widely held as to the ability of these rivalry models to model adequately a process which has such disconcerting properties. Therefore, the third option may represent a cul-de-sac as far as developing useful extensions of the Schumpeterian paradigm is concerned. Obviously, if the models begin to generate empirical analysis and interesting results, these opinions would have to be revised.

In the next section we shall consider how recent empirical studies have provided useful clues as to the reasonableness of the second option discussed above, that is extending the Schumpeterian tradition to recognise the implications of internal and external markets.

2.7.4 Internal markets, external markets and innovative activity

A number of empirical studies of the Schumpeterian approach have incorporated aspects of relevance to some of the theoretical cases we discussed earlier. In particular, attention has focused on the possibility that the large firm may provide internal capital-market opportunities and, if diversified, also internal technology-transfer opportunities. Kamien and Schwartz report a number of studies that included one or other of these considerations. The results were generally disappointing and may have discouraged further reformulation of the traditional Schumpeterian perspective.

Kamien and Schwartz identified seven studies that had tackled the internal capital market aspect. Typically the studies looked at the effect of firms' high liquidity or current profits in a given time-period on R&D or patenting activity, frequently lagged. Overall, the studies produced no conclusive evidence that liquidity or profitability affected innovative activity. They also reported five studies that incorporated some measure of firm diversification as a possible determinant of innovative activity, whether measured on an input or output basis. Again, no strong support was found for the hypothesis, findings often reporting mixed and unclear results.

A difficulty with these studies is the tendency to treat the possibility of internal markets as simply extending the Schumpeterian argument as to the supposed benefits of large monopolies. In fact, the behaviour of internal markets in the diversified corporation is likely to reflect very different considerations from Schumpeterian conjectures as to the effect of product-market structure.[22] The sophisticated strategy-formulating and operating efficiency advantages of the internal capital market discussed earlier may not be easily captured by simply adding a variable measuring short-term cash-flow capability to regression equations. Scherer (1980a: 422–3) also suggests that data limitations have so far inhibited proper testing of the diversification hypothesis.

A further problem is that these extensions typically do not recognise the possibility of external markets as options that may facilitate innovative activity. In sectors where external capital and technology markets are important, such neglect may have a distorting effect on analysis. For example, if venture capital, government support for R&D, joint ventures or licensing are important in specific sectors, these may represent substitute innovation-enabling devices to the internalised support provided by Schumpeterian product-market monopolies or internal resource markets. If these possibilities were included in empirical analysis, a fuller and fairer picture of patterns of innovative activity may be generated. In fact, a number of recent studies have compared the characteristics of internal and external markets in innovative activity. The studies have been concentrated in the multinational literature and have typically looked at the choice between technology transfer using licence agreements and joint ventures on the one hand, and internal market using overseas subsidiaries on the other. They provide useful guidelines as to the desirability of widening empirical analysis to recognise external market considerations. We shall briefly summarise some major findings before discussing possible implications.

Size of firm was a frequent consideration in these studies. Telesio (1979) found that smaller firms were more likely to use licensing rather than multinational expansion as a means of exploiting its in-house skills, Contractor (1981) suggests that smaller firms may prefer to use joint ventures as a means of obtaining access to foreign markets, since they have more limited managerial, marketing and financial capability than larger firms. As far as incidence of licensing itself was concerned, Contractor (1983), in a study of 241 US firms in 1000 licence agreements, found that it was positively related to company size, but that small to medium-sized companies comprised a larger fraction than expected of international technology transfers.

Berg and Friedman (1977) found that complementary/overlapping technologies play an important role in joint ventures by chemical firms, implying that this form of co-operation allows technical economies and synergies to be exploited in this industry. Mariti and Smiley (1983) conducted an analysis of co-operative agreements between firms using a transaction-cost framework, and found that exchange of technological information, followed by transfer of technological information, was the most frequent reason cited for the agreement. Mansfield and Romeo (1980) studied the transfer of technology overseas by 31 US-based firms and found that the mean age of technologies transferred through licences and joint ventures tended to be significantly higher than the mean age of technologies transferred through the internal market to subsidiaries. Although Mansfield and Romeo do not discuss this finding fully, one possible reason could be fear of loss of proprietary knowledge if joint venture of licensing were adopted for newer technologies.[23] They also found evidence that UK subsidiaries perceived their technological capabilities had been enhanced by such transfers, though the effects were not typically seen as extreme or dramatic. Odagiri (1983), in a study of 370 Japanese manufacturing firms, tentatively concluded that firms' innovativeness and growth conditions appeared to influence the decision whether to conduct internal R&D or rely on patent licences.

In a study of 1376 international technology transfers by 32 US-based multinationals, Davidson and McFetridge (1984) found a number of interesting and significant differences in the characteristics of internal and external technology transfers. These include confirming Mansfield and Romeo's (1980) findings that newer technology tended to be transferred in-house via the internal market rather than through inter-firm co-operative agreements, and also that R&D-intensive firms were more likely to rely on internal markets rather than external agreements for technology transfer. Also, the balance of relative probability of internal versus external transfer appears to have been moving towards the latter in recent years, *ceteris paribus*, consistent with Davidson and McFetridge's argument that there has been an increase in international competition in high-technology industries.

They discuss the possibility that transaction costs of co-operative agreements have been reduced by such competition. Amongst other effects they argue it has increased choice, reduced monopoly power and reduced the 'locking-in' effect and associated problems of opportunism when there are limited alternatives to a particular inter-firm agreement. Burgelman (1983) has also conducted an analysis of factors which may contribute to *internal* entrepreneurial activity within the firm, or internal corporate venturing. The possibility that entrepreneurship itself may be a feature of internal markets is an interesting one, and further extends the possible range of internal markets.

These studies are particularly interesting because a frequent motive for licence and joint venture appears to be an intention to circumvent the Schumpeterian scale barrier to innovative activity. Scale in this respect relates not only to sufficient R&D resources, but also to production, marketing and financial resources. Yet a frequently reported barrier to inter-firm co-operative agreements appears to be transaction cost and property-right problems. Schumpeter's emphasis on the need for the innovative firm to be able to appropriate a sufficiently high proportion of gains from innovation may be particularly relevant here. The studies tend to concentrate on internal and/or external market considerations and, to that extent, usually cover one or two of the three legs of the extended programme discussed earlier. We would expect, if the third (product-market structure) leg was included in further studies, that it might further illuminate actual patterns of behaviour. For example, if a particular sector was characterised by low economies of scale in R&D and severe problems in appropriating monopoly rents from innovation, we would expect most innovative activity to be internalised. On the other hand, high levels of R&D economies and few problems in appropriating innovation monopoly rents might encourage inter-firm co-operative agreements.

The empirical results reported here provide interesting signposts for redefining further empirical analyses of innovative activity. They tend to recognise explicitly transaction cost and property-right problems and incorporate them in their underlying theoretical frameworks.[24] While it may be possible to extend the game-theoretic oligopolistic rivalry theories also into this area,[25] the empirical studies have instead typically drawn on theoretical perspectives in which bounded rationality and genuine uncertainty are central concepts.

In the next section we shall discuss how we may draw on these empirical contributions and existing theoretical frameworks to suggest guidelines for future research in this area.

2.8   THEORETICAL DEVELOPMENT AND POLICY FORMULATION

It might be helpful to review what has been argued in the previous sections. In the first section we suggested that Schumpeterian and neo-Schumpeterian perspectives were limited and partial in their treatment of the impact of economic organisation on innovative activity. In particular, three alternative planks were identified as being of potential relevance to theoretical and empirical analysis: product-market structure, internal capital and technology markets, and external capital and technology markets. Different aspects of possible efficiency problems in the respective forms of economic organisation were identified and discussed. In the second section, it was argued that there is sufficient empirical evidence, especially in the area of inter-firm co-operative agreements, to reinforce the theoretical argument that the Schumpeterian perspective requires substantial rewriting and modification.

However, the connection between theory and empirical research has been occasionally *ad hoc* in this respect, with researchers not always relating their studies to wider theoretical frameworks. There has also been compartmentalisation of research activity; for example, the development of game-theoretic rivalry models appears to have built up their own momentum unimpeded and unhindered by recent empirical research, while the empirical research into the implications of external markets for innovative activity has been largely left to researchers into multinational enterprise. There is a general consensus that the notion of technological rivalry is important, but reservations may be expressed as to the usefulness of its expression in the game-theoretic literature. It will be suggested below that there are mutually sympathetic theoretical frameworks that may help in putting meat on the skeleton of the extended research programmes discussed earlier. This may be helpful in indicating how theory development, empirical investigation and public policy problems may be better integrated. We shall start by considering how there may be complementary insights provided by research into business policy and some of the new theories in industrial organisation.

2.8.1 Business policy and industrial organisation

There have been noteworthy developments in the managerial business policy literature in recent years that may have implications for the study of technological change. Before we consider these, it would be useful to consider what is usually implied by the study of business policy.

Rumelt (1984) emphasises that the central organising concept in the business policy literature is strategy, and that the concept is empirical rather than theoretical, stemming from numerous field studies and historical analyses. He argues that the basic strategic concept is that the firm's competitive position is defined by a bundle of unique resources and relationships, and general management's problem is to adjust and review these resources as time, competitors and change erode their value. He summarises the precepts of the business policy literature, not as a theory but as a set of broad empirical observations:

1   The general managers of the firm make choices, and some of these choices are considerably more important (having more impact on performance) than others.
2   Strategic choices are not necessarily explicit but may be characterised by infrequency, uncertainty, the irreversibility of commitments and multifunctional scope, and they are usually non-recurring.
3   The most critical strategic choices exhibited by the firm are those concerned with the selection of the product-market areas in which the firm will compete and the basic approach to these businesses.
4   Similar firms facing similar strategic problems may respond differently.
5   Firms in the same industry compete with substantially different bundles of resources using disparate approaches. These firms differ because of different histories of strategic choice and performance, and because managements appear to seek asymmetric competitive positions.

                                                        (Rumelt 1984: 558).

Thus, the description of competitive rivalry in the business policy literature encompasses concepts of heterogeneity, asymmetry, history, uncertainty and novelty. It is a description of rivalry which contrasts dramatically with the description of rivalry in the game-theoretic literature. Rumelt also contrasts the business policy precepts with those of traditional neoclassical theory, and the tendency for that paradigm to assume away (1) transactions, (2) bounded rationality, (3) technological uncertainty, (4) constraints on factor mobility, (5) limits on information availability, (6) markets in which price conveys quality information, (7) consumer or producer learning, and (8) dishonest and/or foolish behaviour (1984: 554). Teece (1984) provides similar criticism of the difficulties in applying neoclassical theory to analysis of strategic management.[26]

   The differences with traditional neoclassical theory[27] are important because it has been suggested that the traditional structure-conduct-performance (S-C-P) paradigm of industrial organisation may provide a useful framework for the business policy literature (Caves 1980; Porter 1981). However, since the S-C-P paradigm is the applied wing of neoclassical theory, it traditionally neglects the same issues and problems assumed away in neoclassical theory. It is not really consistent with the core observations of the business policy literature.

Two other modern developments in the industrial organisation literature, managerial theory and contestable markets, are also limited in their applicability to technological change. In managerial theory (Baumol 1959; Williamson 1964; and Marris 1964), the only form of bounded rationality permitted is typically a limited one related to separation of ownership and control, and transactional problems in writing and enforcing managerial employment contracts; otherwise optimising behaviour on the part of managers obtains. The managerial literature has stagnated somewhat in recent years, and Williamson now regards his previous managerial modelling as a special case of his more general markets and hierarchies approach. The literature has also been overtaken by the more technical principal-agent literature in recent years. The contestable markets approach (Baumol *et al*, 1982) is an extension of neoclassical theory which has formalised some concepts such as synergy (economies of scope in this literature) at the expense of some richness and variety. It is not yet clear if and how contestable markets theory could be applied to problems of technological change, especially in view of Rumelt's comments above.

However, there are theoretical developments in the industrial organisation literature which may be regarded as being in broad sympathy with each other and the business policy literature. For example, the theory of the growth of the firm as developed by Penrose (1959) represents one such strand, and her work helped provide the foundations for what is now generally described as resource-based economics. Penrose described the firm as a pool of unique productive resources providing a bundle of potential services. In this approach, the nature and character of managerial resources both facilitates and limits the nature of corporate growth. The availability of unused productive services provides opportunities for expansion, diversification and innovation. The behavioural theory of the firm as developed by Simon and Cyert and March[28] represents another relevant strand in this literature. The behavioural school emphasises bounded rationality and decision-making processes in conditions where maximising behaviour is unattainable. Satisficing rather than maximising, objectives expressed as individual aspiration levels, and methods for resolving internal conflicts are important concepts here. It is the history, nature and aspirations of the individual in interaction with the environment that determines behaviour.

A recent development in this literature is the evolutionary theory of the firm of Nelson and Winter (1982).[29] This theory incorporates features from earlier analysis, such as Schumpeter's, the theory of the growth of the firm and behavioural theory. In this approach the firm is regarded as a system of limited economic capabilities stored in routines in which much knowledge is tacit and not articulated. These distinctive and limited skills, with possibly limited imitability options as far as competitors is concerned, contribute to the determination of the strategic development of the firm. History and irreversibility are important features of evolutionary theory.

A fourth literature, the transaction costs or markets and hierarchies approach, owes its roots to Coase (1937), but its modern development to Williamson (1975). Some of the relevant concepts were introduced in the earlier theoretical discussion on the behaviour of external markets. The transaction cost approach is concerned with comparative analysis of the efficiency implications of alternative methods of organising economic activity. The starting point is bounded rationality on the part of decision makers; markets have transaction costs associated with the costs of creating, maintaining and policing exchange agreements due to contract costs and costs associated with actual or potential opportunism on the part of contracting agents. Hierarchial alternatives such as firms may exhibit organisational costs as in the delay, loss and distortion of hierarchial information transmission and through pursuit of managerial sub-goals. Non-standardisation of assets, resource idiosyncrasy or task-specificity have important transactional implications that may influence the mode of economic organisation chosen[30].

While each of these literatures represents a distinct strand in its own right, the direct correspondences or potential complementarities outweigh the difference. Bounded rationality, true uncertainty, non-replicability, heterogeneity and firm-specific resource characteristics are integral to each of these theories or at least consistent with them. If we compare these basic constructs with Rumelt's analysis of the foundation of business policy, we can see that they are in general sympathy with the empirical observations of that literature also.

The foundations of the new theories contrast sharply with traditional economic theory by redefining the starting point for theoretical and empirical analysis. In the traditional approach, perception of profit opportunities leads to derived demand for factors of production; opportunity dictates resources. In the new theories there is a revised sequence (analogous to Galbraith's revised sequence of producers' sovereignty displacing consumers' sovereignty)[31] in which resources dictate opportunities. For example, routines (evolutionary theory), distinctive competencies (business policy literature),[32] synergies (Ansoff),[33] organisational slack (the behavioural school), unused productive resources (Penrose), firm-specific advantages (the 'eclectic paradigm' of multinational enterprise),[34] endogenous technological information (Dosi and Orsenigo 1985), contribute to the determination of the form and content of organisational change.

As far as any basis for contributing towards theories of technological rivalry is concerned, these theories tend to emphasise resource characteristics and innovation potential at the level of the firm. While some extensions of the Schumpeterian paradigm identified industry-specific characteristics such as technological opportunity as potentially important determinants of innovative activity, these approaches go even deeper and signpost firm-specific characteristics as central to questions of strategy and competition.[35]

There is a second major perspective which is likely to be important in any analysis of technological change, and that is the effect of bounded rationality on transaction costs and property rights. Approaches in the Schumpeterian tradition have typically not been greatly concerned with transaction-cost problems. However, both from the point of view of economic efficiency and corporate strategy, there are likely to be strong complementarities as far as the concepts of creative destruction and transaction costs is concerned. A Schumpeterian world of creative destruction unimpeded by transaction costs is unlikely, but, if transaction costs could be ignored, then efficiency problems would be trivial. If there were no transaction costs in capital, labour or product-markets, then the Schumpeterian process of creative destruction could take place frictionlessly with new technologies replacing old, and obsolescent bundles of resources being broken up with the components being smoothly reallocated to the next best alternative usage. Similarly, a transaction-cost world without Schumpeterian creative destruction would not be likely to pose major or interesting problems. In the absence of technological change, transactors in all markets would tend to be faced with familiar, replicable, standardised problems and minimal transaction costs. It is the existence of technological change which frequently creates problems of uncertainty, novelty and inequalities in information possessed by transactors, and associated transaction costs. In reality, it is the combination of both creative destruction and transaction costs which may generate and delineate important problems for corporate strategy and economic efficiency in technological dynamic environments.

The empirical analyses reviewed in the previous section, especially those concerned with joint ventures and licensing, illuminated problems of uncertainty, opportunism and strategic advantage which we might expect to be exacerbated by conditions of creative destruction. In this respect the marriage of the analysis of costs of governance with evolutionary theory may be particularly fruitful; the latter literature has spawned a branch of research concerned with the development of new technologies[36] that could benefit from fusion with analysis of costs of governance.

In the next section we shall consider possible relationships between theory development, further empirical analysis and policy formulation in the light of the discussion so far.

2.8.2   Theory development and implications

It is unfair to criticise Schumpeter for too narrow an expression of his thesis on the determinants of innovative activity. He wrote at a time when the industrial structure was characterised by specialised single-product firms, in which there was a one-to-one correspondence between the firm, its product and technology. Technologies could be shared between firms, but the firm itself was typically definable in terms of its associated product and technology. A steel firm produced steel products using steel-making technology. In such circumstances, concentrating on product-market structure was understandable, especially to the extent that technology was locked up within corporations and not exposed to the scrutiny of external markets as in outside financing, joint venture and licensing.

However, since World War II there have been major changes in the nature of corporate strategy that pose problems for the application of a simple, unsophisticated Schumpeterian model of the competitive process. As far as the evolution of internal markets are concerned, multinationalism, diversification, conglomerateness and the M-form internal organisation are all relevant phenomenan. As far as external markets are concerned, the growth of joint ventures and licensing agreements are obvious examples; however, there have also been major innovations in external capital markets, with the development of venture capital and the Unlisted Securities Market in the UK being examples. Government financing of R&D is another related issue, especially in defence industries.

We can illustrate selectively some of these recent developments by using examples drawn from the European aerospace in the matrix in Figure 2.1

Figure 2.1   Some issues in European aerospace

SINGLE / MULTIPLE	FIRM	PRODUCT	TECHNOLOGY
FIRM	/////////	CONCORDE	GE/SNECMA CFM 56 AERO ENGINE
PRODUCT	ROLLS-ROYCE	/////////	THE TURBO JET PRINCIPLE
TECHNOLOGY	AEROSPATIALE	AIRBUS A310	/////////

The matrix illustrates how complex interactions of multiple firms, multiple products and multiple technologies have replaced the simple single firm/product/technology relationship of Schumpeterian analysis. Rolls-Royce is a partly diversified firm producing multiple products; Aerospatiale is a highly diversified firm utilising and generating multiple technologies. The GE/SNECMA joint venture involves multiple firms, while both Concorde and the Airbus involve multiple firms and multiple technologies. A single technological paradigm like the turbojet has generated multiple products. The matrix is only intended to be illustrative, it is not definitive or complete. For example, Airbus Industrie is a multiple firm/multiple product/multiple technology combine.

It is this complex maze of rich interactions between combinations of firm, products and technologies that must be analysed if patterns of technological change are to be properly understood. The newer theories of industrial organisation may provide tools whereby such phenomena can be analysed. In particular, the concepts of corporate competencies, transaction costs and property-rights problems discussed earlier are likely to be fundamental issues in making sense out of this maze. The role of technological paradigms or trajectories, such as the turbojet above, is also likely to be a critical consideration. In addition, there may be insights and useful interpretation provided by using historical analysis in some cases. For example, Mowery and Rosenberg (1982 and 1985) provide analysis of technological change in the aircraft industry that tends to reinforce and complement transaction cost and evolutionary interpretations of how technological change may take place. The historical approach may be of particular relevance in a research area characterised by long time periods, irreversibility, novelty and heterogeneity.

The various strands of the newer theories on industrial organisation may contribute to analysis of such issues. In doing so, the implications of the concept of creative destruction are likely to undergo reinterpretation; for example, the development of guided missiles led to the replacement of many functions provided by existing military aircraft. However, while creative destruction was observable at the level of the technology, the firms that came to dominate the new technology tended to be those, like Boeing, that had been dominant in the obsolescing technology.[37] Creative destruction at the level of the technology may not be creative destruction at the level of the modern, diversified firm. Diversification, adaptability and distinctive competencies are all strategic issues that affect creative destruction at the level of the technology and the firm differently.[38]

These approaches and techniques may help to fill in the agenda implied in the extended research programme discussed earlier. As such they may incorporate Schumpeterian features such as product-market structure and creative destruction. However, the traditional Schumpeterian perspective itself is too limited to cope with the fundamental transformations that have characterised the evolution of modern industrialised economies.

2.9 SUMMARY

It has been advocated here that there is an urgent need to extend explicitly the Schumpeterian research programme to include both the effects of internal markets in the diversified firm and external markets in finance and technology. The Schumpeterian traditional product-market structure orientation now has to be augmented by efficiency considerations in intra-firm and inter-firm transfers of finance and technology. If these latter sets of markets provide effective enabling and incentive effects, product-market structure ceases to occupy the dominant position argued for it both by Schumpeter and his traditional critics.

In those circumstances, analysis of product-market structure must be integrated with analysis of the behaviour of internal and external markets. There is evidence that there may be efficiency problems associated with each of these strands of an extended research programme, and there is evidence that industry and firm effects may be significant and powerful. It has been suggested that opportunities exist for synthesising and integrating insights and analytical tools provided by a set of broadly sympathetic frameworks in business policy and the newer theories of industrial organisation. It is hoped that the discussion has helped to illuminate some guidelines that may be useful in reassessing the Schumpeterian tradition as well as in reinterpreting existing empirical analysis and possible redirections.

NOTES

1. An earlier version of this chapter was previously published as 'industrial structure, rivalry and innovation: theory and evidence', chap. 2 in P. Earl (ed.) (1996) *Management, Marketing and the Competitive Process*, Cheltenham: Edward Elgar; reprinted by kind permission of Edward Elgar, 8 Lansdown Place, Cheltenham, Glos GL50 2HU, UK.
2. Kamien and Schwartz describe the inefficiencies associated with monopoly managements' laziness as X-inefficiency, after Leibenstein (1966). However, it is more useful to regard laziness in this context as dynamic inefficiency. Leibenstein's analysis of X-inefficiency was really concerned with welfare effects under conditions of static technology, comparing this source of inefficiency with allocative inefficiency.
3. Fama identifies three potential sources of inefficiency; (1) transaction costs, (2) information not available to all investors, and (3) investors differ in their ability to interpret available information. Consistent with Williamson's (1975) interpretation of transaction costs, we regard all these potential sources of inefficiency as transaction costs.
4. The implications of separation of technological and economic indivisibility have been pursued in Teece (1980) and Kay (1982).
5. While the existence of efficient capital markets may contribute to X-inefficiency and dynamic efficiency, allocative inefficiency may still of course obtain, if profit maximising behaviour is adopted by the firm.
6. In fact, the conclusion resulting from a number of different studies in recent years is that market imperfections in general should not be sustainable as long as there is an absence of transaction costs resulting from deficiencies in information. Coase (1960) pointed out that, if property rights were clear and well defined, then efficient resource allocation will obtain through internalisation of externality effects, as long as transaction costs are absent. Demsetz (1968), Calabresi (1968) and Dahlman (1979) each contribute analysis indicating that monopoly and public goods can be regarded as sub-categories of externalities, and consequently elimination of their associated inefficiencies is possible if negotiating costs are indeed zero. See Kay (1984) for further discussion.
7. For further discussion on information asymmetries on market exchange, see Akerlof (1970). Williamson (1975) describes information impactedness as a condition in which information asymmetries are com-

bined with opportunism; it is the presence of potential opportunism that makes information asymmetries particularly problematic in efficiency terms.

8. The terms 'risk' and 'uncertainty' are often used interchangeably in this literature. We do not wish to enter into a debate on the applicability or otherwise of Bayesian interpretations of risk here. However, given the novel and non-recurring nature of innovation, we are using the Keynesian or Knightian concept of true or genuine uncertainty as non-quantifiable, non-measurable uncertainty. Innovation is not amenable to quantitative probability estimation techniques as in playing roulette or in actuarial analysis.

9. Bounded rationality is limitations on the capacity of the human mind to collect, assimilate, interpret and act on information in an objectively rational fashion. It reflects both the intention to be rational and information barriers to such a goal. See Simon (1957) for further discussion.

10. The moral hazard problem is frequently encountered in insurance markets. For example, if an individual insures a bicycle, it may encourage negligence (carelessness and indifference over securing against theft) or even fraudulent behaviour (selling the bicycle and claiming insurance).

11. This leads to a discussion of whether institutions should award R&D contracts on the basis of cost-plus (in which case the risk and uncertainty is borne by the contracting institution) or fixed price (in which case the risk and uncertainty is borne by the firm undertaking the R&D). In conditions of high levels of uncertainty, moral hazard and opportunism, the party expected to bear the risk may face very high transactions costs.

12. Contrary to Williamson's claim (1975: 13–16) moral hazard does not necessarily imply opportunism; carelessness and neglect need not be associated with deliberate deceit.

13. This cannot really be regarded as a defect or an omission on the part of Schumpeter, who wrote during an era of essentially single producer firms. The large corporation had usually evolved as such through horizontal and vertical integration, not diversification. Even Galbraith's later neo-Schumpeterian analysis appears more relevant to the large, functionally organised, vertically integrated firm than to divisionalised diversifiers; for example, his concept of the 'technostructure' implies a degree of cohesion and interaction more appropriate to a simple, specialised, functionally organised or U-form corporation, than to a complex, diversified, divisionalised of M-form corporation. The technostructure is 'an organised collection of individuals whose function is to bring to bear specialised knowledge in the development of corporate strategy. They direct the corporation and decide its policy' (Kay 1984: 130). The boundaries extend to all those who contribute information to corporate decision making, from manager to blue-collar worker (Kay, 1984: 202). Such a description appears difficult to apply to the M-form, in which fragmentation of managerial cabals, separation out of functional influence and creation of divisional profit centres are intended to create competitive internal markets orientated towards pursuit of profit without significant distortion due to pursuit of managerial sub-goals.

14. A fuller analysis of efficiency considerations would compare U-form to M-form as well as M-form to external markets. See Williamson (1975: 132–54) for comparative analysis in this area.

15. Most usually this is on a product group basis, but can also be process or geographical region.

16. A good example of a firm which exploits such diversification advantages is the 3M Corporation. Smith (1980) cites the example of the development of a non-woven fabric composite material by the company; applications were first explored in disposable diapers, then as seamless cups in bras. Expense provided a barrier in those areas, but a viable commercial application was finally discovered in surgical masks for doctors and nurses. With 45 000 products and 41 divisions in 1980, 3M was sufficiently diversified to provide a rich internal market for technological opportunities.

17. Though, of course, market structure may affect allocative efficiency. Here we concentrate only on exploitation of innovative profit opportunities.

18. This is not to understate the difficulties of empirical measurement and testing of the Schumpeterian thesis. For a thorough analysis of these issues, see Kamien and Schwartz (1982: 49–53).

19. Technological opportunity was typically defined as the extent to which the underlying scientific base facilitated innovation possibilities.

20. Kamien and Schwartz deal with decision-theoretic and game-theoretic models. In the former, many environmental variables are taken to be fixed, including intensity of rivalry; it is game-theoretic models that made the concept of rivalry and oligopolistic interdependence explicit and central to analysis.

21. The early 1980s saw a sharp rise in interest in modelling innovative behaviour using game-theoretic approaches. Dasgupta et al (1982) used a dynamic formulation to analyse the effect of market structure on R&D activity. Gilbert and Newbery (1982) provided a game-theoretic approach to the maintenance of monopoly power in innovation; Reinganum (1982) modelled optimal R&D resource allocation; Telser (1982) analysed optimal sequential search in research activity; Fethke and Birch (1982) analysed optimal timing of innovation; Wright (1983) modelled the patent search process; Brander and Spencer (1983), Tandon (1983) and Spence (1984) considered aspects of dynamic efficiency problems in innovative activity; De Brock (1985) considered the effect of rivalry on optimal patent life; Reinganum (1985) developed a game-theoretic rivalry model in which the possibility of a sequence of innovations is recognised. After this the literature expanded rapidly with considerable numbers of studies being produced. See Tirole (1988) for discussion of some of these.

22. Williamson (1975: 176–207) considers some implications of internal markets for technological innovation. One difficulty in Williamson's analysis in this context is that the only form of diversification recognised in this work is conglomerateness. To the extent that internal technology transfers may utilise market or technological links among the firm's product markets, limiting analysis of diversification in this fashion may be unsatisfactory.

23. Though they do discuss later the possibility that any overseas technology transfer (including to a subsidiary) may run the risk of loss of proprietary knowledge.

24. See also *The Economist* (1984) for an analysis of European high-technology joint ventures. They suggest that the problems and barriers encountered in making these agreements work relate to transaction cost problems of the type discussed above, especially opportunism or potential opportunism.

25. Tandon (1982) has used such an approach in analysing compulsory licensing as a means of dealing with the monopoly problem of patents, and Wilson (1977) introduced licensing as an option in a formal strategy rivalry model. Ordover and Willig (1985) tested various models of the effect of market power on innovative activity in research-orientated joint ventures and mergers.

25. Useful reviews of what constitutes the business policy field are also given by Bourgeois (1980), Jemison (1981), Leontiades (1982) and Bower (1982).

26. These arguments have also influenced the development of resource-based economics.

27. Neoclassical theory is concerned with the behaviour of markets not firms. Kay (1984) discusses the limitations of the traditional theory for the analysis of corporate strategy.

28. See especially Simon (1976) and Cyert and March (1963).

29. See also Nelson and Winter (1974), Winter (1984) and Iwai (1984a and b).

30. See Chapter 4 here and Kay (1997) for critiques of this approach

31. Galbraith's (1972) revised sequence derives from informational weakness on the part of consumers and shareholders. The managers are able to impose their own goals on the economic environment.

32. Hitt and Ireland (1985) include a brief survey of previous studies of distinctive competence in this literature. They summarise distinctive competence as representing those activities in which a firm or part of a firm does better relative to its competition.

33. Ansoff's concept of synergy refers to economies derivable from shared resources.

34. See Dunning (1981) for a statement and analysis of the eclectic paradigm in the theory of multinational enterprise.

35. The commercial aircraft industry is characterised by fierce technological rivalry, but the competition is determined by very different starting points as far as the relevant companies are concerned. For example, Newhouse (1982) quotes an aerospace industry analyst who remarked that, if he was building the Great Pyramids, he would get Lockheed to design them and Boeing to build them. Boeing's distinctive competence in manufacturing and Lockheed's in design are essential elements of the competitive process in this industry. Behaviour like this appears more consistent with the picture of rivalry portrayed in the newer theories of industrial organisation, than with the game-theoretic concept of rivalry.

36. In addition to Nelson and Winter (1982), see also Dosi (1984), Saviotti and Metcalfe (1984) and Sahal (1985) for analysis of how technological

regimes/paradigms may be specified and analysed. Such analysis may provide useful input into tracing the pattern and implications of any process of creative destruction.

37.   Simonson (1964) provides an analysis of the process of creative destruction in this industry.

38.   Simonson (1964) argues that airframe manufacturers' technological competencies in some aspects of the new technology (for example, in frame construction, power plants and guidance systems), combined with marketing competencies in selling to the government, frequently gave the aircraft manufacturers a competitive edge over electronic companies in the construction of larger missiles, despite the latter's control of what was widely regarded as the dominant, leading-edge technology.

3 How Economists Can Accept Shackle's Critique of Economic Doctrines Without Arguing Themselves Out of Their Jobs[1]

3.1 INTRODUCTION

The methodology of mainstream neoclassical economics deals with knowledge deficiency problems in a deterministic manner and as 'refinements to the theory of economic action rather than rudiments of it' (Coddington 1975: 151). For Shackle (1972), such an approach to the subject is unacceptable, since its deterministic nature is fundamentally at odds with his argument that, to be meaningful, choice must make a difference to the unfolding skein of events. Central to his view of the nature of choice is clearly a rejection of the concept of equilibrium and of the assumptive fiction that co-ordination is achieved, on a once-and-for-all basis, via the costless efforts of an omniscient auctioneer. If choices are meaningful in Shackle's sense, the skein of events contains many surprises, many incentives for agents to rethink their views of things and change their behaviour. For example, the workings of a multiplier process falsify expectations and these surprises may then spark off euphoric or depressing super-multiplier effects. In markets for financial assets, 'bulls' and 'bears' cannot both be right in their predictions, while in product-markets the creative exercise of marketing and R&D personnel's imaginations may continuously send out waves and backwashes in keeping with Schumpeterian notions of creative destruction. If one accepts Shackle's alternative starting point, one must sacrifice notions pertaining to 'given' preferences and technologies and, with them, the stable functions upon which IS-LM macro models[2] and orthodox value theory are built.

Few economists have been prepared to begin their analyses by focusing on the origins of choosers' beliefs and how they change, and then to use these choice-theoretic foundations as a basis for the study of non-equilibrium dynamics. Instead, the received wisdom has been that Shackle's contribution is eloquently presented but unduly nihilistic and, ultimately, self-denying. This chapter considers the validity of the conventional charge against Shacklean work by asking whether unpredictability and novelty are destructive of economic theorising in general, or whether we can make sensible statements about a world in which Shacklean notions of surprise and uncertainty are pervasive, even paramount. Our position is that it is, in fact, possible to reconcile a lack of faith in the usefulness of much model building based on a deterministic or probabilistic view of the world, with a belief that it is possible to develop useful explanatory theories of economic behaviour. Central to this reconciliation is a Shackle-inspired view of how one should see the role of the economists, and it is to this that we shall first proceed.

3.2   PREDICTABILITY AND POLICY FORMATION

It was very much with Shackle's (1967, 1982, 1973, 1974) 'fundamentalist' interpretation of Keynes's vision in mind that Coddington (1983: 61) made the following observation about the kind of Pandora's box opened for economic science by 'root and branch' adherents to a subjectivist position:

> If subjectivist logic is followed to the point of becoming convinced that there is nothing for economists to do but to understand certain (praxiological) concepts, then the only problem that remains is that of subjugating one's conscience long enough to draw one's salary in exchange for imparting this piece of wisdom. One could, of course, having got into this state of mind, spend a good deal of time and energy in trying to convince those who engage in macroeconomics, econometric model building, general equilibrium theory and so on, of the folly of their ways. But, that task accomplished, there would be nothing left but for the whole profession to shut up shop.

A similar stance concerning the policy contribution of fundamentalist Keynesians is taken by Cross (1982), who characterises, via a 'non-diagram', the position of those economists who emphasise the unpredictability of events. The 'non-diagram' shows a point in space depicting the current configuration of variables, with arrows leading off in all directions to depict what may happen next; there are no lines representing particular functional relationships.

It is by no means obvious that the pursuit of a subjectivist position has to be quite so 'indiscriminately destructive' (Coddington 1983: 50) as it is often taken to be. In particular, it is not obvious that, if one allows the future to be unknowable before its time and undetermined by past events, one has necessarily to jump to the polar opposite from perfect foresight and proclaim that we can say nothing about anything. The Shacklean perspective certainly does involve a rejection of the notion that economists should seek to make *single-line* predictions of what *will* happen. However, it does not deny that an economist might be able to contribute to the process of policy formation by providing insights on the *range of things* that *could* happen. To be sure, economists might frequently be surprised by what does happen in actuality, but they may be serving a useful role if they are less bemused and make less costly errors of advice concerning economic matters than would someone who lacked their special expertise.

It would appear that the economist who has accepted the Shacklean perspective can contribute to the process of policy formation in a variety of ways, all of which have a good deal in common with the functions served by those strategic thinkers in large corporations, whom Jefferson (1983) has characterised as 'scenario planners'. The economist can actively attempt:

1   to *highlight* the areas of uncertainty and delimit the bounds of lack of knowledge, given the existing structure of the system, so that the policy makers can have some appreciation of what disasters they might have to cope with or what opportunities they might be able to grasp (providing they make advance preparations) if they implement particular changes;
2   to *propose* improvements to the design of the system so that it is better able to cope with dangerous threats and creative opportunities as they materialise;
3   to *discover* ways of modifying or eliminating the incidence of surprises in the environment.

The economist seeking to undertake these tasks has only to admit defeat in situations where there are far too many potential sequels to policy choices.[3] The obvious question that follows from this is: 'How often should we expect the utter defeat of such an economist, who faces up to Shackle's vision of the scheme of things and does not shunt knowledge problems aside in a cavalier manner in order to make tightly specified predictions?' The answer is inevitably uncertain, but in the following sections of this chapter we hope to provide a basis for concluding that quite often the Shacklean economist may end up with something constructive to say.

3.3 SURPRISE, UNCERTAINTY AND EMERGENCE

Quite how unpredictable the subject matter of economics appears to be will vary according to the level of abstraction at which the economist attempts to make sense of it. Economic sub-systems, like smoke particles in a demonstration of Brownian Motion, may be moving around in a manner which seems to lack any pattern, yet higher-level economic sub-systems, like a puff of smoke drifting through the air, may be more stable and manageable and consequently explicable. For example, one could well imagine that an economist might end up 'failing to see the wood for the trees' if he sought to arrive at conclusions about possible sales in a market by looking at the behaviour of individuals who were each adapting in a complex manner to their own, individually perceived views of the environment. However, if the economist confined himself to market-level data[4] they might succeed in avoiding bewilderment in respect of possible future developments in that market.

In other disciplines, there has been considerable debate from an instrumentalist standpoint about the relative merits of reductionism and holism.[5] This is a debate from which economists have generally excused themselves, despite the emerging crisis in the profession. We view this as unfortunate, since the issues this debate raises may help indicate real opportunities for economic analysis and scenario construction.

Despite its professed concern with developing predictive models, traditional economic analysis remains, in principle if not always in practice, firmly and exclusively reductionist in treating as axiomatic the notion that the behaviour of the world can be described from the bottom upwards, in terms of aggregates. Shackle has rightly argued that the legitimacy of this approach is highly questionable, particularly in the context of attempts to understand speculative markets where traders are trying to out-guess each other's behaviour. However, the important point to be recognised in this connection is not so much that widespread crowd behaviour in the market place undermines traditional economic analysis, but that the 'problem' of non-decomposability can be a starting point for *novel questions* and possible solutions. Thus chemists do not have constantly to bear Heisenburg's Uncertainty Principle in mind, ecologists do not have to incorporate physio-chemical relations in their models, and a gravitational model of the solar system can safely ignore the complexity and variety of the natural world on Earth.

Such a holistic perspective has already been adopted by structuralists and systems theorists in their model building in other social sciences, yet most economists have tended to avoid anything which threatens 'bottom-up', aggregative models and decomposability. Neoclassical economists seem to be prepared to confine themselves to the questions which suit their methodology instead of displaying a willingness to embrace alternative methodologies. But one *can* grasp the nettle of undecomposability by employing non-reductionist methodologies – for example, we have made attempts to show how systems or structuralist approaches can provide insights on resource allocation questions that recognise the pervasiveness of unpredictability and uncertainty at lower levels. This work has encompassed consumer budgeting processes and the evolution of preferences in a social setting (Earl 1983a, 1983b, 1984a), corporate and organisational evolution and innovation (Earl 1984b; Kay 1979, 1982, 1984) and monetary policy (Dow and Earl 1982, 1984). Within these hierarchical research programmes it becomes apparent that, at higher levels, new questions, concepts and issues emerge, displacing those associated with lower levels. It is, therefore, only natural that new theoretical approaches and models should also emerge, displacing those associated with lower levels.

3.4 SCENARIO WRITING WITH KEYNESIAN UNCERTAINTY

Even after attempting to analyse problems at a variety of levels, the economist may, nonetheless, still feel that it is desirable (for example, in order to avoid oversights and spot potential for kaleidic change) to try to understand behaviour in the context of unpredictable change at the level at which such change takes place. If this level concerns that of individual decision makers, the economist should not be unduly perturbed if they happen to recall Keynes's famous comment to his critics on what he meant by 'uncertainty':

The sense in which I am using the term is that in which the prospect of a European war is uncertain, or the price of copper and the rate of interest twenty years hence, or the obsolescence of a new invention or the position of private wealth owners in the social system in 1970. About these matters there is no scientific basis on which to form any calculable probability whatever. We simply do not know.

(Keynes 1937: 214[6])

Shackle's rejection of expected utility theory and his emphasis on the flimsy expectational foundations of many decisions was, of course, both affected by, and is often juxtaposed with, this passage. It is easy to read from it the suggestion that people often have to take decisions while lacking any reasons for believing less in some possible sequels than in others. In such situations people are unable to form useful potential surprise curves, let alone probability distributions, and even Shackle's theory of deliberation in the face of uncertainty breaks down.

But all is not lost in such contexts. The possibility that decision makers may be unable to choose rationally does not necessarily ensure that the economist cannot offer reasoned advice which concludes that wide ranges of conjectured sequels should not be taken seriously. In fact, the recent work of Heiner (1983) leads us to the view that the behaviour of economic agents may be *less* surprising,[7] the greater the uncertainty with which they have to deal.

The basis for Heiner's rather paradoxical-sounding contention is as follows. Suppose that decision makers are very highly informed about the structures of the choice problems. If this is the case, they can confidently select complex, tailor-made solutions to them, on the basis of very detailed chains of reasoning. The economist trying to comprehend and anticipate their behaviour will not be able to obtain, far less handle, all the idiosyncratic information enjoyed by the multitude of their subjects. Consequently, it will seem to them that the successive choices of individuals lack consistency. Now consider situations where decision makers face choice-problems of great complexity and uncertainty: here, they will have no basis for choosing *particular* complex solutions. Rather – as Keynes (1937: 214), himself was quick to recognise) – their choices will tend to be made at a rather high level of abstraction, using tried and trusted *general* 'recipes for success'. The repeated use by individuals of such 'programmes' for dealing with situations in which they 'simply do not know' will enable the economist to discern some degree of consistency between their successive choices, which may provide a basis for fairly confident advice about what they could and could not reasonably be expected to try to do. In so far as the economist has access to resources for fieldwork investigations of how their subjects may be segmented into groups with common sets of programmes for dealing with complex problems, they should be able to construct useful scenarios about the bounds to possible market-level behaviour.

Choice environments that preclude 'rational' choice clearly pose major problems for orthodox forms of economic analysis. However, it would appear from the foregoing discussion that such problems can be overcome by making a switch in methodology in the direction of behaviour research and studying the procedures that decision makers actually use for coping with Keynesian uncertainty.

3.5 ORGANISATIONAL STRATEGIES FOR COPING WITH SURPRISE AND UNCERTAINTY

It might well be argued that a knowledge of decision-making units' repertoires of action programmes is of limited use to the scenario-writing economist who cannot successfully anticipate the environmental shocks with which the decision makers will have to deal. Even the most creative scenario writers may on occasion recognise that they are being asked to deal with environments that are full of surprises – actual events which they fail to consider as possibilities. However, an inability to specify or define stimuli in advance does not necessarily mean that the economist cannot draw up scenarios concerning how particular systems may fare, and which policy measures might usefully change their fortunes. The economist should at least be able to classify and order environments in terms of key characteristics – for example, stability/turbulence, static technology/dynamic technology – before considering ways in which the decision makers might seek to cope with different patterns. Even though their individual events may be unpredictable, different kinds of turbulent environments may display particular regularities or patterns, signalling the need for appropriate system design or procedure if the decision maker is to operate and survive in their own particular, turbulent environment. Thus although the economist may, like their subjects, be unable to predict the unpredictable, at a higher level of abstraction it may be possible to expect the unexpected, as Boulding (1968) has suggested.

The task of the economist preparing for surprise and reacting to it in respect of environments that are classified in one way or another as 'surprise rich' may be likened to that of policy makers called upon to deal with aspects of mental illness. People with mental disorders may act unpredictably and thereby seem a menace to the rest of the community; their unpredictability may actually be the only consistent feature of their personalities. But individual societies still manage to evolve *specific* social, legal, psychiatric and police systems and procedures to deal with such problems. Likewise, while speculative behaviour in financial markets may be directionally unpredictable, economic advisers standing on the sidelines may still be able to devise policies – such as 'lifeboat' buffer loan agreements between the Central Bank and major clearing banks, and deposit insurance schemes – to deal with the kinds of problems, such as the failure of financial intermediaries, in which it is prone to result.

The economist may have a good deal to learn from the study of how organisations, like societies, develop devices and methods for dealing with surprising events. One method is to design the system deliberately so as to enhance its prospects for adapting to change in a flexible manner. Burns and Stalker (1961) explicitly recognise Shackle's work on potential surprise as a precursor to their own which is concerned with the appropriateness of different organisation designs for coping with alternative environments. In the light of case-study investigations, they argue that 'organic systems' (characterised by continual adjustment and redefinition of tasks, 'authority' residing in expertise rather than hierarchical position, and predominantly lateral rather than vertical communication and delegation of authority and control) tend to be more appropriate for rapidly changing conditions that generate fresh problems and unforeseen circumstances. By way of contrast, a mechanistic system (characterised by precise specialisation and division of labour and vertical hierarchical relationships emphasising superior/subordinate responsibilities) may be more suitable for stable conditions. Child (1977: 90) sees matrix management systems – discussed in detail in Child 1977, chap. 4 – adopted by many modern firms as potentially enjoying many of the advantages of the 'organic' system described by Burns and Stalker. Such findings have an obvious significance for the economist called upon to comment on a possible rescue plan for a 'lame duck' corporation; if it has a mechanistic structure and the environment is turbulent, the chances of saving it may be slim in the absence of a major restructuring operation, and established practices may be something the existing personnel would find very hard to abandon.

Another broad strategy commonly employed for coping with turbulent environments is to devise methods of localising and limiting the danger posed by external threats, even if the source or form of the threat cannot even be approximately specified in advance. If individual sub-systems can be decoupled from the overall system without threatening the latter's integrity or survival, then this may form the basis of system design in such environments (and, if it does not, the economist may consider proposing incentives, regulatory changes or direct intervention to redesign the system accordingly). Following Simon (1969), we would expect that, after a period of environmental turbulence, the surviving systems would be found to be those that had exhibited a good deal of decomposability. However, since decoupling is not without its costs, we would only expect to find organisations adopting decoupling strategies, in areas where previously they had sought the benefits of integration, at the time of the onset or expectation of a period of turbulence.

The following rather disparate collection of examples should help clarify what we mean by decoupling, as well as indicating how common it is. Firstly, we note that in some cases the development of revolutionary political parties has been characterised by the adoption of a cellular system, in which small groups of activists operate independently without clear knowledge of the identity of members associated with other cells. Even if one cell is uncovered and broken up, their self-contained and limited knowledge means that the survival of other cells may not be directly threatened by exposure. The development of modular production systems is a related strategy in so far as it facilitates decoupling and reassembly: the progressive upgrading of a system of hi-fi 'separates' (as distinct from a 'music-centre') and the adaptability of a module-based degree course are cases in point, for they permit the decision maker to change direction in response to changing circumstances as time unfolds; he or she is not locked into an inflexible strategy. The conglomerate strategy may provide similar advantages in the managerially controlled firm: the decomposability of a strategy based on unrelated product markets means that both divestment of old divisions and formation of new divisions may be undertaken in isolation without strategists having to be too concerned with any relation of the part to the whole. Thus the conglomerate may exploit the flexibility and adaptability features of modular design. It is commonplace to argue that a diverse collection of product-markets helps generate earnings stability by averaging out the performances of various differently fluctuating but ongoing activities. Less widely appreciated, however, is the fact that the decomposability of a conglomerate firm means that if any part of its operations is threatened – say, with obsolescence – the unrelatedness of the part with the whole limits the possibility that the rest of the system also will be threatened. Thus the conglomerate may limit the damage posed by external threats to sub-systems, just as in the case of the political cell system.

It may seem paradoxical to identify desirable survival properties associated with some decomposable systems, in view of our argument that non-decomposability may be an important feature of economic systems. In fact, the conglomerate is a special case, and usually decomposability will only have limited applicability in its description: for example, the absence of product-market linkages between groups may facilitate decoupling of individual divisions, while the existence of linkages between product markets within divisions may inhibit decoupling of individual products. The conglomerate is typically a complex multi-level organisation whose system description may alter as we move between levels.

Further, the conglomerate is only one type of diversified system that may be set up – with or without the participation of the economic policy maker – to deal with turbulent environments. For example, Rumelt (1974) describes the development of the 'related-linked' strategy which has recently become significant in US industry. An example of this kind of strategy would be a manufacturer of industrial clothing who diversified into ladies' clothes and then into toiletries and cosmetics. In the first move, there are likely to be technological links (shared production techniques, R&D and so on), while the second move is more likely to exploit marketing links (for example, shared distribution channels, advertising and image). Thus the firm is built around a series of market or technological links between groups of products and yet no single link dominates the corporate strategy. While decoupling may be inhibited due to these linkages, the diversified nature of such a strategy should, as in the conglomerate, help to localise and limit most external threats.[8]

Organisation design is, therefore, an important device for dealing with unstable and unpredictable environments. We would hope that, as they seek to piece together scenarios and policy advice, organisational matters are rarely far from the economist's mind (or, for that matter, the corporate planner's). Consider, for example, how monetary policy acquires an altogether different complexion once it is seen not merely in terms of debates about the appropriate type and size of money-supply target, but also from the perspective concerning the structure of links between the financial institutions involved in the process of credit creation. Once one recognises the layered nature of modern financial systems – where scrambles for liquidity can take place in the context of one bank's assets being another's liabilities – it becomes less easy to countenance the withdrawal of lender-of-last-resort facilities as a means to achieving a monetary base target. The organisational perspective thus helps in the generation of cautionary scenarios, yet it may help also to provide justifiable grounds for optimism: for example, a layered financial system *might* turn out to be sectorally segmented in a way which ensured, say, that industrial production and employment were largely immune from a property-market crash.[9]

Organisations seeking to maintain flexibility when confronting a turbulent environment have yet other defence mechanisms that protect and insulate them from unpleasant shocks: they can hold cash, engage in multiple sourcing of inputs, lease rather than buy and avoid long-term contracts. These kinds of behaviour can be anticipated in alert organisations and promoted in sleepy or impulsive ones. As Loasby (1967) warns, flexibility and adaptability may be impaired if formal planning leads to an over-enthusiastic commitment of resources; it may be rational to defer some decisions until the future unfolds, and devices such as the above may enhance responsiveness in unpredictable environments. One would expect organisations confronting treacherous but foggy landscapes either to make tentative explorations in a variety of directions (see Waddington 1977) and avoid crucial, large-scale experiments until they can see how the land lies, or, like Eisenhower, to utilise the 'delay principle' (see Ansoff 1979: 53) and defer decisions altogether until all essential information is available or the fog has cleared. The economist should not be ashamed to offer policy advice that involves similar kinds of behaviour: procrastination can have its efficiency advantages.

3.6 ANTICIPATING SURPRISE

The previous section was concerned with ways in which economists, like economic systems themselves, may seek to prepare for surprises and react to them. The decision-making systems were those portrayed as passive in the face of external developments; they did not actively attempt to change or eliminate unpredictable developments in their environments, though their strategies might facilitate the generation and development of benign surprises internally (for example, a firm's structure may be such that it creates a conducive atmosphere for R&D). Our essential theme was that system design can be adjusted to cope better with creative opportunities and dangerous threats as they materialise.

However, another line of attack is to focus on policies to modify or eliminate the incidence of surprises. For example, cartelisation and collusive or co-operative behaviour are means by which economic systems may be able to pre-empt future dangers of competitive attack. Cyert and March (1963) describe the process of neutralising competitors' threat as one of creating a 'negotiated environment'. Uncertainty, surprise and threat are bargained away. Much of the descriptive literature on monopoly behaviour can be interpreted in this fashion, displaying a richer and more complex decision-making process than is typically contained in neoclassical models of monopoly and oligopoly. By recognising the prevalence of such attempts to preclude surprises, the economist is not merely able to narrow down the range of possible occurrences in the contexts in which the attempts are taking place, but is also able, once more, to pursue similar approaches in the kinds of policies they recommend.

In fact, at the level of government policy making, many proposals can be interpreted as intentionally reducing the possibility of unpleasant or destabilising surprises. Friedman's development of monetarism can also be, at least partly, interpreted as intending to reduce the surprise potential of environments faced by economic decision makers. Friedman sees stable monetary growth as a means of engendering confidence and predictability by eliminating this area as a major source of possible surprise and instability.[10] Indexation and indicative planning are two other policy measures that have been at least partially justified in similar fashion in so far as they deal with potential sources of ignorance and uncertainty.

Successful pre-emptive policy 'strikes' are, of course, contingent upon creative thinking about what could happen. It is here that many economists would tend to highlight the nihilistic message in Shackle's critique of deterministic model building; for he seems to suggest that, although creative thinking can only take place within the limited set of reference points that decision makers *already* have at their disposal, the number of new possibilities which they could nonetheless dream up is immense. In his most recent book, Shackle makes this point particularly vivid by likening the reference points to alphabetic elements and then noting (1979: 21) that a small set of alphabetic elements can generate a huge dictionary. From this standpoint, it would seem unreasonable to hope that the economist (or the corporate planner) would be very successful in trying to anticipate the creative thoughts of decision makers. There would appear much scope for missing ideas that came to their minds and for becoming paranoid about those that did not.[11]

A possible way round this problem emerges in the work of Ansoff (1979), who developed an analysis of corporate response to strategic surprises (novel, unexpected, rapidly developing environmental threats having a potentially significant effect on the organisation's performance), based partly on the earlier work of Cyert and March. He argued that many potential strategic surprises could be avoided or better dealt with if organisations develop techniques to recognise and act on 'weak signals' from the environment. Ansoff's work implies that the degree of potential surprise associated with many developments could be reduced if devices for recognising and amplifying weak signals (early hints and clues) can be introduced. The analyst might then be more confidently able to pin down the channels down which creative thinking could be proceeding. For example, Ansoff points out that in the early 1940s there was a general sense of expectation of important break-throughs and developments in electronics; the early post-war period made it clear to experts that the break-through would materialise as the transistor; and so on. Recognition of weak signals at an early stage would allow the organisation to prepare for subsequent development, just as exploration can be made safer with the aid of scouting parties.

Ansoff's analysis is interesting, though he does not really deal with the problem that weak signals of impending shocks are easier to identify with the benefit of hindsight. *Ex ante* anticipation of future shocks requires sorting out significant signals from background noise, and this trick is not easily achieved. For example, it is easy to detect weak signals in the aerospace industry in the early post-war period to the effect that the future of commercial aviation lay in VTOL and SST developments, less easy to detect that jumbo jet travel would soon dominate.

3.7 COGNITIVE AND STRATEGIC BARRIERS TO KALEIDIC THOUGHTS AND ACTIONS

Shackle's emphasis on the potential for discontinuous shifts in economic systems – potential which arises from the creative powers of human minds – seems to rest uneasily with the inertia that one observes in much individual and organisational behaviour. In some degree, this may be explained by the use of programmed decision methods instead of deliberative approaches to choice; by simple procrastination instead of abrupt reactions to perceived environmental changes; by the existence of constraining long-term contracts (other than those which are so onerous in the fact of a disturbance that they involve bankruptcies – see Minsky, 1975); and, more generally, by the existence of various forms of slack which help make the system 'shatter-proof' and dampen the effects of disturbances which might otherwise have been amplified (cf. Leijonhufvud 1973).

In this section we wish to emphasise two further possible explanations of inertia, an appreciation of which may enable the economist better to argue when and where discontinuous shifts of behaviour might, and might not, be reasonably expected. First we note that decision makers will have strong incentives to resist changes wherever they are dealing with highly integrated systems that are highly specific in their purpose. The costs of change when such systems are threatened with obsolescence will be such as to make worthwhile attempts to force the environment back into conformity with the system's capacities. If such Procrustean efforts fail, of course, the non-decomposability of the obsolete system then guarantees precisely the kind of revolutionary, kaleidic shift discussed in Shackle's work.

For example, for someone who has an old car that is becoming increasingly prone to unreliability, a decision to make a commitment to the purchase of a new one may be revolutionary in nature. Often it will follow a long period during which expensive repairs are made to the old car because each time an individual part wears out it threatens to immobilise the car, both physically and as a saleable item. Each repair involves the decision maker in staking his judgemental capabilities on the possibility that further breakdowns are not just around the corner. The business history literature is full of parallel examples of periods of last-ditch stands, followed by revolutionary upheavals (see Earl 1984b: chap. 5). An especially pertinent case involving a highly integrated production process concerns the Ford Motor Company at the time of the obsolescence of the Model T. In his attempt to keep the product viable, once he conceded that further price cuts no longer increased market penetration in a profitable manner, Henry Ford reluctantly went against his own principles and advertised it. When eventually production was abandoned and the changeover to the Model A and a general policy of frequent model changes was undertaken, the 18-month disruption involved $200 million losses for Ford, 60 000 workers being laid off in Detroit, with 15 000 machine tools being replaced and another 25 000 totally rebuilt. In the process, too, many of the workers' skills were rendered obsolete in so far as they related to the task idiosyncrasies (cf. Williamson 1975) of producing the Model T rather than those of coping with assembly-line methods in general. But despite the far-reaching physical upheaval entailed in Ford's belated attempt to match his production system with a more turbulent, styling-dominated market, forces of inertia remained. As Selznick (1975: 110) points out, only after World War II was an in-depth reorganisation completed; initially, necessary changes in orientation and in the hitherto lowly status of sales and public-relations functions failed to materialise.

The mention of Henry Ford's 'principles', and of the difficulties his company had in achieving changes in orientation, relate to our second point: the fact that a creative mind can throw up many fantastic new potential hopes and fears, even from a limited collection of existing perspectives, does not mean we should jump to the conclusion that such a mind will deem them *believable* conjectures. Central to Shackle's potential surprise analysis is an assumption that choosers seek to discriminate between rival possible sequels on the basis of how easily they can be disbelieved – that is to say, according to the grounds they can imagine for arguing that events could not happen. In the potentially kaleidic mind a tension therefore exists, between creative processes that open up possibilities and creative processes that, by throwing up possible objections, seek to close off possibilities. In the midst of this there appears to be a problem of infinite regress: objections to possible sequels are themselves possible sequels that must be able to stand up to objections if they are not to be disbelieved.

For his part, Shackle did not, so far as we are aware, devote much attention to the means by which degrees of disbelief come to be assigned to particular sequels, nor to the infinite regress problem we have just raised. Rather, he preferred to take potential surprise curves as already existing in the minds of decision makers, though only as tentative constructs, possibly ripe for imaginative revision. This has left the path wide open for critics such as Coddington (1983: chap. 4) who make accusations of nihilism after characterising Shackle's (and other fundamentalist Keynesians') analyses using the ideas of 'the spontaneous and erratic workings of individual minds ... to drive a wedge between behaviour and circumstances' (Coddington 1983: 53).

A natural counter to this charge, and one which deals with the infinite regress problem, is to argue that assignments of degrees of disbelief can be traced back to a self-imposed hierarchy of *rules* according to which the decision maker organises their view of the world. That is to say, individual minds are to be seen, not as erratic, but as *judgemental systems* for processing creative suggestions. On the surface, behaviour may at times seem without consistency, but it is actually constrained by an underlying set of procedures. If the economist can access the structures of judgemental systems employed by representative members of segments of the decision-making population, they may be able to infer which possibilities they would find unbelievable if they imagined them. Thence they could narrow down the bounds of their possible choices and anticipate, with some degree of confidence, their inertia in particular areas.

This view of the mind as a system of judgemental rules which also generates creative suggestions subject to an existing set of reference perspectives is one which we take from the work of the psychologist George Kelly (1955). Like Shackle, Kelly is at pains to depict choice as a forward-looking, theory-testing exercise, with choices being made among images that decision makers construct for themselves. Kelly (1955: 59), too, emphasises that people have a finite number of blinkers through which they attempt to make sense of the world. But he goes beyond Shackle when he stresses that an individual's theories are interrelated in ways which are relatively immovable, so that any newly imagined ways of construing events are tested for admissibility (rather like submissions in a courtroom proceeding) against these prior tenets. As he puts it (1955: 20), 'the structure we erect is what rules us'. New thoughts that threaten to destroy existing expectations will be deemed inadmissible, unless, that is, a failure to admit them would actually clash with the maintenance of expectations that have been assigned an even higher ranking in the person's hierarchy of ideas.[12]

If a person's expectations and theories are related in this hierarchical manner, with one notion often being used as a judgemental reference point for many others, then the spillover effects of admitting a particular new notion may be considerable. The situation is rather akin to that which a neoclassical economist would face if they had to give up the notion of maximising behaviour as one of the central, 'hard-core' assumptions of their research programme.[13] Thus, we would expect that the more subordinate implications are attached to a particular notion (or 'construct', in Kelly's terms), the more a person will resist accepting new ideas that entail their changing the notion. This has been found to be the case in work by Hinkle

(1965) and Crockett and Meisel (1974), where subjects' attitudes were investigated using developments of research techniques pioneered by Kelly. These research techniques[14] could equally well be used by economists seeking to uncover the bounds of their subjects' abilities to believe new notions and thence their resistance to making kaleidic shifts of behaviour.[15] In fact, some of these techniques are already in use in market research.

A Kelly-inspired view of expectations does not preclude the notion that people will make Shacklean shifts of outlook as a result of creatively exercising their imaginations. But it does suggest that such changes – and associated changes of outward behaviour – will occur mainly at the sub-system level. Ideas with really dramatic damaging implications for a person's outlook will only be admissible if a *failure* to admit them would, by virtue of the higher-level contradictions this entailed, result in even more alarming implications. Otherwise, they will tend to be ruled 'out of court' as 'unbelievable'. Thus, for example, most of us may find it easier to imagine we might select tea instead of coffee, than to imagine we might one day find ourselves in the dole queue or choose to give up our possessions and opt for a monastic way of life. Thoughts that contradict our beliefs concerning social institutions or our own self-images will be particularly hard to accept as serious possibilities, for so much of our daily outlook is contingent on these core constructs.

To conclude this section, it is instructive to note that Kellian psychologists have analysed thought-disordered schizophrenia as being due to successive attempts by sufferers to introduce decomposability into their judgemental systems. By severing links between ideas, they seek to reduce the implications of expectational falsifications in a surprising world. Unfortunately, such a policy leads to completely inconsistent thinking if applied repeatedly: lacking any anchor points – any principles – for forming beliefs, the sufferer believes one thing one moment, another the next. In his outlook he is as flexible as corporate planners who have sought to deal with the possibility of unpleasant environmental surprises by moving in the direction of a conglomerate activity set or, in the extreme, to becoming simple portfolio investors who only own parts of any production system. Such planners can make rapid and kaleidoscopic changes of activities via the stock market; they are not constrained by linkages when they want to shed interests. But, taken to extremes, strategies that pursue decomposability can result in confusion rather than the ability to deal with surprises. An individual suffering from thought-disordered schizophrenia can find themselves at the mercy of events due to the fluidity in their outlooks. Their mind is the prototype of the 'spontaneous and erratic' mind in Coddington's critique of subjectivism, while, as Adams-Webber (1979: 66; emphasis added) observes, 'the experience of such [a person], in so far as we can imagine it, must seem hopelessly *kaleidoscopic*'. Investors, whose eagerness to diversify is on a par with the ability of schizophrenics to take on new perspectives, often encounter analogous problems: the more activities in which they are involved, the less insight they can have into any of them. This, coupled with their reluctance to exploit scope or synergy (or, in the 'portfolio investor' extreme, to direct operations at all) means they may be unable to generate performances which match those achieved by specialists, even if the business environments in which they participate are in some degree turbulent.[16]

3.8 CONCLUSIONS

From the standpoint of conventional economics, it is not easy to see Shackle's emphasis on the centrality of ignorance and uncertainty in economic affairs as providing anything other than a means whereby economists might argue themselves out of their jobs. A Shacklean adherence to a hard line on the non-quantifiable nature of uncertainty and the pervasiveness of ignorance and surprise naturally leads to an emphasis on the unpredictable and subverts the principle and practice of economic model building that has evolved as the accepted basis for modern economic analysis.

From the standpoint of behavioural economics, Shackle's critique of orthodoxy seems to serve a constructive, not nihilistic role. It clears the ground for alternative approaches to pattern finding and theory building by economists, who, we have argued, may use the following escape routes as means to delimit the bounds of possible sequels to particular policy and environmental disturbances:

1 *holistic* analysis where higher level systems are more stable than sub-systems;
2 the practical study of *procedures* employed by decision makers as bases for choice in situations of Keynesian uncertainty;
3 attempts to classify environments by type (for example, 'surprise rich', 'surprise poor') and then to analyse the relation between system and environment;

4   recognition that decision-making units do not simply react to unpredictable change in their environments, creating predictability, order and control out of potential chaos;

5   attempts to assess the extent and structure of linkages between physical structures, and between ideas, for these constrain what can be undertaken and thought, and provide a basis for anticipating either inertia or kaleidic shifts and the amplification of disturbances.

The first escape route leaves much or all of the uncertainty behind at lower levels while the remainder may, at best, enable policy makers actively to exploit the opportunities presented by unexpected developments, or at worst, permit a damage limitation exercise. These escape routes all approach the problem laterally rather than directly: instead of attempting to predict the unpredictable, they find devices which permit the uncovering of behaviour relations and patterns in human activity.

NOTES

1.   This chapter is co-authored with Peter Earl and was originally published in the *Journal of Economic Studies*, 12, (1985): 34–48). This was an issue of the journal devoted to celebrating the work of George Shackle, and the article is reprinted here by kind permission of the publishers, MCB University Press.

2.   See Shackle (1982).

3.   Of course, how many believable sequels are 'far too many' to be tolerable will vary according to how open-minded and reconciled to uncertainty the economist is, and/or who their paymaster happens to be.

4.   In the manner of, say, Houthakker and Taylor (1970).

5.   Cf. Koestler and Smythies, (1969) and Hofstadter, (1979: 310–36).

6.   See also Keynes (1936: 161–2) concerning animal spirits and investment behaviour.

7.   At least to an economist familiar with contributions to the literature of behavioural theory, such as those by Simon (1957, 1969, 1979) and Steinbrunner (1974: chapt. 3).

8.   See Kay (1982 and 1984) for further discussion.

9.   See, further, Dow and Earl (1982: chaps. 11 and 12).

10.   However, his failure to examine the structure of relationships between monetary institutions results in his blindness to the possibility that monetary base control could actually run counter to the stability of the monetary system.

11.   The latter would be a stronger possibility the more that decision makers actually behaved in a programmed manner and themselves avoided trying to dream up possible scenarios before choosing.

12. In the latter case, the new ideas would be admitted at the cost of the rejection of the lower-level notions that they contradict.
13. Lakatos' (1970) well-known hard-core/protective belt separation in his views of scientific research programmes is very similar to Kelly's view of the use of a hierarchy of ideas by an individual seeking to form expectations in everyday life. In both cases some notions are deemed to have priorities over others, for maintenance in the face of anomalies.
14. Described in detail in Adams-Webber (1979).
15. See Earl (1984a) for some suggestions of how these techniques might be applied and some contexts in which they might be particularly revealing.
16. See, further, Earl (1984a: 115–19.

4 Markets, False Hierarchies and the Evolution of the Modern Corporation[1]

4.1 INTRODUCTION

Transaction-cost economics, or the markets and hierarchies framework, has emerged in recent years as an important new approach for dealing with a variety of problems in industrial organisation. Although Coase (1937) provided an early statement of the role of costs of using the market in encouraging firm organisation to replace market exchange in certain circumstances, the development of transaction-cost economics as a coherent and systematic industrial organisation framework did not take place until the 1970s. The rediscovery, development and refinement of transaction-costs as a possible analytical tool is due in large part to Oliver Williamson, whose outline of the framework is contained in three works. The initial statement, *Markets and Hierarchies* (1975; henceforth M&H) provided an integration and synthesis of some earlier applications of transaction-cost economics in areas such as internal labour markets, vertical integration, conglomerates and the economics of internal organisation. Recently, his *Economic Institutions of Capitalism* (1985; henceforth EIC) has further extended the boundaries of transaction-cost economics, remaining broadly consistent with M&H and integrating many of its earlier arguments in the text. In addition, *Economic Organisation* (1986; henceforth EO) is a selected set of essays, some in transaction-cost economics and some from an earlier period in Williamson's work. For our purposes, EIC may be taken as a definitive and current statement of Williamson's approach to economics though both of the other works extend the analysis in significant respects.

We recognise the seminal contribution made by Williamson in this area. His work has rightly attracted considerable interest both inside and outside economics, and has acted as a direct or indirect stimulus to much recent research activity on the organisation and behaviour of the modern corporation. However, in this chapter we suggest that there are critical problems in transaction-cost economics as interpreted by Williamson. It is argued below that transaction-cost economics as at present constituted displays critical flaws that may impede and even prevent the realisation of its ambition to provide a useful explanatory framework in industrial organisation.

In Section 4.2 we briefly outline Williamson's transaction-cost approach. In Section 4.3 we look at problems associated with the contractual basis of Williamson's framework, and then go on to look at conceptual limitations and associated problems with the approach in Section 4.4. In Section 4.5 we look at substantive issues and problems raised by Williamson's analysis of the evolution of the modern corporation before finishing with a short concluding section.

4.2 THE TRANSACTION-COST APPROACH

Although many complex and sophisticated structures can and have been built on transaction-cost principles, its foundations are simple and straightforward. Three concepts form the basis of transaction-cost analysis: bounded rationality (cognitive and language limits on individuals' abilities to process and act on information), asset specificity (specialisation of assets with respect to use or users), and opportunism (self-interest seeking with guile).

If bounded rationality, asset specificity and opportunism co-exist, this may pose efficiency problems for the market mechanism. Interestingly, if *any* of the three conditions do not exist, then, Williamson argues, the market mechanism will still allocate resources effectively; contracts face trivial problems of governance and execution. Firstly, if there are no bounds on rationality, all future contingencies may be anticipated and incorporated into contractual agreements. Unbounded rationality excludes the possibility of unexpected events not allowed for in the contract, and so both or all parties may settle all problems from the outset. Contract may therefore be relied on to settle issues arising from problems of opportunism or asset specificity. Secondly, if asset specificity does not exist, then bounded rationality and opportunism are not serious problems. If assets can be easily transferred in and out of alternative uses then mistakes can be quickly and simply rectified and opportunism does not have continuing or lasting effects. Finally, if opportunism is not a problem, then asset specificity and bounded rationality are not serious impediments to the working of the market mechanism. For example, if the transacting world is populated by saints rather than opportunists, a simple promise to deal with future unexpected problems and surprises in a mutually fair and equitable manner should be sufficient to ensure the smooth functioning of the market mechanism (EIC: 30–2).

Therefore, if any one of these conditions – bounded rationality, asset specificity, opportunism – does not exist, contract can be relied upon to deal with resource allocation problems smoothly and effectively. At first sight, this would appear to create a fairly strong case in favour of the apparent power and flexibility of the market mechanism. However, Williamson argues persuasively that situations in which all of these conditions exist are significant and pervasive problems in economic organisation. In these circumstances the market imperative is replaced by a broader imperative: to '*Organise transactions so as to economise on bounded rationality while simultaneously safeguarding them against the hazards of opportunism*' (EIC: 32; italics in original). At this point the analysis evolves into comparative analysis of alternative governance structures for organising transactions. For any given economic activity there usually exists a wide range of potential institutional forms within which it can be organised, ranging from centralised hierarchies at one extreme to traditional market contracting at the other, with mixed or intermediate modes in between. The issues then becomes one of which institutional form is the most efficient in terms of organising the specific activity.

The comparative basis of the analysis involves the recognition that all forms of economic organisations are likely to encounter problems in handling and processing the information involved in resource allocation if all these conditions of bounded rationality, asset specificity and opportunism are present. For example, market transactions may involve expensive legal contracting, time-wasting haggling, and costly monitoring, all of which may constitute transaction-costs. One solution may be to internalise the activity and so reduce transaction-costs. Internal monitors such as supervisors or boards of directors are likely to be better informed (through experience and improved access to better quality and quantity of information) and in cases where individual performance can be ascertained, have available a more immediate direct range of rewards and penalties than may be available in the market place. Therefore, internal organisation of the transaction may be more efficient than market contracting in some circumstances to the extent it reduces bounded rationality problems and curbs opportunism. Consequently, the existence of transaction-costs may encourage expansion of corporate boundaries through merger, takeover or internal expansion.

However, such internalisation is unlikely to be costless. In practice, enlargement of the bureaucracy through internalisation is likely to lead to impairment of incentives (EIC: 131–62). Markets involve what Williamson calls high-powered incentives such as profits and losses. These incentives may be blunted or sacrificed by internalisation. Promises to act efficiently made by internal actors in the resource allocation process are not costlessly enforceable. The bureaucracy may be more permissive and forgiving with respect to inefficient activity than is the impersonal world of the market place. Williamson argues that efficiency will tend to encourage the appearance and continuance of the least cost alternative in different cases. Comparative analysis of firms and markets also permits the analysis to be extended into related areas of state intervention such as in antitrust policy and allocation of franchises.

These concepts and principles constitute the basic foundations of transaction-cost economics. In the next three sections we shall discuss analytical difficulties associated with Williamson's approach, starting with the transactional nature of hierarchy in his framework.

4.3 TRANSACTION AND HIERARCHY IN WILLIAMSON'S APPROACH

In the beginning there were markets' (EIC: 87). Williamson deliberately uses this perspective as a starting point from which to analyse the problem of parties to the transaction, 'designing governance structures related to their contracting needs'. Only when market problems such as transaction-costs create pressures for internalisation might the transaction be removed from external market exchange (EIC: 87). Thus, 'one of the attractive attributes of the transaction-cost approach is that it reduces, essentially, to a study of contracting (EO: 197). This perspective is carried to the logical conclusion of analysing hierarchy in contractual terms, 'if one or a few agents are responsible for negotiating all contracts, the contractual hierarchy is great. If instead each agent negotiates each interface separately, the contractual hierarchy is weak' (EIC: 221). While Williamson acknowledges that hierarchy may also be analysed in decision-making terms (EIC: 221), it is the contractual interpretation of hierarchy which tends to infuse subsequent analysis of hierarchy in EIC.

The problem with using *contracting* as a basis for analysing hierarchy is that it extends exchange-based perspectives for analysis of economic organisation from external markets into internal organisation. As far as we are concerned here, this leads to two major difficulties: inconsistencies in the use of concept of transaction, and distortion of the concept of hierarchy. We shall discuss both in turn.

Williamson does not define transaction in M&H or EIC, presumably because the concept is felt to be so obvious as to be self-explanatory. Instead, the reader is referred to John R. Commons' argument that the transaction should be regarded as the basic unit of analysis, though what Commons meant by transaction is not precisely defined (M&H: 2, 254, EIC: 3, 6).

Williamson does define transaction in EO, but his definition falls into two parts, which are not necessarily mutually consistent:

'The costs of running the economic system to which Arrow refers can be usefully thought of in contractual terms. Each feasible mode of conducting relations between technologically-separable entities can be examined with respect to the *ex ante* costs of negotiating and writing as well as the *ex post* costs of executing, policing, and when disputes arise, remedying the (explicit or implicit) contract that joins them.

A transaction may thus be said to occur when a good or service is transferred across a technologically-separate interface. One stage of processing or assembly activity terminates and another begins.
(EO: 139)

Arrow's cost of running the economic system are transaction-costs (EO: 136), and the first concept of transaction introduced above is a contractual or exchange-based interpretation entirely consistent with Commons' definition: '*actual* transactions occur, of course between those who actually exchange products. The *potential* transactions are those which *may* not occur, since the parties are on the market and ready to exchange but do not' (1968: 65; italics in original).

However, the second definition of transaction as transference across a technologically separable interface is not necessarily the same thing at all. We can illustrate this with some examples, starting with a simple Robinson Crusoe-type example.

Suppose Crusoe needs to have farming implements fashioned so that he can cultivate crops. The manufacture of implements and the cultivation of crops constitute technologically separable activities. The transference of the tools from the fabrication stage of utilisation in agriculture is therefore a transaction according to Williamson's second interpretation. We assume Crusoe's sojourn passes through three phases. During the first phase he is alone and makes all his own tools as well as farming his own crops. For the second phase, Man Friday arrives, Crusoe exerts authority over him and instructs him to make tools to assist Crusoe in his farming. At the beginning of the third phase, Man Friday rebels and refuses to co-operate unless Crusoe teaches him how to read English. Man Friday gets English lessons and Crusoe gets tools. The three phases can be characterised as those of autonomy, authority and exchange, respectively. In each case transactions in the sense of transferring a product (tools) through technologically separable interfaces (from fabrication to use in cultivation) takes place. Yet only in the third phase is there any evidence of Williamson's first definition of transaction as an agreement to exchange.

It is not difficult to conceive of other examples. Suppose, for example, we have three farmers whose farms are run by professional farm managers. The three farmers share co-operative rights in a tractor. For simplicity, we assume the only contracts the farmers have to concern themselves with are the employment contracts for the respective farm manager and the terms and conditions under which each farm can utilise the tractor.

Unfortunately, the farmers are extremely opportunistic and the tractor contract proves highly expensive to all concerned; negotiating, policing and enforcing the contract takes up much more time and wastes the resources of each of the parties. One farmer decides to buy out the other two; the overall effect is the switching of farm ownership and farm managers' employment contracts to the farmer and the tearing up of the tractor co-operative agreement. The tractor is allocated to farms in much the same fashion as before.

The net effect is therefore the *elimination* of the transaction in the contractual sense and the *preservation* of the transaction in the physical transference sense. As in the first two phases of the Robinson Crusoe example, the two interpretations are not consistent. Unfortunately, examples of this type are commonplace. Mergers to deal with transaction-costs involved in such problems as cross-licensing of R&D, joint venture agreements, and vertical relationships may all be intended to eliminate the transaction in the contractual sense but to preserve it in the physical sense. It is true that some of these may be expressible in internal market terms as in transfer pricing, but to presume that they automatically will be is to reduce the markets and hierarchies issue to external markets versus internal markets. In practice, autonomy and authority (fiat) may represent genuine alternatives to external markets and internal markets.

In fact, Williamson generally plumps for the contractual interpretation of transaction, as is obvious from the discussion above. This has a number of distorting effects on subsequent analysis. Both markets and hierarchies are presumed analysable as exchange systems in which contracting parties have a fundamental propensity to behave opportunistically. This is evident in M&H, in which the transactional properties of external markets are compared and contrasted with those of internal markets in labour, capital and intermediate products. The concept of the firm as hierarchically organised is to some extent developed when the multidivisional form is discussed in Chapter 8, but here the analysis is comparative only in so far as alternative hierarchies (U-form and M-form) are compared. Thus the comparative basis of Williamson's analysis is really internal markets versus external markets, or hierarchy versus hierarchy, not market versus hierarchy. Even the analysis of hierarchy becomes finally reducible to a question of markets when Williamson concludes that the superior efficiency of the M-form is due to its ability to create an internal capital market. Consequently, M&H is about markets, not markets and hierarchies. This perspective is carried to its logical conclusion in EIC, where hierarchy itself is defined in contractual, exchange-based, terms (p. 221).

Thus, the view here is that markets and hierarchies in Williamson's approach may be more appropriately described as involving false hierarchies. An economics background and perspective naturally lead to an emphasis on prices, markets and exchange; unfortunately, when this mental set is carried over to an analysis of hierarchy it may lead to the misconception that hierarchial relations may be adequately reducible to exchange-based terms. It is this misconception which runs the danger of incurring the inconsistencies and distortions of analysis discussed above.

4.4   SOME CONCEPTUAL LIMITATIONS OF WILLIAMSON'S TRANSACTION-COST ECONOMICS

As discussed in Section 2, Williamson argues that the existence of significant transactional problems in the market place requires the simultaneous presence of the three phenomena: bounded rationality, opportunism and asset specificity (EIC: 30–32). We accept the role of bounded rationality as a necessary starting point, but question the roles assigned by Williamson to the other two concepts. In particular, opportunism is too narrow a motivational basis for adequate description of economic relations while asset-specificity is neither necessary nor sufficient for problems of economic co-ordination to arise.

Williamson's reliance on opportunism extends the distorting bias of exchange-based analysis into the motivational arena. This is exemplified by his analysis of Japanese economic relations; 'the hazards of trading are less severe in Japan than in the United States because of cultural and institutional checks on opportunism' (EIC: 122). This interpretation of the Japanese system implicitly assumes that (1) individual opportunism is still the driving force in economic relations, (2) culture operates only as constraint. This contrasts strongly with other analysts' observation of Japan's emphasis on 'group rather than individual, on cooperation and conciliation aimed at harmony, on national rather than personal welfare' (Patrick and Rosovsky 1976: 53). In fact, Williamson does appear to observe these effects in his informal description of the Japanese system (EIC: 120–123), yet he argues that 'the same principles that inform make or buy decisions in the United States and in other Western countries also apply in Japan' (EIC: 122), with opportunism retaining its place centre stage.

To analyse all economic relationships as definable in terms of opportunism runs the danger of cultural and institutional myopia. Williamson associates 'obedience' with Utopian literature and social engineering, and dismisses it as involving the unwarranted assumption of 'mechanistic orderliness' (EIC: 49–50). The fact that 'obedience' is an observable phenomenon naturally associated with many hierarchial situations is obscured by his insistence on analysing hierarchy in exchange-based terms, a perspective more easily reconcilable with individualism and opportunism. Yet, in the case of Japan recurrent themes of group harmony as opposed to individualistic self-interest suggest that obedience would be a more reasonable behavioural assumption than is opportunism. It is not possible to reconcile this with Williamson's analysis, since the substitution of opportunism with obedience would effectively eliminate the existing transaction-cost framework, as is obvious from the discussion in Section 2 above. Further, as Kuran points out (1988: 149), there is a tendency towards *ex-post* rationalisation in Williamson's work in so far as his claim that efficient organisational adaptations do not always obtain is inconsistent with the dominant methodological assumption of his work, which is that social arrangements are efficient adaptations to problems of transaction-costs.

As far as the concept of asset specificity is concerned, its existence is not a prerequisite for the existence of transactional problems, despite Williamson's claim to the contrary. Indeed, there is evidence that asset specificity can actually facilitate and encourage market exchanges. For example, in an early study Blois (1972) found a number of cases where dependence of suppliers on single large customers enables the latter to use their buying power to extract special arrangements and concessions from suppliers. The subsequent economies were in many cases comparable to those realisable under vertical integration[2]. Blois also found that some areas involving high technology and special services provided transactional defence and protection for suppliers and customers (1972: 265–6). That *mutual* dependency and specificity of transactional relationship should help generate orderly and well-behaved markets is a persuasive and indeed obvious idea. If the ultimate weapon of termination of relationship involves Mutual Assured Destruction (or at least, Mutual Assured Severe Damage), then joint specificity of transactional relationships may reduce the likelihood of opportunistic threats and concomitant transaction-costs. If both parties are sitting on the same branch, a threat to saw away the branch may reasonably be disbelieved.

Asset specificity may well help to create transaction-costs,[3] but the actual effects are likely to be more complex than Williamson recognises. However, what is even more serious is the neglect of a parallel issue in many cases, that transactional difficulties are created not by the specificity of transactional relations between parties but rather the converse, asset non-specificity.

The problem arises because Williamson (EIC: 31–2) argues that if asset specificity is absent in contractual situations, then discrete market contracting is efficacious, markets are fully contestable,[4] and characterised by ease of entry and exit between markets due to non-specificity of assets. However, this ignores the fact that non-specificity of assets may frequently create property-right problems. Suppose firm *A* has an invention and offers to license it to firm *B*. Firm *C* observes the transaction, poaches the idea, and appropriates a proportion of the rent that would otherwise have accrued to firm *A*. Devices such as patenting may be less than adequate to protect the intellectual property rights of firm *A*, and consequently the licensing contract may pose significant transaction-costs for the contractors in so far as the absence of asset specificity is here expressed in the form of appropriability problems. Once property-rights problems are recognised, non-specificity of assets to the transaction in question may create rather than resolve transactional problems.[5]

A common device to try to deal with such appropriability problems is internalisation of the transaction, and there has been much analysis documenting this solution, most notably in the area of multinational enterprise, as we shall see in the next section.

Thus, while opportunism and asset-specificity may be significant issues influencing transactional considerations, the status accorded them in Williamson's development of his framework is unwarranted, and is likely to lead to problems of analysis. In the next section we shall examine how specific problems do in fact arise in Williamson's analysis of three major issues in industrial organisations: the rationale for conglomerate diversification, the evolution of the M-form corporation and the nature of multinational enterprise.

4.5   THE CONGLOMERATE, THE M-FORM AND MULTINATIONAL ENTERPRISE

While Williamson has successfully demonstrated the significance of transaction-costs principles for a wide variety of economic phenomena, there are problems associated with his specific interpretation of transaction-cost analysis, as we have discussed above. In turn, there are difficulties when the approach is applied to the study of particular micro-economic phenomena, and we shall consider this with respect to his analysis of the conglomerate, the M-form structure and multinational enterprise (the MNE) respectively.

4.5.1   Conglomerateness and transaction-costs

Williamson (M&H: 155–75; EO: 154–78), provides an explanation for the existence of conglomerates based upon M-form principles and failures in the external capital market. As such, it appears to offer a means of resolving the apparent paradoxical existence of firms operating in unrelated product-markets with no obvious synergy benefits.

Williamson argues that the conglomerate may constitute a miniature capital market superior in performance to the external capital market. Firstly, *internalisation* of the capital market might enhance the quality and quantity of information available to providers of funds and give more direct control over auditing and the rewarding/penalising of performance. The advantages of internalisation in this respect were discussed earlier, in Section 2. Secondly, *divisionalisation* encourages creation of profit centres as basic elements in an M-form (multidivision) structure. Divisionalised profit centres organised around product, terri-tory or process may allow the creation of an internal capital market within the firm. Divisions can be assessed in terms of profit contribu-tion; the development of this uniform, measurable standard facilitates divisional comparability and may have beneficial incentive effects on managers.

Williamson argues that the combination of internalisation and divi-sionalisation advantages permits the conglomerate to operate as a miniature capital market with associated attractive efficiency advan-tages. This is offered as a rationale for the conglomerate.

In fact, there is nothing wrong with the argument when it is offered in terms of why the conglomerate may be more efficient than the external capital market. Consistent with the general internal markets versus external markets orientation of M&H, this is how the analysis is developed. The idea that capital market failure may encourage inter-nalisation and divisionalisation is persuasive. The problems arise when this is offered as a rationale for the evolution of the conglomerate. In this context, Williamson is comparing the wrong things. Instead of analysing why the conglomerate may be superior to the external capital market, transaction-cost economics has to explain why it may be superior to the specialised firm. By Williamson's own chosen crite-rion of efficiency there must be some advantage that conglomerate-ness has over specialisation that encourages this strategy to evolve at the expense of the specialised firm. Unfortunately, the internalisa-tion/divisionalisation thesis contains no such advantage. We can illus-trate this with reference to a simple example.

Suppose we start off with a grouping of nine independent firms – say, three aerospace, three chemical and three electronics. The firms have all been facing capital-market problems, possibly because the growth of the respective firms has tended to encourage separation of ownership and control – this is consistent with Williamson's analysis of the growth of specialised U-form or functionally organised firms [M&H: 133–6]. The firms can all be characterised in terms of manage-rial teams wasting existing funds and being unable to attract new funds. Creation of a miniature capital market could contribute towards the mitigation of some of these effects, and Williamson's internalisation/divisionalisation argument is helpful in explaining how this might be achieved. Amalgamation of firms by merger or takeover is an obvious device for this purpose.

However, Williamson's internalisation/divisionalisation advantages are neutral as regards which pattern of amalgamation should be

adopted. Suppose one strategy involved the amalgamation and divisionalisation of the three electronics firms, while a second involved a
combination of three firms, one from each sector. Both strategies
could create internal capital markets and separate independent profit
centres around the former corporate boundaries. Both the specialised
electronics-based strategy and conglomerate strategy could extract the
miniature capital-market advantages associated with the multidivisional forms. In these respects at least, there is nothing to choose
between them. Unfortunately, this apparent neutrality of effect is
superficial. When the specialisation/conglomerate choice is examined
further, there are in fact sound transaction-cost reasons why the specialised strategy would appear to be generally superior. These are
related to problems of performance comparability and the possibility
of internal trading respectively.

Firstly, similarity in technology and markets between divisions facilitates profit comparison between divisions and may improve the
profit-centre operation of the internal capital market, as Williamson
recognises (EIC: 140). In principle it is easier to infer efficiency from
performance within the sectors than it is between sectors.

Secondly, if there are complementary markets or technologies
between divisions as a consequence of specialisation as in the electronics case, these may open up the possibility of internal trades or
deals to exploit synergistic possibilities. The independence of the divisional profit centres need not be compromised, but the existence of
internal senior management 'umpires' may reduce the internal transaction-costs of such deals compared to external options such as
leasing, joint venture or licensing. In particular, opportunistic behaviour may be more easily rectified or prevented. The same transaction-
cost arguments used to justify the internal capital market can also be
utilised in considering other internal markets involving inter-divisional
transfers of informational, human or physical resources. Williamson's
own transaction-cost tool-kit provides arguments for specialisation
rather than conglomerateness. In short, there is no advantage that
may be provided by the conglomerate in Williamson's analysis that
could not also be provided by more specialised strategies. In addition,
specialisation may provide additional efficiency gains over conglomerates. Consequently, Williamson does not explain why the conglomerate should evolve in preference to alternative corporate strategies.

What is overlooked in this analysis is that the conglomerate is a
relatively rare phenomenon even among large firms (Rumelt 1974;
Channon 1973; Dyas and Thanheiser 1976). Even highly diversified

firms tend to exploit market and technological linkages between product-markets. What is missing from Williamson's analysis are positive reasons for choice of conglomerateness rather than specialisation in the cases where it is does obtain. One such explanation is provided by Kay (1982, 1984) in terms of specialisation dangers; as well as providing synergies and economies, specialisation may provide vulnerability to environmental threats in turbulent, rapidly changing and uncertain environments. The conglomerate strategy is one option that may be adopted by corporate management in such circumstances. Management avoid market and technological linkages, not for internal efficiency gains but because they do not wish to tie the fate of the firm to a limited set of market and technological opportunities.

A further comment is warranted with respect to Williamson's general neglect of related diversification. This may appear strange, considering that such diversification is easily the more common strategy, the conglomerate being a comparatively rare phenomenon. Most diversification exploits some scope economies, such as shared resources in marketing, technology and production.

In fact, Williamson's theory cannot explain the multiproduct firm in general, not just the conglomerate in particular. By definition, related diversification is built around internalisation of assets *shared* in different product markets. Williamson's explanation of internalisation depends entirely on the opposite: asset specificity, or *specialised* use or user. If his theory is applicable, then it can only be with respect to the limit (and unusual) case of the single-product firm.

4.5.2   The evolution of the M-form corporation

The evolution of the M-form corporation has been a major area of study in transaction-cost economics (M&H: 132–54; EO: 65–77, 151–4; EIC: 279–94). As well as providing a basis for analysis of the economics of internal organisation, Williamson has extended this analysis into investigation of conglomerate diversification and multinational enterprise. However, we suggest here that there are problems with Williamson's explanation of the M-form innovation. According to Williamson, U-form firms – that is, those organised by functional specialism such as R&D, marketing, production and finance – eventually run into control-loss and strategy-formulating problems as they expand in terms of size and diversity. Since all problems involving more than one function have to be co-ordinated and decided on at senior management level, centralisation of decisions results in a high level of organisation costs. Centralisation creates control-loss problems by requiring information to pass through numerous levels before it is acted on; congestion and limited capacity, as far as information processing at senior management level is concerned, exacerbate these problems. Short-run, urgent operating crises may push out long-run strategic decision making at this level. If senior management attempt to ease the information capacity problem by involving functional heads in top level decision making, pursuit of sub-goals by these functional heads may distort the profit orientation of the corporation. For these reasons there may be severe efficiency problems accompanying the growth and expansion of the U-form corporation.

Williamson argues the M-form, divisionalised corporation mitigates these problems. By giving divisions responsibility for inter-functional operating problems, control-loss problems are reduced since most decisions can be taken lower down the system. Top management are freed to concentrate on long-run, strategic problems, while the creation of divisional profit centres may facilitate the creation of an internal capital market.

These arguments are quite reasonable in isolation. The difficulties with Williamson's subsequent analysis relate to his explanation of the origins of the M-form. He suggests that with the expansion of the firm, 'the ability of the management (in the U-form) to handle the volume and complexity of the demands placed upon it became strained and even collapsed ... the U-form laboured under a communication overload while the pursuit of sub goals by the functional parts (sales, engineering, production) was partly a manifestation of opportunism' (EIC: 280–1). Therefore, 'faced with the need either to retrench or to develop a new set of internal contracting relationships, organisational innovators devised the M-form structure' (EIC: 295).

At this point it is important to identify exactly what Williamson is saying: expansion of the U-form eventually leads to crisis and collapse and the development of the M-form to solve these problems, 'eventually the U-form structure defeats itself and results in the M-form structure to solve these problems' (1971: 350). The evolution of the M-form is regarded as an evolutionary process operating according to natural selection criteria (EIC: 296), and indeed Williamson sees transaction-cost reasoning in general as relying on the competitive process to winnow out the most efficient mode of organisation over the long run through a process of natural selection (EIC: 22–3; including footnote).

Williamson's argument, at first sight superficially plausible, is in fact severely flawed and indeed inconsistent. To suggest that the U-form somehow 'defeats itself' through over-expansion, leading to crisis and collapse and the M-form innovation to solve these problems, is to put the cart before the horse. A genuine natural-selection argument would see the M-form innovation generating crisis and collapse in the (inferior) U-form, rather than U-form collapse generating the M-form innovation. Natural selection selects from *present* competitors, it does not generate future competitors; it filters out inferior forms by creating inefficiency problems as a consequence of competition from superior forms *after* the appearance of the latter, not before. As Alchian points out, 'even in a world of stupid men there would still be profits' (1950: 213) and the same could be said of a world of U-form corporations before the introduction of the M-form innovation. This still leaves us with a puzzle: if the M-form was not around to create initial crisis and collapse in the U-form structures, what did cause such problems?

In a sense that is a problem outside the scope of this chapter, our main point here is that evolutionary arguments have been misapplied by Williamson. However, it is instructive to consider how natural selection arguments should be applied in this context, if they are to be applied at all. Before the introduction of the M-form, the only competition a given U-form faced was from other U-forms or smaller, more specialised firms.

If a given U-form is competing unsuccessfully against other U-forms, the selection process should lead to appropriate substitutions and redistributions within the U-form population. If the U-form is competing unsuccessfully against smaller, more specialised firms (which may or may not be U-form), the selection mechanism should generate and sustain limits to growth in favour of smaller, more specialised firms. This is the process one would expect with Williamson's weak-form selection mechanisms in which the relatively fitter survive, without there being any reason to suppose that they are the fittest in any absolute sense (EIC: 23, footnote). Williamson's crisis induced M-form innovation is analogous to giraffes deciding to develop long necks to get to the high branches; neither are consistent with natural selection. Consequently, neither the initial U-form collapse nor the subsequent search for new forms (rather than selection from existing forms) are explained by Williamson.

Gregory Dow (1987) discusses Williamson's interpretation of competitive processes as a feedback mechanism generating natural selection of efficient forms. Dow concentrates on difficulties associated with Williamson's use of selection concepts in the context of diffusion of organisation forms, but, as we have seen, there are severe problems when Williamson attempts to explain organisational innovation such as the M-form development. In this context, it is important to note that evolutionary or natural selection theories are classified as contributing to functional explanation and are distinguished from theories of intentional explanation, which is the more common method of explanation in the social sciences (Elster 1983: 49–50). If rationality is presupposed, theories of intentional explanation involve either optimising or satisficing decision-making criteria (1983: 69). Williamson's approach is remarkable and unusual in modern micro-economics in that it does not utilise either decision-making criterian or process and so there are no guidelines by which intentional explanation could be pursued. Such a neglect could be sustainable if functionalist natural-selection explanations were adequate, but as we have seen, they are not. Consequently, there is an absence of sound theoretical foundations on which to build Williamson's argument that the efficient mode of organisation will win out.[6]

4.5.3 The nature of multinational enterprise

Williamson also argues that his transaction-cost framework can be applied to the analysis of multinational enterprise. This would appear to represent a reasonable extension in so far as a technological transfer mechanism such as licensing (market) and multinationalism (hierarchy) are amenable to analysis in comparative institutional terms.

Williamson again argues that asset-specificity represents the motive for internalisation and substitution of market-exchange relations with corporate hierarchy.

> A more harmonious and efficient exchange relation – better disclosure, easier reconciliation of differences, more complete cross-cultural adaptation, more effective team organization and reconfiguration – predictably results from the substitution of an internal governance relation for bilateral trading under those recurrent trading circumstances where assets, of which complex technology transfer is an example, have a highly specific character.
>
> (EIC: 294)

However, a survey by Contractor (1981) of empirical analyses of licensing as a preferred strategy to MNE does not provide support for

Williamson's argument. Indeed there is evidence that *specificity* of transactional relationships may encourage the licensing (market exchange) option in some circumstances, as we would expect from our earlier discussion in Section 4; reviewing the empirical evidence, Contractor concluded, 'the disadvantages of licensing arising from licensee independence are often removed if the licensee is kept dependent on trademarks, foreign market access, technical improvements, etc.' (1981: 78). Contractor also cites evidence that licensing may be preferred if *non*-specificity of assets in the form of appropriability problems is not liable to be a severe problem, either because products are in the mature phase of the product life cycle or because technological change is so rapid that potential competitors appropriating informal leakages due to market exchanges would find it difficult to catch up anyway.

Consistent with this, it is *non*-specificity of assets and problems of protection of property rights that is frequently cited as a major transactional problem contributing to the creation of multinational enterprise through internalisation (Casson 1979; Dunning 1981; and Caves 1982). In recent commentaries on this literature, Coombs, *et al.* emphasise the role of internalisation in preventing leakage of information to other firms (1987: 161), while Casson concludes that 'because knowledge has the characteristics of a "public good" the firm with privileged knowledge tends to become multinational' (1987: 29). These transactional non-specificities are neglected by Williamson.

In practice, the technological transfer process and associated transactional problems are influenced by the forms in which both asset specificity and asset non-specificity are expressed. Galbraith and Kay (1986) argue that analysis of multinationalism requires prior recognition that the technology transfer process involves a bundle of specific and non-specific assets. Such interpretation is based on insights drawn from the available theoretical and empirical analysis of multinational enterprise neglected by Williamson. Once this literature is recognised it becomes clear that Williamson's interpretation of transaction-cost economics does not explain the evolution of the modern multinational enterprise but instead reflects his general neglect of the relationships between technology, transaction-costs and institutional arrangements as noted by Englander (1988). This underlines the argument of the previous section, that Williamson's theory rests on comparative statics and cannot be used to describe dynamic, evolutionary phenomena, despite his claims to the contrary.

4.6 CONCLUSIONS

In Coase's original article he argued that the 'distinguishing mark of the firm is the supersession of the price mechanism' (1937: 389). Coase's article makes clear that this is taken to mean the replacement of external exchange relationships with internal organisation and hierarchy. 'If a workman moves from department Y to department X, he does not go because of a change in relative prices, but because he is ordered to do so' (Coase 1937: 387).

Unfortunately, Williamson's approach distorts Coase's insight by representing the comparative institutional foundations of transaction-cost economics as being internal markets vs. external markets, whether these be capital markets, labour markets or intermediate product markets. The comparative static and non-dynamic nature of the approach, as well as the hints dropped by Williamson in EIC that it may be possible to develop his arguments into a theory of optimal institutional choice, suggests that his framework is rather closer to the neoclassical tradition than Williamson is prepared to admit.

Representing the firm as a series of internal markets monitored by internal umpires is to create a false construct of hierarchy. It is true that internal markets and internal prices do exist, but to use these as a representation of internal organisation is as credible as an anthropologist attempting to unravel the sociology of an Indian tribe by relying solely on their smoke signals. In fact, market, internal or external, is a very rare and occasional device as casual census of resource allocation decisions and actions taken in the course of producing a typical final product serves to illustrate. Whether it is Coase's workman moving among departments under instruction, or my own autonomous attempts to move from sentence to sentence in constructing this chapter, economic activity rarely encounters market interfaces.

The construction of false hierarchies in Williamson's framework is a prelude to fundamental problems of analysis. His explanations for the evolution of the conglomerate and the M-form corporation are untenable even within the terms and constructs of the framework, since his capital-market failure and natural selection arguments are logically flawed. His explanation of the development of the multinational is sustained only at the expense of neglecting the considerable wealth of theoretical and empirical analysis which suggests that non-specificity rather than specificity of assets is a fundamental influence on the choice of internal organisation over market-exchange agreements in this area.

If there is a way forward from these difficulties, it may involve taking an initial step backwards and re-reading Coase's original article. Coase argued that 'Within the firm ... in place of the complicated market structure with exchange transactions is substituted the entrepreneur-co-ordinator, who directs production. It is clear that these are alternative methods of co-ordinating production' (1937: 388). It would resolve the ambiguity over the nature of transaction discussed earlier, and would be sympathetic to Coase's original analysis,[7] if the term 'transaction' was reserved for exchange relationships, and comparative institutional economics was seen as being concerned with costs of co-ordination, not just transaction-costs however defined. Co-ordination-cost economics would then genuinely encompass costs of organisation as well as exchange costs and help set a proper agenda for a comparative institutional research programme.

Co-ordination-cost economics in the Coasian tradition would recognise wider behavioural imperatives than opportunism and draw upon insights from the property-rights literature as a corrective to Williamson's mistaken view that asset specificity is a necessary prerequisite for transactional problems.[8] As far as the substantive failures of analysis discussed here are concerned, some alternative solutions and perspectives have been suggested above, and it is hope of that future analysis could develop these further, as well as integrating valid insights and interpretations from the rest of Williamson's analysis.

NOTES

1. Reprinted from *The Journal of Economic Behaviour and Organization*, 17, N. M. Kay (1992) 'Markets, false hierarchies and the evolution of the modern corporation,' 315–33, with kind permission from Elsevier Science, NL, Sara Burgerhartstraat 25, 1055 KV Amsterdam, The Netherlands.
2. Blois notes that in many cases the only significant difference between quasi and full vertical integration is that large customers can extract special requirements due to buying power, while the vertically integrated firm extracts compliance through legal power.
3. Williamson in EIC: 104 discusses the empirical literature relevant to his analysis of the role of asset specificity in generating innovation costs and influencing choice of institutional form. Englander (1988) sees asset specificity as a refined version of Williamson's earlier concept of information impactedness.
4. Contestability theory presumes that asset specificity is insignificant. See Baumol *et al.* (1982) and Baumol (1986), as well as Williamson's discussion (EIC: 31, footnote).

5. In EIC Williamson only discusses the property-rights literature in passing (pp. 27, 29).

6. Williamson's analysis of the M-form innovation is in fact Lamarckian rather than Darwininan; Lamarck argued that life is generated, continuously and spontaneously, in very simple forms. It then climbs a ladder of complexity, motivated by a 'force that tends incessantly to complicate organisations'. This force operates through the creative response of organisms to 'felt needs' (Gould, 1982: 77). Gould in fact acknowledges that human cultural evolution is analogous to Lamarckian evolution rather than Darwininian natural selection (1982: 83–4) This could be taken as encouragement to model organisational evolution in a Lamarckian fashion, but doing so would require modelling of 'creative responses' and 'felt needs', and, as we have seen, Williamson does not incorporate decision criteria for such intentional mechanisms in his evolutionary approach. For an approach that does, see Nelson and Winter (1982).

7. In fairness to Williamson, it should be pointed out that this ambiguity is not resolved in Coase's original paper either.

8. The existing multinational literature already deals with the second perspective in a wide variety of contexts.

5 The Economics of Trust[1]

A Review of *Studies in the Economics of Trust* by Mark Casson[2]

'I don't want to be in the war any more.'

'Would you like to see our country lose?' Major Major asked.

'We won't lose. We've got more men, more money and more material. There are ten million men in uniform who could replace me. Some people are getting killed and a lot more are making money and having fun. Let somebody else get killed.'

'But suppose everybody on our side felt that way?'

'Then I'd certainly be a damned fool to feel any other way, wouldn't I?'

Joseph Heller, Catch-22.

5.1 INTRODUCTION

Anyone who writes a two-volume series sub-titled *The Economics of Trust*, as Mark Casson has done, must face up to something akin to what might be described as 'Yossarian's Dilemma' – except that for Yossarian in *Catch-22* there is really no dilemma since there is only one rational choice. He is Homo Economicus in an n-person Prisoner's Dilemma. If everybody obeys, his best strategy is to defect and free-ride on others' sacrifices. If nobody obeys, his best strategy is still to defect and protect himself. Whatever everybody else's strategy is, Yossarian's best strategy is to defect. In game-theoretic terms, defection is a dominant strategy for Yossarian, as it would be for all other rational participants with his payoff function. Major is aware that individual defection aggregates as collective defection or anarchy, and that this poses certain problems for collective well-being. However, this does not shake the logic of Yossarian's position, but merely serves to extend and reinforce it. Even if it was pointed out to Yossarian that everybody's chances of collective survival would be greater if they all fought together rather than if

93

they all chickened out, this would not alter the logic of Yossarian's position. Whatever everybody else does, his best strategy would still be to defect.[3]

In *Catch-22*, defectors like Yossarian are the sane ones, it is the rest of society that has gone mad – or, more accurately, the rest of the aggregate, since in Yossarian's world there is no society. Suspicion and paranoia are endemic; trust, belief and faith are parodied (this was written at the time of the McCarthy era in the USA); and if we wish to see what a world in which trust is betrayed or negated might look like, then *Catch-22* serves as an excellent blueprint. The wonder is not that such a world can be conceived of; the wonder is that, given Homo Economicus and the rationality of opportunism (Williamson 1985), it is not a standard model for social relations. Most societies, most of the time, do not behave as the characters do in *Catch-22*. Even in the USA (the archetypical individualistic society and home of *Catch-22*) the majority of respondents to a questionnaire delivered not long after McCarthy answered in the affirmative when asked if most people could be trusted (Putnam 1995: 73).[4] A real-life Yossarian is still likely to believe in something, whether it is family, friends or a higher power. The contemporary power of *Catch-22* is that in showing what the world could be like, it raises the question of why it is not like that in the first place.

A game-theoretician might argue that it may be more useful to analyse games such as the Prisoner's Dilemma as repeated games. A standard game-theoretic way to solve games such as the Prisoner's Dilemma when they are repeated is to use backward induction. I first came across backward induction in a riddle that fascinated me when I was a child, though I did not know then that this was called 'backward induction'. At morning assembly a headmaster announces that today there will be a surprise fire drill at the end of one of the eight class periods. However, it is obvious that the alarm cannot be left to the end of period 8, because by then there would be no choice left and the alarm would no longer be a surprise. But ruling out a last period alarm means that, if it has not been sounded by period 7, then everybody knows it *must* be sounded at the end of that period – which means it also would not be a surprise, ruling out that option. However, if both period 7 and 8 alarms are ruled out, it follows from similar reasoning that it cannot be left until the end of period 6 ... and so on, the same logic holding for period 5, then 4 and so forth. By backward induction it can be shown that there is no time at which a surprise fire alarm can be rung. Funnily enough, despite backward induction, the teachers at my school kept on trying to surprise us with fire alarms, and we kept on acting as if we were surprised. But they were only teachers who probably did not know they could not surprise us and we were only children who did not know we were not surprised.

The structure of finite repeated games such as the Prisoner's Dilemma can also be uncovered using backward induction. Whatever has happened in earlier plays, the rational strategy for both players in the last play of a repeated Prisoner's Dilemma is to defect and confess. But if the outcome of the last game is *certainly* confess-confess, it no longer figures in strategic calculations. The second last play now effectively becomes the last play, the rational strategy for both players is again confess-confess, which means the third last play effectively becomes the last play – and so on, until confess-confess is revealed as the only feasible strategy at each stage of a repeated game (Rapoport and Chammah 1965: 28–9). As Dasgupta (1988a: 66–7) points out, even if a car salesman promised to stay in business for 50 years, backward induction suggests that, if it were rational for him to cheat on his last sale, it would be rational for him to cheat on all the preceding sales. It may be interesting to know, as Dasgupta points out (1988a: 67), that honesty and trust may be rational in the case of infinitely repeated games (though usually as one of many possible solutions), but even in the long run we all play games of less than infinite duration.

As with *Catch-22*, so with the Prisoner's Dilemma. Over 1000 experimental studies of the Prisoner's Dilemma have been carried out. The classic study by Rapoport and Chammah (1965) conducted a large number of tests of the Dilemma with number of runs typically equal to 300. They found that the rational strategy predicted by game-theory (their equivalent of confess-confess) was typically only chosen in a minority of cases. By the end of the experiments, co-operative choices were typically reaching a level of about 60 per cent. Their results have been supported by several subsequent investigators (Colman 1982: 116). Unfortunately, even though game-theory models such as the Prisoner's Dilemma are common currency in textbooks at all levels of economics teaching, findings such as these are rarely referred to. The fundamental question is, if game-theory cannot generally explain behaviour in such simple cases, why should we trust its explanations of more complex and realistic situations (such as cases involving uncertainty as in games with finite but indefinite horizons)?

The experimental findings of the Prisoner's Dilemma require explanation. The three obvious candidates are these: (1) the experiments were badly carried out, (2) subjects were being irrational, (3) the Prisoner's Dilemma is a bad model of behaviour. Explanation (1) can be rejected. The experiments were generally carried out by experienced researchers and the experimental results of Rapoport and Chammah in particular have been generally confirmed (Colman 1982: 116). Explanation (2) may be worth entertaining, but this threatens to open up a can of worms for game theorists. In Prisoner's Dilemma subjects are generally drawn from university populations and can be assumed to have a higher level of intelligence than the average member of society. The structure of the Prisoner's Dilemma is also simpler than for many more complex (and realistic) games, so if subjects generally make irrational choices here, it does not bode well for the applicability of non-co-operative game-theory in other contexts. However, there is still the third explanation (3) and the possibility that the Prisoner's Dilemma does not provide a good explanation of how people behave. The most simple and obvious explanation as to why it does not provide a good explanation of behaviour is that the assumption of simple self-interest is flawed and that players trust each other not to pursue this tactic, and reciprocate this trust. We might also conclude that this is a concept worth exploring and that it has been unjustly neglected by economists. This appears also to be the conclusion also of Casson (1995a: 13), when he concludes that the cohesiveness of social groups in the face of problems such as the Prisoner's Dilemma is difficult to account for in terms of traditional concepts of economic man. If there is an inconsistency between theory and behaviour, it suggests that the basis of theory should be questioned rather than outmoded models perpetuated, and much of Casson's work in his two-volume series is concerned with pursuing the former agenda.

At this point an immediate objection may be made that this breaches the assumption that players are being rational. That may or may not be so, but the circumstances in which trust is rational is something that raises issues that go well beyond the limited confines of the Prisoner's Dilemma itself. The relation between self-interest, individual rationality and collective rationality has been the subject of considerable philosophical debate (e.g., see Colman 1982: 254–69). Whether trust is rational is a subsidiary question to the fact that it appears to be widely observed and reciprocated, both under controlled laboratory conditions as in the Prisoner's Dilemma experiments, and in society as a whole. Trust appears to be a wide-spread phenomenon even if it is difficult to reconcile with individualistic perspectives of economic and social behaviour. To the extent that it subverts simple individualistic self-interest, it also clearly has potentially significant implications for resource allocation, though whether this balances out as beneficial or deleterious cannot be settled *a priori*. One person's deal-smoothing 'trust' may be another's anti-competitive collusion.

5.2   WHAT IS TRUST?

A problem with trust is that it is a concept with wide currency, but which is not so easy to pin down. I might be said to 'trust' the milkman to deliver my milk, and he may 'trust' me to pay him. But if either of us breaches the bargain, we can forget about future benefits from future exchanges. In such cases, adhering to the agreement can hardly be said to differ in any meaningful respect from simple self-interest. If this is all trust is, it may influence tactics but it really represents just an extension of conventional notions of self-interest. The concept has to offer something more than this if it is to justify appearing in the titles and sub-titles of economic treatises.

One route to approaching this problem is to explore what the concept is generally taken to reflect, and how it contrasts with self-interest. First of all, we can note the definition of 'self-interest' in the *New Shorter Oxford English Dictionary* (NSOED): '*Self-interest n.* one's personal profit, benefit, or advantage; regard to or pursuit of this, esp. to the exclusion of regard for others.' However, the corresponding definition for trust is less straightforward. There are a number of legal and obsolete definitions, reducing the relevant definition for our purposes to an equally short but more ambiguous account: '*Trust n.* Faith or confidence in the loyalty, strength, veracity, etc. of a person or thing.'

The 'etc.' is problematic, implying as it does a fairly open (and incomplete) definition. If we tried to unbundle this definition further, it would seem reasonable that confidence in strength would more likely refer to trust in a thing (such as a bridge), while loyalty, veracity, and so on would more likely refer to people (though dog owners may wish to add their own sub-clauses). The 'etc.' is only a crude indicator that certain concepts such as trust may be more complex than the simple behavioural postulates we are used to in economics. If you are being self-interested, NSOED tells us that you can ignore other people's interest, and if you are being opportunistic, it also tells us you may ignore principles. Even honesty and truth in NSOED are relatively uncomplicated in that their execution does not necessitate making judgements on the possible actions or beliefs of others. However, trust is more complicated. Trust appears to imply an attitude (and implied behaviour) on the part of one person on the basis of qualities (and implied behaviour) on the part of at least one other person. The qualities required of the others would appear to be virtuous (loyalty, veracity and so forth), and would appear to imply that associated actions would be offered at some cost to the individual or individuals without regard to any obvious compensatory gains on their part (otherwise the actions would tend to reduce to rational self-interest). Also, compared to self-interest, uncertainty appears to have a necessary role to play. If all future actions and events were known with certainty, trust would be redundant.

The question of whether or not trust is a quality of individuals or of circumstances is one in which economists may help make a contribution. For example, Fukuyama (1995: 51) sees the breakdown of the nuclear family as symptomatic of breakdown of trust in many Western societies. However, an economist might point out that this could have been influenced by the lowering of exit costs from marriage in many of these societies. In previous generations, unhappily married couples might have been forced to stay together for a variety of economic and social reasons that made divorce impracticable, such as father's essential role as breadwinner, mother's as childminder-housekeeper, transaction costs of divorce and social ostracism. The influence of each of these factors has moderated somewhat in many Western societies in recent years. There are a variety of ways that exit costs could be reimposed that include subsidising marriage, taxing divorcees, and a lump sum tax on divorce decrees (whether manufactured domestically or imported). While this might make marriage a less contestable market and discourage hit-and-run operators, the removal of realistic alternatives in such cases makes it questionable whether 'trust' in any meaningful sense has been raised. Rather than just suggesting that marriage breakdown is symptomatic of breakdown of trust, a more balanced interpretation might acknowledge that low marriage turnover in the context of high exit costs might have helped conceal a high incidence of low trust relationships.

5.3   TRUST AND EFFICIENCY

Casson is one of the few economists to make a serious attempt to recognise the role of trust in economic behaviour (1995a and b), though McMaster and Sawkins (1995) show that there has been recognition of the efficiency-enhancing attributes of trust in the economic literature for some years. Casson argues that trust can be efficiency enhancing; for example, absence of trust can lead to misallocation of resources (e.g., 1995a: 28) and high-trust societies can reduce transaction costs relative to low-trust societies (e.g., 1995a: 90–1). The role of trust in reducing transaction costs associated with policing and monitoring is so well accepted that it might seem almost a truism. It is not invisible hands or competitive ethics that appears on my Scottish pound note, but a promise from the governors of the bank no less, and anyone expecting to find exhortation to opportunism or self-interest on dollar bills might be disappointed to find an expression of trust (albeit to a higher entity than the Federal Reserve authorities). Clearly, here is a concept with considerable potential mileage, which is one reason why we should be so careful about treating it at face value – on trust, as it were. Casson is an honourable, respected academic who is careful to be fair and honest in what he writes. But if Casson says trust is efficient, does this mean that we should also trust what he says? The role of scepticism is a valuable and indeed an integral part of academic transactions and is complementary to trust. If we mistrusted every statement an academic makes, we would be continually checking and rechecking (and checking and rechecking the checkers) to the extent that intellectual progress would be painfully slow and halting. On the other hand, if every statement was accepted uncritically, we would still probably be a profession of sun-worshipping flat-earthers. Intellectual progress depends on a particular blend of trust and scepticism with the reviewing process itself test driving theses both before and (as in this case) after publication. We should not be surprised if economic progress was to be characterised similarly by a blend of trust and scepticism.

So, putting on my test driver's goggles, I will steer Casson's vehicle in the direction of some testing terrain. To the east we can see a society based on family loyalties and kinship networks with individuals having ties of duty and obligation to group interests. To the west we see a highly individualistic society in which these kinship systems are much weaker, and social capital in the form of trust has broken down to a great extent; corruption is so widespread that almost anything from politicians to university degrees can be, and have been, bought and sold easily. Which would be the better bet as a base for economic growth?

In fact, the two societies are sketches of early eighteenth-century Highland and Lowland Scotland respectively (I lied about the east and west to influence your expectations, and you probably trusted me). Clan comes from the Gaelic *Clann*, meaning family or kin. It is interesting to note that this term, used by Fukuyama as well as Ouchi[5] to describe contemporary high-trust co-operative systems (e.g., many Japanese corporations and Chinese social structures), comes from a failed social system in Adam Smith's homeland: the Highland clan system largely disintegrated after the 1745 rebellion.[6] It is tempting to speculate on a counterfactual world in which Bonnie Prince Charlie did not stop at Derby, Culloden never happened, the clan system recolonised the Lowlands of Scotland, and the young Adam Smith experienced at first hand the social and economic possibilities of kinship and networks. This Adam Smith might well have observed in 1776, 'It is not from the self-interest of the butcher, the brewer or the baker that we can expect our dinner, but from their regard to their obligations to kith and kin.'

Unfortunately, there is little evidence to support any contention that this alternative Celtic world would have been more economically successful than the one that actually occurred. In a major questionnaire study of individualism/collectivism at work involving 40 countries and 116 000 individuals, Hofstede (1984) found a 0.82 correlation at country level between his estimate of degree of individualism and GNP.[7] Argyle (1991: 75) points out that the most interesting exception to this pattern is Japan, though Chinese societies and Korea are also exceptions. As Argyle notes, individualistic societies have less conformity, co-operation and social support, while collectivist societies tend to have more identification with group interests and subordination of individual goals to group interests, and there are higher degrees of conformity and co-operation (1991: 72–3). With the striking exception of some of the South-east Asian economies, it seems that what are generally characterised as low-trust economies have been more successful than what have what have been generally characterised as high-trust economies. High trust may be a good thing in moral terms, but the evidence so far suggests that in the global economy it does not necessarily help to pay the rent.

One of the most important features of trust is that it tends not to be a free good. Firstly, it can take considerable time and other resources to build up trust and, while it may be easily breached, it may again take considerable time and other resources to restore trust (Fukuyama 1995). A corollary is that it may not be worthwhile or feasible to invest the time and resources required to create trust in certain circumstances. This may help explain why international business collaborations are often characterised by severe transaction costs at the level of individual ventures, and why firms often cluster their collaborative agreements in a few selected partners.

Cooperation between firms of different nationalities is unlikely to be able to replicate the internal cohesion and shared values of a Toyota or Mitsubishi – or even a Daimler-Benz or an ICI. Trust is easier to foster when management share communities, schooling, culture and values; this is not an option generally available to firms considering international co-operative ventures. In such circumstances, pleas to foster trust may have limited validity, and management may have to reconcile themselves to default tactics involving high transaction costs and reflecting low trust. Also, preferring to cluster your collaborative agreements with few rather than many partners does not reflect trust, but is instead an indicator of its absence. Both partners may be more willing to enter into specific collaborative arrangements if they have other ventures in common with the same firm that can be used as hostages to encourage and ensure good behaviour if necessary. If we wished to find indirect evidence that trust is difficult and costly to create from scratch, we need look no further than the high transaction costs typically associated with international joint venture activity, and the evolution of alliances as an umbrella for multiple collaborations.

Secondly, while trust may economise on costs of monitoring existing relationships, this may be at the expense of additional costs associated with relationships at the entry and exit stages. What happens if the system has made a mistake, or changing circumstances signal a need to re-evaluate the present relationship? Low-trust societies usually have well-established exit solutions for dealing with problems of incompetence, obsolescence, decline and senescence. These solutions are usually as simple as they are inequitable, but they are often not solutions that can easily be adopted by high-trust societies, at least not without some modification and social tension. Trust may encourage flexibility *within* relationships at the expense of flexibility *of* relationships themselves, impeding the formation of new relationships and the termination of old ones.

5.4   LEVELS OF TRUST

The notion of trust has further layers of complexity when attempts are made to unravel its meaning and importance. For example, when we analyse the foci of trust identified by Casson (and other authorities), there appear to be at least three distinct types or levels. Firstly, there is what we might describe as trust at the level of the *event*, in which individuals may trust that certain actions executable by another individual may (or may not) occur in, for example, a Cournot type game (Casson 1995a: 18). Secondly, there is what might be described as trust at the level of the *individual*, as when an individual has a reputation for non-exploitation, integrity and fairness (Casson 1995a: 19). Thirdly, there is what might be described as trust at the level of *society* as when groups or societies can be identified as high trust or low trust (e.g. Casson 1995a: 172–4). Thus, Casson characterises Japan as a high-trust society with strong co-operative social relations, while he characterises the USA as a low-trust society in which the legal system has had to play a significant and expensive role to compensate for failures of trust. Social trust may also be reflected at the level of groups or organisations (e.g., some firms, voluntary organisations, clans of various kinds).

The problem for conventional economics is that it is only comfortable dealing with the first form of trust, even if the possible conflicts with self-interest are set aside in each case. Trust could be imputed in the case of event-based trust as a change in the subjective probabilities that an event will or will not occur; for example, if another player promises to co-operate even if it is against his or her immediate self-interest, and the first player revises his or her expectations accordingly. Thus Dasgupta defines trust 'in the sense of correct expectations about the *actions* of other people that have a bearing on one's choice of action when that action must be chosen before one can *monitor* the actions of those others' (1988a: 51; italics in original).

Conventional economics faces more difficulties in dealing with the second level of trust; that is, trust in individuals. The question that naturally raises itself in this context is, trust with respect to what? The temptation is to define trust in this context also with respect to some defined task, which can bring us into the territory of principal–agent problems and back to the notion of event-based trust. Dasgupta (1988a: 53) also comments 'trust is based on reputation and that reputation has ultimately to be acquired through behaviour over time in well-understood circumstances'.

The type of well-understood circumstances Dasgupta envisages are specified events in a game-theoretic context, as when a salesman develops a reputation for honesty in selling cars. The idea of trustworthiness as some abstract quality which can be embodied in individuals can be endowed is not one that comes naturally to economists *qua* economists, especially given the dominant role that self-interest plays in the discipline. Of course, conventional methods could be found to impute it – e.g., if we inferred a premium in the internal or external labour market for some worker deemed 'trustworthy' – but this is very much a side-door method that reduces trust to the status of just another quality such as strength, productivity or intelligence. It does not really recognises that trust can change the characteristics of relationships as well as the characteristics of individuals or events.

However, it is the third level of trust; trust at the level of society or groups that can help characterise them as high- or low-trust associations, that poses particular problems for conventional economics. The idea of a disembodied notion of trust floating around somewhere in the social ether is not one that economists naturally warm to, to say the least. True, possible social or cultural factors may be alluded to in asides in economics when conventional explanations have failed, but this usually seems a defeat for economic reasoning rather than an integral aspect of it. As Casson points out, culture has traditionally been regarded as an exogenous factor in economic analysis. However, while there is absolutely no justification for recognising the third level of trust if one believes that economics is about methodological individualism, there may be every justification for doing so if one believes that economics is about what influences the allocation of resources. As Casson argues, the third level of trust appears to have profound implications for the development of economies.

It is worth noting in passing here that conventional economics already has a unit in which co-operation and trust would seem to be implicit: the terms 'consumer' and 'household' are typically used interchangeably, even though the former clearly refers to an individual and the latter may comprise such a tightly defined group that it can effectively be treated as a single unit for many purposes. As Casson points out (1995a: 32), economics has not fulfilled its claim to explain key features of family behaviour in purely economic terms. It is difficult to see how the concept of the household 'unit' can be legitimated without recourse to some co-operative glue such as trust. Conventional economics usually deals with the issue of how individualism can be reconciled with the concept of the household by ignoring it. An anthropologist might find the next step from 'household' to 'clan' a not particularly dramatic one, especially in societies in which the households already comprise large, extended families.[8] It might seem that there is a greater conceptual distance between the notions of the individual and the household than there is between those of the household and the clan. The former comparison involves a *qualitative* shift of focus from individualism to kinship relations, while in the latter shift the major differences tend to lie in the *degree* to which kinship relations impact on resource allocation. However, for a modern economist, the latter step is the step from economics to sociology, and, again, there lie dragons.

5.5   TRUST, CULTURE AND LEADERSHIP

One of the important features of Casson's approach is that he brings cultural aspects centre stage in the analysis of economic activity. He argues that 'economists can no longer afford to regard culture simply as an exogenous factor impeding the modernization of primitive societies' (1995a: 31). This is certainly the case but it is important to acknowledge that our models and theories have always been influenced by cultural factors, even when they are presented as universal treatises. Adam Smith wrote at a time when the Scottish economy was characterised by fragmented, small-scale industrial activity, individualism was a thesis which was developing partly in reaction to a repressive church regime, and the 'public interest' had been subverted by a Scottish establishment whose corruption was remarkable even by the permissive standards of the eighteenth century. The *'Wealth of Nations'* is a product of its time and culture, and we should not be surprised that Smith emphasised atomistic competition, private self-interest and public corruption. This was not a product of armchair reasoning or abstract modelling: it was what he saw around him. Twentieth-century economics is the codification and embodiment of eighteenth-century Scotland.

These points are important in the context of Casson's discussion of the role of culture. Casson defines culture from an economic standpoint as 'a shared set of values, norms and beliefs' (1995a: 89). However, what about individualistic versus collectivistic societies? Presumably the latter reflect a higher level of shared values, norms and beliefs. Does this mean the former are low-culture societies and latter high-culture (in the economic sense)? Casson sees culture as generally having a benign influence on economic efficiency:

> [C]ulture sustains shared values and beliefs and thereby engineers mutual trust within a group. Trust economizes on information costs ... it is sufficient to know whether someone belongs to the same group to know whether the information they supply is likely to be true or not.
>
> (1995b: ix)

> A culture that encourages good behaviour towards other people, honesty and integrity, for example, is likely to improve the coordination of different individuals' decisions: for example by reducing transaction costs. This may be termed the moral aspect of a culture.
>
> (1995a: 163)

There is nothing wrong with these points as they stand; the question is, at what price are these gains achieved? Shared values, beliefs and norms may certainly facilitate exchanges by reducing transaction costs. They may also induce conformity, reduce variety, dull innovativeness and stifle entrepreneurship. For example, immigrant Scots frequently played strong entrepreneurial roles in the development of North America, and immigrants from the Indian sub-continent have played similar roles in East Africa. The performance of the migrants in these respects frequently compare favourably with their peers in the home country: Scots in Scotland and Indians in India have tended to exhibit weaker tendencies as far as formation of a strong entrepreneurial class is concerned. The obvious culprit is not the absence of culture but its presence. A traditional saying in Scotland is 'ah kent yer faither' (I knew your father), meaning do not get too big for your boots, remember the society you came from: no doubt there is an equivalent saying in Punjabi or Gujarati. However, a Scot in America, or an Indian in East Africa, might have to travel a long distance before somebody could say that to him. It would seem reasonable to conclude that culture can both stimulate and inhibit entrepreneurship; if a society values equality of *opportunities*, it is likely to stimulate entrepreneurship, while, if it values equality of *outcomes*, it is likely to inhibit it. A culture (such as traditional Scottish society) that values both versions of egalitarianism simultaneously is likely to provide a complex mix of conflicting signals and incentives.

A related issue which plays a major role in Casson's analysis of culture is the role of leadership. This is something which I frankly found puzzling at first. Culture appears to be a generalised contextual phenomenon in Casson's analysis and it is not immediately obvious what central role leadership has to play in such discussion. It appears that the reason that leadership plays such a significant part in Casson's work is that he sees it as a major element in change; parallels are drawn with the entrepreneur (1995a: 117–20) and the role of leaders in effecting cultural change (e.g., within the corporation: 1995a: 198–205) is also discussed. In a sense the institutional perspectives of markets (and entrepreneurs) and hierarchies (and peak co-ordinators) provide natural frames of references to invoke the role of leaders (whether as entrepreneurs or peak co-ordinators) in the process of resource allocation in Casson's analysis. However, I wonder if the role of leadership is perhaps overstated in the discussion of the role of trust and culture. If I trust my colleagues to cover for me if I have a cold, and they trust I am not malingering, it is not clear where leadership comes into this equation. Casson also argues that the reconciliation of individual freedom with a high degree of trust can only be achieved through effective leadership at the level of both the nation and the firm (1995a: 162) and gives Japan as a model of a high trust society (1995a: 174), Yet this is a nation in which the corruption of politicians has become 'a national scandal' in recent years (Fukuyama 1995: 15). To the extent that Japan has remained a high-trust society, it would seem to be despite the country's leaders rather than because of them. Trust may be a social characteristic that may be less directly linked to the function of leadership than Casson claims.

A related point is that the notion of necessary *intervention* (by a leader? a government?) is also implicit in economists' notion that trust is a public good, and so will tend to have market failure characteristics that may lead to an under-investment in trust (Dasgupta 1988a: 64). However, the economists' perception here raises more problems than it solves, since the usual economists' solutions to public good problems do not seem to hold in the case of trust. The public good problem is that a society will *not* spontaneously organise the provision of such a good or service. Defence is a classic example, and Yossarian would likely be a classic free rider if he was asked to voluntarily pay his contribution to the war effort rather than through taxes. Without intervention, the free rider would lead to the good not being provided at all, never mind being under-provided. How, then, do societies like

Japan develop a public good associated with being a high-trust society and not dissolve into a society of Yossarians? Why has the free rider not wiped out the trusting fools if trust is indeed a public good? This is surely a perverse kind of public good that can somehow be spontaneously generated and sustained without apparent intervention and conscious government regulation.

Instead, Fukuyama (1995) suggests that trust may emerge as an aspect of 'spontaneous sociability', a form of social capital which can refer to the emergence of a wide range of intermediate communities distinct from the family or those formed by the government (1995: 27). These may include, *inter alia*, corporations, voluntary organisations and community structures. Fukuyama points out the most useful kind of social capital associated with spontaneous sociability is not the ability to work under authority but the capacity to form new associations and to co-operate within the terms of reference they establish (1995: 27). The idea of 'spontaneous sociability' is not inconsistent with the notion of leadership, but Fukuyama's perspective is on group characteristics rather than individuals such as leaders. This may be as we should expect; a corollary of letting 'trust' chip away at the self-interest aspect of the notion of individual self-interest is that it may invite reconsideration of whether the individual itself is the appropriate unit of analysis. It is at least worth noting that notions such as entrepreneur and leadership are carry-overs from the methodological individualistic perspectives of conventional economics. Even notions of market failure such as public goods depend on an individualistic conception of the economic process. This is the baggage that all of us who trained as economists carry with us into our analysis of social science phenomena, especially those who come from individualistic cultures. The danger is that we may place to much emphasis on the role of individuals (leaders, entrepreneurs) and miss the fact that groups themselves may spontaneously evolve characteristics that are not attributable to (or maintained by) the actions of specific individuals, especially if that spontaneity takes place at the level of the evolution of society as a whole and not specific organisations.

5.6   LAST WORDS

As Casson acknowledges above, the trick is to reconcile individual freedom with high degree of trust: the problem is that there may be trade-offs between the two and that trust may be costly and indeed inefficient compared to alternatives. What Casson and Fukuyama have helped to do is to open up the agenda to a concept which has traditionally been largely neglected in economics, or dismissed as 'sociological'. If there are questions raised by their contributions, this is all to the good and to be expected, and reflects the innovatory nature of their analysis. Trust is a fascinating concept, not only because it appears to have strong efficiency implications but because it is not always clear as to what these are. It is clearly a more complex concept than straightforward self-interest, and as Casson indicates, it is likely that further exploration of its implications will draw economists into methodological issues which they have traditionally avoided. In economics, trust has been as neglected as opportunism has been oversold. If opportunism has been a Leitmotif for late twentieth-century economics writing, it may well be that work such as Casson's will help make trust a theme for the beginning of the twenty-first.

NOTES

1   Originally published in *The International Journal of the Economics of Business*, 3(2) 1996, pp. 249–60; reprinted by kind permission of the publisher, Carfax Publishing Ltd, PO Box 25, Abingdon, Oxfordshire OX14 3UE

2   Vol. 1, *Entrepreneurship and Business Culture*, and Vol. 2, *The Organization of International Business*, Aldershot: Edward Elgar.

3   It is assumed that the reader is broadly familiar with the logic of the Prisoner's Dilemma. If not, most first-year economics textbooks carry an explanation of it.

4   Reported in Fukuyama (1995: 310). In this longitudinal study Putnam found that the proportion answering in the affirmative to the question fell from 58% in 1960 to 37% in 1993. Fukuyama takes this as an indicator of the decline in social trust in the US over that period.

5   See, for example, Ouchi (1980).

6   The Scottish clan system and the Zabaitsu – described by Ouchi (1980), as a form of industrial clan – shared similar fates in being systematically broken up by the incoming victors. However, whereas the Zaibatsu successfully reformed, the Scottish clans did not. The different military occupations were characterised by very different social, economic and political circumstances, especially the goals of the occupying military authorities and the persistence of occupation in the respective cases.

7   Reported and discussed in Argyle (1991: 74–5).

8   Traditional Chinese society may provide a good example of this. Beyond the extended family (which could encompass five generations)

there were typically further concentric circles of kinship relations with great economic significance. The most important of these was the lineage, clan or family of families, in which all claimed common descent from a single ancestor. The economic function of lineages was to widen the circle of kindship beyond the family and so extend the number of people who could be trusted in an economic enterprise (Fukuyama 1995: 90–1).

Part II Strategies

INTRODUCTION

Part II is concerned with the strategies pursued by firms and looks at R&D (Chapter 6), diversification (Chapter 7), multinational enterprise (Chapter 8) and joint venture activity (Chapter 9). They build on the analysis of Chapter 4 in that transactions costs of one kind or another tend to influence the analysis in each of the cases. The role of surprise as discussed in Chapter 3 is especially important in Chapter 7, and the discussion of technological change in Chapter 2 is also relevant to Chapters 6 and 7 in particular. The analysis of multinational enterprise in Chapter 8 is in part a spin-off from the earlier diversification work of Kay (1982 and 1984).

The work on joint venture (Chapter 9) was also partly inspired by earlier work such as the paper on Boeing's diversification strategy (Chapter 7). It became apparent in looking at Boeing and its rivals that much of the strategic effort of such large diversified companies in the post-war period was increasingly being diverted away from mergers and acquisitions and into joint venture and other collaborative activity. The paper that makes up Chapter 9 was a subsequent attempt to consider why this was the case.

111

6 The R&D Function

Corporate Strategy and Structure[1]

6.1 INTRODUCTION

The purpose of this chapter is to examine the R&D function, its strategic problems and internal organisation, from the perspective of economics. We shall analyse the economics of R&D activity in terms of four basic features or characteristics, and then consider the implications of these characteristics for function, strategy and structure. We hope to show that these characteristics are recurring features of analysis, often underlying a wide variety of issues and problems that have frequently been treated independently of each other in separate literatures and approaches. We start by examining the four characteristics, before examining in turn their implications for R&D activity, strategy and internal organisation.

6.2 THE CHARACTERISTICS OF R&D ACTIVITY

The four characteristics or features that have central importance for the economics of R&D activity are non-specificities, lags, uncertainty and costliness. *Non-specificity* in this context is relevant at the level of the product and the firm. Much R&D is not product-specific in so far as a particular piece of work may feed into a variety of end products, the R&D generating technological synergies, or economies of scope. Also, much R&D activity is not firm-specific, generating externality and property-right problems. Both questions are likely to be very important for the firm; low product-specificity may allow the firm to spread R&D costs over a variety of product lines, while low firm-specificity may signal a weak or low competitive advantage for the firm in its R&D activity.

Lags and delays are a typical feature of R&D activity, a given piece of R&D often taking many years before it is embodied in commercial ventures, if at all. In themselves, lags are not necessarily an intractable problem, but they may directly contribute to other problems such as dangers of losing proprietary knowledge (low firm specificity), cost and uncertainty.

Uncertainty is also a pervasive problem, uncertainty in this context meaning unmeasurable or non-insurable uncertainty (Knight 1921), in contrast to predictable or measurable risks of an actuarial nature. Uncertainty here can be classified into general business uncertainty, which refers to all decisions concerning the future; technical uncertainty, which is concerned with achievement of specified performance and cost level; and market uncertainty, which refers to the possible achievement of a commercially viable product or process. R&D work can be faced with problems of uncertainty of all three types (Freeman 1982: chap.7).

Cost levels and associated resource commitment also tend to pose problems, though these can vary from sector to sector. The barriers to entry, or even to continuance, posed by high and/or increasing R&D economies of scale and scope have become a major issue in some sectors like aerospace and automobiles. Just as lags may not pose insuperable problems in certain circumstances, so also cost level itself should not be a problem if there are no significant problems of knowledge and information in the market place. Such issues do become important, however, if R&D cost levels exceed the internal financing capability of the firm, and there are information barriers to external capital market financing of corporate projects.

The impact of these factors generally varies as a project moves from basic research through applied research into development and then final introduction or innovation. Generally, non-specificities, lags and uncertainty tend to decrease, while cost levels and associated resource demands tend to increase, as a project moves downstream through the various stages towards final innovation. As far as non-specificities are concerned, both product- and firm-specificity of R&D tends to increase as a project moves towards final launch. For example, in laser R&D, basic research may be ultimately applicable to a wide range of applications in laser technology, applied research is likely to be concerned with a narrower range of potential applications – say in measuring devices – while resulting development work is liable to be limited to a specific measuring device or highly related group of devices. This tendency for product-specificity to rise as a project moves through the various R&D stages may also create parallel tendencies for firm-specificity to rise in the same direction; the extent of external applications due to leakage of technical information is likely to be directly related to product non-specificity. Thus, externalities may be more important for earlier, upstream research activity, especially basic research. Any tendency for firm-specificity to vary in this fashion may be reinforced to the extent that development work reflects tacit knowledge that may not easily diffuse externally, and also to the extent that basic research involves appropriability problems such as inapplicability of patent protection.

The other features tend to vary in a more obvious fashion as projects move along basic research, applied research, development, to introduction. Lags to final innovation will tend to be cumulative through the various stages and will tend to shorten towards and through development (Kay 1979: 23–4). Uncertainties tend to increase the further a stage is removed from final innovation (Freeman 1982: 150), and so degree of uncertainty in its various manifestations is likely to diminish as a project moves through its various stages to completion. Finally, the cost of R&D activity tends to increase as projects move from earlier stages through to development and from laboratory experimentation to prototypes and pilot plants (Mansfield 1968: 78).

In the next section we shall examine how these characteristics individually and collectively contribute to important issues and problems in R&D management and behaviour.

6.3   THE FOUR CHARACTERISTICS AND R&D BEHAVIOUR

It follows therefore that non-specificity, lags, uncertainty and costliness are each common features of R&D, though the relative importance of respective characteristics may vary with technology, firm or even time period. The extent and significance of the first three characteristics will tend to diminish as projects move from earlier upstream stages towards eventual innovation, while costliness of projects and associated resource commitments frequently increase in the same direction. Any reasonably innovative project is likely to encounter issues of non-specificity, lags, uncertainty and cost that could have important implications for their competitive position in the market place. For example, are product-specificities low enough to provide synergies and spread R&D costs? Are firm-specificities strong enough to avoid appropriability problems? Are lags short enough to facilitate first-mover advantages? Are uncertainties sufficiently controllable to guide resource direction and reassure the capital market? Will cost considerations be low enough to permit internal financing?

Not only will questions like these vary in importance from project to project; they will vary in importance as projects and related or derived projects move downstream towards final completion. In this section we explore the implications of these general issues for a number of problems in R&D behaviour.

6.3.1   The financing of R&D and the importance of uncertainty

Uncertainty is a dominant characteristic influencing the financing of R&D both at project level and at the level of the R&D function overall. To start with, very little R&D work is financed by the external capital market, most being internally financed (Freeman 1982: 149). However, this may conceal a greater level of capital market response to R&D activity than is apparent at first sight, since the external capital market may be strongly influenced in their overall level of support for the company by general R&D performance, as well as signals relating to the proposed activity.

One element that may impede efficient linking of external capital and internal R&D is possible conflict of interest in information disclosure as far as capital market and product market is concerned. Improving the quality and detail of R&D plans available to the capital market may have a detrimental effect on a firm's competitive advantage in the product market. These conflicts may constitute limiting factors on the potential efficiency of external financing, and the problems may be exacerbated to the extent that corporate actors are liable to indulge in opportunistic behaviour and misrepresentation. If, despite these problems, external financing is undertaken – say, by government agencies – uncertainty creates problems in contract design. A cost-plus system would leave the sponsoring agency vulnerable to moral hazard and opportunism, while fixed-price systems might make it difficult to find R&D-conducting firms willing to bear the uncertainties and associated costs. The frequently observed optimistic bias in estimating R&D costs and lag times (Freeman 1982: 151–6) is also attributable to uncertainty either because no allowance is made for uncertainties, 'bugs' and surprises, or because project estimators may opportunistically abuse a knowledge advantage to gain project approval by deliberately underestimating costs and lags.

Uncertainty also creates time-cost trade-offs; if a target is required urgently, as in cancer research, many tasks may have to be carried out simultaneously, increasing the chances of duplicated learning, dead-ends and diminishing returns (Mansfield 1968: 72; Freeman 1982: 151). If the target can be approached more slowly, many R&D tasks can be carried out sequentially, permitting transference of learning and experience, with consequent economising on resources. Finally, the same problems of uncertainty encountered in this problem area also impede construction of R&D budgets in a rational, aggregative, bottom-up fashion. As a consequence, most large firms allocate annual funds to the R&D function on a rule-of-thumb basis such as percentage of sales (Mansfield 1968: 62; Kay 1979: 72–7). The actual budget rule often evolves through decision makers learning what is the 'appropriate' budget for their firm (Freeman 1982: 163).

6.3.2 Basic research: the extreme case

The further upstream a project is located in the basic research-applied research-development-introduction progression, the more lags, uncertainties and non-specificities assume importance in the resource allocation process. This is especially the case for basic research activity. The lags and uncertainties involved may discourage private investors (Freeman 1982: 168) and these problems are likely to be compounded by the existence of non-specificities in the form of externalities. Consequently, government intervention or support for basic research is likely as a result of these market failure problems, though government support for basic research has traditionally been biased towards support for universities rather than corporations. For those firms that do conduct basic research, the diversified firm is likely to have an advantage, since a broad portfolio of businesses means that the various unpredictable and unexpected results are more likely to be internalised within corporate businesses (Nelson 1959).[2] The 3M Corporation is an example of a highly diversified firm which has a successful track record of exploiting radical, innovative opportunities in this way, often within divisions unrelated to those that developed the original idea.

Demand-pull[3] theories of innovation are likely to be less relevant the further upstream a project is located. If demand-pull theories are relevant at all, it is likely to be in the development stage when work is close to completion, less uncertain, and more specific and precise in its output; Freeman (1982: 103) points out the pull of the market operated as a complementary force to technological momentum in many cases where the market demand was *urgent* and *specific*. The further back towards basic research a project is located, the more supply-side science and technology-push arguments are likely to be relevant.[4]

6.3.3   Winners and losers

Being first to introduce a new product or process does not guarantee success, and indeed the four characteristics of R&D may combine against the first-in. The first-in may incur severe problems of uncertainty, delay and cost, while non-specificities may contribute to rapid leakages of technical knowledge externalities to potential competitors. Mansfield (1985) produces evidence to show that information on technical developments typically leaks out very rapidly to competitors in a wide range of technologies. The second-in may exploit such non-specificities to cut down on the uncertainties, delays and costs incurred by the pioneer. The pioneer may have first-mover advantages, but these factors may erode them partially or totally. Sperry's loss of an early lead in commercial computer development to IBM was a major example of this type.

Consequently, the link between a firm's own R&D and its subsequent growth is highly tenuous at best, though for a given industry as a whole there is typically a stronger and observable relationship between industries' R&D and industry growth (Freeman 1982: 164). The instabilities associated with firm level tend to smooth out at industry level, while many of the externalities will work themselves out within industry boundaries, strengthening the link between industry R&D and growth.

6.3.4   Implications of possible recent changes in the characteristics

The cost factor has become an even more important influence in some sectors in recent years. Previously, merger and takeover represented strategic devices for spreading escalating R&D costs and exploiting internal economies. In some sectors, such as aircraft and automobiles, mergers and takeovers may have reached saturation point for nationalistic and antitrust reasons. Joint ventures and licensing agreements have grown in importance in recent years and, in at least some cases, represent attempts to spread R&D costs when merger is not feasible or desirable. R&D consortia or clubs have also evolved for similar reasons in some sectors, such as electronics.

The creation of R&D consortia or clubs may provide co-operative gains for the participating members in the form of technological advantages that would have been difficult or too costly for individual members to develop alone. We would expect such co-operative ventures to emphasise more upstream non-product-specific activity, since research of this nature is more likely to benefit the group as a whole, or a significant proportion of its members. More downstream product-specific development activity might lead to possible direct competitive conflict between group members and could have a zero-sum quality for participants in the venture. Consequently, Nelson (1984) suggests that such ventures are more likely to be appropriate for the exploitation of generic research programmes applicable to a variety of subsequent development programmes. Some evidence of this is provided by Peck (1986), who cites the example of MCC, a private microelectronics and computer technology joint R&D project involving 21 US companies. Its research programmes are generally consistent with Nelson's definition of generic research; Peck gives as an example the VLSI/CAD programme in MCC which does not design specific circuits but instead seeks to develop methods of computer designing circuits (1986: 220).

Another possible change that may have significance for the conduct of research is that the perceived lag between conduct of basic research and eventual commercial application may have shortened in some cases, such as certain areas of biotechnology. Scientific norms of openness and active dissemination of research results may be compromised if commercial applications are expected in the relatively near future; the compartmentalisation of the historically distinct traditions and norms of science and commerce has traditionally been facilitated by the existence of buffers in the form of long lags weakening the profit implications of basic research for individual researchers.

Therefore, the four characteristics, and changes in these characteristics, have fundamental implications for the conduct of R&D activity. In the next section we shall see that these same characteristics have similarly profound implications for corporate strategy and internal organisation.

6.4   STRATEGY AND STRUCTURE IMPLICATIONS

In this section we shall look at some implications of the four characteristics for the strategy and structure of individual corporations. We shall devote more attention to problems of structure or internal organisation, since many of the problems relating to strategy have already been introduced and discussed in the previous section. Freeman (1982) provides a synopsis of strategy types that incorporate or reflect a number of problems discussed in the last section. As far as analysis of strategy itself is concerned, Freeman (1982) produces a useful basis for analysing different types of R&D strategy.

The *offensive* strategy will be appropriate if there are particular advantages to being first in with a particular innovation. Here protection of property rights (especially non-specificities) and lags required for competitive response are critical elements in deciding whether or not to adopt an offensive strategy.

The *defensive* strategy is still likely to involve a high level of R&D, but the firm is prepared to react and follow offensive innovators, possibly with some degree of product differentiation. Obviously, if an offensive innovator finds that non-specificities benefit other firms in the form of externalities, this facilitates defensive strategies, and, as we saw in the previous section, such circumstances may be the norm rather than the exception. The ability to respond quickly and reduce lags is also important. As Freeman points out (1982: 178), a science-based firm's R&D strategy may contain mixtures of offensive and defensive strategies. IBM was an example of a company which grew by successfully and consistently pursuing a defensive strategy, mobilising considerable technical and marketing resources to respond to external technological threats.

The *imitative* strategy does not attempt to match the offensive and defensive innovators in terms of skills and is prepared to follow some way behind if it enjoys particular advantages in terms of cost, tariffs or supplies.

The *dependent* strategy is usually followed by smaller firms with subordinate sub-contracting roles in which they do not initiate new products but accept specifications and conditions imposed by dominant firms. Component manufacturers in the automobile industry have typically adopted such a role, though there are interesting signs that even in this sector the threat from Japanese manufacturers is likely to lead to merger and consolidation among parts-makers. Amalgamation would help create the critical mass necessary to take a more active and leading role in component and sub-system innovation (*The Economist*, 23 May 1987, p. 80).

The *traditional* strategy is based on absence of technological innovation in a market which is benign and slow changing, while the *opportunist* strategy is based on entrepreneurial perception of niches that may not require substantial in-house R&D.

The four characteristics discussed earlier may all influence the possible strategies a firm will choose. For example, cost, uncertainty and lags may dissuade smaller, specialised firms from adopting offensive or defensive strategies, while non-specificities and second-in advantages discussed earlier may persuade firms to adopt a defensive rather than an offensive strategy. On the other hand, if it is possible to disengage the relatively cheaper upstream inventive stages from the more expensive downstream development work, small firms may have a comparative advantage on these cheaper, earlier stages. Large firms may be better placed to indulge in costly full-scale development (Freeman 1982: 137; Williamson 1975: 142). The role of structure or internal organisation in R&D activity is also influenced by the four characteristics. Williamson (1975), building on Chandler (1962), provides an analysis that will help introduce basic ideas which we can then develop further using our earlier analysis of the four basic characteristics.

Williamson contrasts the functional, or U-form, structure which is more appropriate for smaller, specialised firms with the multidivisional, or M-form, structure which is likely to evolve in large diversified firms. In a specialised firm, the similarities and synergies between groups of products are so strong that functional specialists are liable to have to spend considerable time talking to each other and co-ordinating plans and schedules. Consequently, it is logical to group them together in a functional home as in the U-form example in Figure 6.1.

The M-form structure will tend to be more appropriate for a large, diversified firm. Divisionalisation creates natural decision units in the diversified corporation, putting together those functions responsible for a product or group of products. The divisions are assigned responsibility for operating and short-term strategic decisions, so as to reduce the number of levels in the hierarchy that have to be crossed before an inter-functional decision is arrived at, reducing delay, loss and distortion of information, and permitting top-level management to concentrate on long-run, strategic decision making.

Figure 6.1   Basic hierarchies

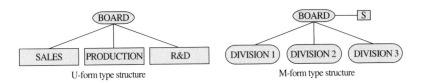

Further, a competitive internal capital market may be created, comparability of divisions being facilitated by the existence of a uniform project yardstick for performance at middle (divisional) levels.

Therefore, the M-form creates a rational structure for the management of large, diversified firms. The problem that R&D poses for this solution is that of all the functions it is the least likely to be amenable to such treatment. We can see why by comparing the characteristics of reasonably innovative R&D work with the characteristics of economic activity appropriate to divisional operations. On the four characteristics of time, uncertainty, non-specificity and cost, reasonably innovative R&D scores badly on the first three counts as far as divisional implications are concerned. Profit-centre operation tends to be short run; divisional managers are not only commonly assessed on the basis of annual performance, they are also typically highly qualified and mobile general managers for whom divisional performance in a few years' time would often represent an externality, and consequently be disregarded. Highly uncertain and long-term returns may also be discounted heavily by a managerial set for whom the penalties for failure may be greater than the rewards for success.[5] The product non-specificity aspect would also reinforce the tendency for divisional management to under-invest in, or neglect, R&D due to externality considerations, if most of the benefits accrue to other profit centres.

The problems of long-time horizon, non-specificity (or synergy) and high uncertainty are more appropriate to levels in the firm responsible for strategic overviews rather than short-term, specific responsibilities as in divisions. The further we move upstream towards basic research activity, the more these problems become exacerbated for divisional management. Therefore, the tendencies towards centralisation of R&D are accentuated the further upstream the R&D is located. This is indicated at 'S' level for the M-form in Figure 6.1. The fourth characteristic, cost, may work against the inclusion of even development work in some divisions if the system under development is extremely costly and complex. Divisions often have extremely limited discretionary access to internal funds, and costly development plans may exceed their discretionary limits. Accordingly, financing decisions, or even the development work itself, may have to be shoved further up the corporate hierarchy.

In those circumstances, it is reasonable to ask why *any* R&D should be conducted at divisional level. Low product-specificity, long lags, extreme uncertainty and high cost all provide barriers to the effective divisionalisation of R&D. If even one of these characteristics is present in a particular R&D project, it impedes divisionalising the project and provides pressure for incorporation at 'S' level in Figure 6.1. Further, even if some projects do not possess any of these characteristics to a significant extent, there may still be incentives to allocate them to 'S' level to avoid diseconomies from splitting the R&D function.

There are, in fact, counteracting pressures to leave some or all R&D at divisional level. Firstly, removing a major function such as R&D from divisional responsibility impairs the internal capital market in so far as R&D cost is now shared between divisions, reducing the extent to which divisions can be treated as independent profit centres. Secondly, in a major study of factors influencing success or failure of innovation,[6] the factor which discriminated most clearly between success or failure was whether or not users' needs were understood (Freeman 1982: 124). Separating R&D from divisional marketing could inhibit the integration of technological possibilities and designs with consumer requirements. Therefore, the location of R&D in the corporate hierarchy is likely to be a complex problem in practice, involving trade-offs between divisionalisation/centralisation advantages and disadvantages. Different companies evolve different solutions to these conflicts. At a relatively early stage in its post-war development, General Electric discovered that its divisions were not innovating largely for the reasons discussed earlier, and responded by reallocating much of its R&D to 'S' level. Du Pont's solution to similar problems was to split its divisions' budgets into two components, one for operations and one for innovations, and monitor the respective components separately.

In fact, the formal hierarchical designs discussed above face potentially severe limitations imposed by the nature of R&D and product life-cycle considerations. Hierarchical bureaucracies of the type described above fall into the category of mechanistic systems as defined by Burns and Stalker (1961).[7] *Mechanistic* systems are characterised by functional specialisation, precise roles, vertical interaction between managers and formal hierarchical relationships. This form was identified by Burns and Stalker as being appropriate to technologically stable conditions. *Organic* systems are characterised by informal lateral relationships, networks rather than hierarchies, continual redefinition of tasks and broadly specified responsibilities. These characterisations are ideal types, and in practice organisations operate along a continuum on which these descriptions represent polar extremes.

Mechanistic systems encounter problems in incorporating innovative decisions on their agenda, and are likely to face extreme difficulties in rapidly changing environments. Since innovation constitutes a break in existing standard operating procedures and programmes, mechanistic structures typically have great difficulty in accommodating relevant decisions within existing routines.

Relevant information is liable to be ignored or mistreated in mechanist structures because it does not fit into existing classifications, or may face delays in being acted on as it is referred up the hierarchy. Even if the system is set up to signal significant data on innovation, in a highly innovative environment this would lead to the senior management fire brigade facing a number of alarm bells ringing simultaneously. Innovation, especially in turbulent environments, is characterised by non-programmable, surprising, routine-breaking information, and the mechanistic structure typically encounters severe difficulties in this area of decision making. The characteristics of R&D uncertainty and non-specificity discussed earlier are particularly relevant here; Burns and Stalker point out that the mechanistic system is designed to deal with tasks that are *precise* and *specific*; uncertain, surprising tasks with a high degree of non-specificity will be ignored or mishandled by such a system.

The organic system, with its absence of pre-set rules, roles and responsibilities, is better equipped to facilitate innovativeness in rapidly changing environments. The form sacrifices the possibilities of static economies from functional specialisation and division of labour, but this can be a cheap sacrifice in conditions of rapid technological change, since these economies may not be obtainable in any case. What it provides instead is flexibility and responsiveness; the non-specificity and uncertainty inherent in innovation finds parallels in the non-specificity and uncertainty typically surrounding relationships and roles in the organic system.[8]

The principles differentiating organic from mechanistic systems in Burns and Stalker's early analysis have been embodied in a variety of organisational designs that have evolved in recent years. For example, project teams or task forces with limited life spans may be set up to deal with innovative opportunities, cutting across formal organisational hierarchies and dealing with non-specificities by focusing on 'the innovation' as the unifying concept. Matrix management is a more elaborate and complex solution displaying both mechanistic and organic features and has been adopted by firms facing turbulent environments, including ITT, Monsanto, ICI and Lockheed. In a matrix structure an individual typically has simultaneous responsibilities to a functional home (for example, R&D, production, marketing) and to a specific project. In principle, the functional line of responsibility provides mechanistic static economies from functional grouping specialisation, while the project line of responsibility provides organic dynamic efficiency gains by focusing and integrating at the level of the particular project or innovation. In practice, dual responsibilities and confusion of responsibilities may inhibit the extent to which firms operating a matrix system can pursue dynamic and static efficiency goals simultaneously.[9]

To summarise, the characteristics that were important in shaping issues at *project* level in innovative activity (that is, uncertainty, non-specificity, lags and cost) have also proved central in analysing problems of R&D strategy and organisation design. Non-specificity, uncertainty, lags and cost are major considerations affecting R&D strategy and the incorporation of R&D within formal hierarchies, while non-specificity and uncertainty are particular features that may encourage adoption of an organic rather than a mechanistic mode.[10]

Thus, probing beneath the surface differences of conventional analysis of R&D behaviour, business and corporate strategy, and organisational form, reveals interesting similarities and parallels in terms of the general relevance of the four common concepts. This encourages optimism as to the possibility of pursuing a policy of integrating the historically separate literatures, to a greater or lesser extent.

This line of possible development finds further justification in arguments by some organisational theorists that work in their field would be enriched and strengthened by the adoption of an evolutionary perspective on the development of organisational forms (McKelvie and Aldrich 1983). They argue that existing studies tend to suffer from over-simplistic assumptions, presuming that organisations are either all alike or unique. They argue that systematising analysis of organisational forms, and introducing notions such as variation, selection and competition into analysis, would create a more coherent analytical basis in this area of study.

Again, at a surface level, McKelvie and Aldrich's argument is symptomatic of the Balkanisation of analysis in this area, since they make no reference to the extensive economic literature on evolutionary approaches to the study of organisation. However, at a deeper level, it suggests the possibility of commonalities and even convergence in terms of methods and frameworks between economics and organisational approaches, possibly complementing and building on the four common characteristics discussed throughout this chapter.

6.5 CONCLUDING REMARKS

Non-specificity, uncertainty, delay and cost are important attributes affecting the economics of R&D activity. This chapter has attempted to show that it is possible to synthesise apparently disparate threads as far as issues in analysis of the R&D function, corporate strategy and structure are concerned. It is argued that analysis of function, strategy and structure should be rooted in the same core issues and problems.

We are also optimistic that it is possible to discern kinship relationships in approaches, such as evolutionary theory, transaction cost economic and organisational decision making[11] in those subjects. If so, it offers interesting possibilities for cross-fertilisation between economic, business and organisational approaches.

NOTES

1. Originally published as 'The R&D function: strategy and structure', in G. Dosi, C. Freeman, R. Nelson, G, Silverberg and L. Soete (eds) *Technical Change and Economic Theory*, London: Frances Pinter, 1988, pp. 282–94. Reprinted by kind permission of Cassell Academic, Wellington House, 125 Strand, London WC2R 0BB, UK.
2. This implicitly assumes that the specialised firm would not be able to appropriate a high level of gains through market transactions; for example, joint venture and licensing. The reasonableness of this assumption may depend on the transaction costs associated with these alternatives in particular industrial environments.
3. The demand-pull approach is most commonly associated with Schmookler (1966). Mowery and Rosenberg (1979) have, however, questioned the legitimacy of many of the demand- or market-pull approaches to empirical interpretation.
4. However, the market still has an important role as an *ex post* selection device. See Nelson and Winter (1982) and Dosi (1982).
5. Freeman (1982: 167) points out that failure of divisional management to look far enough ahead was one consequence of the short-time perspective in profit-controlled divisions. Hayes and Abernathy (1980) identify the short-term orientation of divisional profit centres as a contributory factor towards what they perceive as the neglect of technological change in the US economy.

6. This was termed the Sappho project and is discussed in more detail in Freeman (1982: chap. 5).
7. Since Burns and Stalker's seminal work, a great deal of theoretical and practical analysis has been undertaken regarding organic system design. Child (1984) provides an excellent coverage of both these aspects.
8. This does not mean that R&D lags are not important in organic as they are in mechanistic systems. They will of course still be of relevance. However, what the organic system does appear to offer is a particularly appropriate system for dealing with the other two characteristics of non-specificity and uncertainty.
9. See, in particular, Nelson and Winter (1982).
10. Williamson (1985) presents a recent statement of his development of transaction cost economics. Kay (1982, 1984) utilises transaction-cost economics to analyse problems in corporate strategy and structure. For an analysis of problems associated with Williamson's existing framework, see Chapter 4 (this volume).
11. For a survey of work in this field, see March and Shapira (1982).

7 Boeing, Corporate Strategy and Technological Change[1]

7.1 INTRODUCTION

The concept of corporate strategy is one which has received considerable attention in the managerial literature in recent years. It is also attracting attention from economists concerned with problems of technological change, reflecting increased sensitivity to the possibilities for, and responses to, innovation.[2]

In this chapter we shall analyse the evolution of Boeing's corporate strategy over the 40-year period from 1945, with special reference to the role of technological change as a major element in this process. We shall briefly summarise relevant literature in both the corporate strategy and industrial organisation fields, before introducing a framework that will be applied to the problem of how Boeing's strategy has changed over a four-decade period. We shall then look at major aspects of Boeing's strategy in the light of the framework developed earlier, and finally present our conclusions as to how it may contribute to the development of corporate strategy.

7.2 CORPORATE STRATEGY

The strategy literature is characterised by a wide variety of definitions and interpretations of the concept. There are, however, common threads that may be tentatively identified in much of the literature.[3] For example, a distinction has been generally made in recent years between corporate strategy which defines the range of the firm's businesses, and business strategy which is concerned with how the firm will compete within each business (Bourgeois 1980). The strategic decision-making process can be characterised as one in which strategy is then formulated to pursue immediate objectives that are consistent with long-term objectives. The particular areas

129

of strategy formulation and strategy implementation have received considerable attention in the literature. The analysis of corporate strengths/weaknesses and opportunities/threats has been reinforced by the concept of distinctive competence; that is, those areas of activity in which a firm or part of a firm does better relative to its competition (Hitt and Ireland 1985). This field has generated a body of empirical analysis that provides valuable insights into the strategic behaviour of firms and industries. However, there are a few reservations that may be relevant to the applicability of this framework.

Firstly, the concept of distinctive competence has real problems of measurement and testability. A distinctive competence generates improved performance on the part of the firm, but to be objectively measurable that competence should be identifiable *independently* of improved performance, otherwise it runs the danger of being tautological. It is not always clear how this could be done, especially since distinctive competencies are almost by definition specific to the appropriate firms and so strategy is non-replicable in scientific-experimental terms (Bourgeois 1980). Further, since distinctive competencies can be associated with functional specialisms, it may be difficult or impossible to separate out different functional competencies as far as their respective contributions to the overall performance of the unit or firm are concerned.

Secondly, distinctive competencies may become obsolete. Singer's distinctive technological competencies in assembling electro-mechanical systems such as sewing machines and calculators was attacked by external technological innovations in electronics. The possibility of obsolescence in competencies is likely to be stronger in some environments than in others, but where it exists it should be an element in the strategic decision-making process. Strengths may become weaknesses in the very long run.

Thirdly, the goals and objectives of the strategic models and frameworks typically appear to have a fairly limited and constrained time horizon. For example, Hofer *et al.* (1980) identify a number of immediate objectives (growth, efficiency, resource utilisation, contributions to owners/customers/employees/society) designed to serve (unspecified) long-term goals. While it is obvious in many cases how these could be consistent with certain measurable and operational long-term goals like profit and market share, it is difficult to see how certain other strategies and goals could be reconciled with such a perspective; for example, diversification strategy to serve long-run survival. Survival may be a goal that it more difficult to operationalise, but in turbulent environments it may be a central preoccupation forced on the firm through choice or necessity.[4] Interestingly, the orientation of the literature towards more immediate and measurable goals is consistent with Hayes and Abernethy's (1980) criticism of the short-term marketing-biased perspective of US business. Whether this is coincidental, or whether there is cause and effect running in either direction between theory and practice, we leave here as an open question.

Fourthly, a further aspect reinforcing the restricted time horizons of much of the business strategy literature is that it tends to emphasise strategic reactive decision-making associated with particular points on the product life cycle; for example, strategy in growing, mature and declining markets. However, there are often generic similarities between product life cycles within an industry or technology groups (for example, food, electronics). To the extent that patterns can be identified, this may serve as a set of signals providing inputs into strategic decision making. Strategic decision making may be anticipatory as well as reactive; for example, if product life cycles are fairly slow changing and predictable then specialisation may be a more tenable option for a firm in such an environment than for one operating in complex, turbulent and unpredictable environments (Kay 1982).

It should be emphasised that these are general comments to which exceptions can be found; however, to the extent that a corporate strategy consensus or paradigm could be said to exist, the above comments may be taken as criticism of that consensus. In the next section we shall consider how the economics literature in industrial organisation may be of relevance to the study of corporate strategy, sounding alarm bells where we believe there is a danger that an inappropriate paradigm may be drawn on. We feel the criticisms we have made above would be reinforced if this approach was taken as representative of work now going on in industrial economics and adopted by corporate strategy theorists.

We shall concentrate on the corporate strategy of the firm as a whole rather than individual business strategy such as the commercial aircraft business or the space business. This reflects our concern in this chapter, not an opinion as to the relative importance of corporate strategy versus business strategy. A complete analysis of Boeing would integrate corporate and business strategies and treat them as complementary problem areas.

7.3   INDUSTRIAL ORGANISATION AND CORPORATE STRATEGY

Porter (1981) argued that the traditional Bain/Mason paradigm of industrial organisation has offered researchers in strategic management a useful model for assessing strategic decision making in industry. In this approach, industry structure determines corporate conduct or behaviour which in turn determines performance. Porter recognised that the traditional structure-conduct-performance (SCP) approach did not make great inroads into the strategic management literature, attributing this to a variety of factors, including differing frames of references in the respective fields as well as some limitations in the SCP approach itself. However, he argued that improvements being made to this established framework make it a much more appealing proposition for analysts of corporate strategy.

We do not agree, because we feel that the SCP approach is fatally flawed by its hereditary link with neoclassical theory in economics. The traditional structure-conduct-performance approach is in fact the applied arm of the neoclassical framework in which monopolies and competitors pursue rational profit-maximising behaviour under conditions of perfect knowledge. As Rumelt (1984: 559) points out, neoclassical theory assumes away (1) transaction costs, (2) bounded rationality, (3) technological uncertainty, (4) constraints on factor mobility, (5) limits on information availability, (6) markets in which price conveys quality information, (7) learning, (8) dishonest and/or foolish behaviour. It is true that some recent developments in oligopoly theory have extended some of the neoclassical analysis, but reservations may be expressed as to how they may actually contribute to strategy formulation.

Neoclassical theory is intrinsically deterministic and characterised by an absence of problems associated with bounded rationality and uncertainty. It could be argued that Rumelt's list of neoclassical theory's neglected issues would serve as a useful starting point for any researcher into corporate strategy. In such circumstances, neoclassical theory and its offspring the SCP approach are congenitally inappropriate for the analysis of corporate strategy. Developments and refinements of the basic paradigm cannot adequately deal with these fundamental defects.[5]

In fact, there are writers outside the neoclassical/SCP tradition in economics who have provided analyses that may be of direct relevance in developing an economic input into the corporate strategy field. For example, Schumpeter (1950) made technological not (neoclassical) price competition a central feature of his analysis, Penrose (1959) developed a theory of firm growth founded on a resource-based analysis of corporate distinctive competencies, while Nelson and Winter (1982) have followed in the Schumpeterian tradition and built on major contributions by Cyert, March and Simon in analysing the role of technological change in corporate decision making. Williamson (1975) is another writer whose work lies outside the neoclassical tradition.[6] His emphasis on problems such as bounded rationality, uncertainty, opportunism, information problems and transaction costs makes his work a potentially very valuable tool-kit for researchers in the strategy field.[7]

In the next section we shall briefly outline an economics-based framework for strategic decision making that is more consistent with these 'alternative' traditions than with the neoclassical approach, and then use it as a basis for analysing Boeing corporate strategy.

7.4 FRAMEWORK FOR ANALYSIS

In the analysis below we concentrate first of all on the question as to whether or not resource characteristics are shared or differ between activities. Where resource characteristics are similar between activities, they may provide synergies (Ansoff 1965). In economic terms, shared characteristics may provide commonalities in resource utilisation permitting economies in resource utilisation to be generated through exploitation of indivisibilities and specialisation/division of labour.

These are well-established and accepted features of strategic decision making. What is perhaps less obvious is that shared characteristics may also provide areas of mutual or common vulnerability to external threats. The resource linkage coin is double-sided; on the one side it may provide economies, on the other it may provide vulnerability. This should represent a basic starting point for any analysis of corporate strengths-weaknesses/opportunities-threats.

We can illustrate this point with a simple example. Yavitz and Newman (1981: 48–9) describe the strategy of Head Ski who diversified into aluminium tennis rackets from their original base in aluminium skis. According to Yavitz and Newman this may facilitate risk spreading to the extent that the two markets' fortunes are not perfectly correlated. We could add that Head should also have been able to exploit synergies due to common resource characteristics in leisure marketing and aluminium technology.

Thus Head could exploit synergies *and* spread risks. Such strategic moves would appear to be straightforward and highly desirable, as well as apparently conflicting with the suggestion above that resource sharing means risk sharing.

In fact, this double-side relationship holds at a deeper, strategic level. For example, if a competitor developed a superior skill in aluminium technology, Head's distinctive technological competence would be attacked across the board, just as in the case of Singer's mechanical assembling being threatened by new electronics technology skills. Also, if leisure tastes switch away from outdoor sports for some reason, both skiing and tennis would be threatened.

It is important to note that common resource characteristics need not necessarily provide economies or vulnerability. Economies may be fully exploited already, and particular common resource characteristics may not be threatened by any specific threats; for example, leisure market characteristics may be fairly stable as far as Head Ski is concerned. The relevant and critical point is that resource commonalities provided both a *potential* source of economies or synergies and a *potential* source of vulnerability, and it is these links that determine the implications of specific corporate strategies for particular firms.[8]

If we could map the pattern of resource similarities and linkages between the products and businesses of an individual corporation, then this would provide a basis for assessing the implications of specific strategies. In this perspective, strengths-weaknesses/opportunities-threats would be analysed in terms of the connections and interrelationships illuminated by mapping the patterns of resource similarities/differences. In earlier works (Kay 1982, 1984), this mapping approach was developed to investigate patterns of diversification, merger, takeovers, aggregate concentration, multinationalism and strategy/structure relations from an industrial organisation perspective. Here we shall develop the technique further to investigate its possibilities for analysis of corporate strategy.

In the diagrams that follow, the relative importance of each business area in terms of sales is associated with the implied volume of each sphere defining the respective businesses;[9] for example, if one sphere has twice the apparent volume of a second sphere, the former represents twice the sales volume of the latter. This scale relationship is maintained within and between diagrams, the sales volume[10] information is measured in constant 1967 dollars[11] so that the relative importance of business activities can be illustrated both at a point in time and as they change over time.

The aerospace business is volatile, with individual product lines and businesses recording often substantial variation in activity when measured on a year-to-year basis. In order to deal with this problem when constructing maps the mean annual sales for individual businesses was taken over selected three year periods. Using individual years would have been less reliable in indicating general patterns in the evaluation of corporate strategy. The three-year periods chosen were 1952–54, 1962–64, 1972–74 and 1982–84, and, as we shall see, serve as snapshot pictures of Boeing's changing strategy.

The other major feature of the diagrams is the linking of the business areas through shared characteristics. As discussed above, the existence of commonalities or similarities in resources between businesses may permit economies or synergies to be exploited as well as define areas of potential vulnerability to specific threats. It is therefore important to establish the strength or otherwise of resource commonalities between respective business areas and we illustrate this in the diagram by way of links or bonds of varying thickness to denote the degree of commonality. It may in principle be possible to derive methods for objectively measuring the strength of linkage or bonding between areas; for example, by conducting detailed analyses and audits of resources and their associated characteristics. Here we rely on subjectively estimating the extent to which resources share characteristics in different businesses. However, a large number of sources were consulted in order to provide evidence for estimation and these are discussed in detail in a later section. We analyse resources in terms of two categories of resources: marketing and technological.

7.5   BOEING'S POST-WAR DEVELOPMENT

Boeing in the early 1950s was a firm heavily specialised in the manufacture of military aircraft. The cessation of World War II had led to a slump in total aircraft industry sales from a wartime peak of $16 billion to about $1 billion in 1947. To some extent the wartime expansion had been facilitated by the temporary entry of non-aircraft firms such as the car manufacturers, and the provision of government-owned facilities; the exit of these firms and the government's assumption of much of the burden of excess capacity went some way to mitigating the consequences of such savage cutbacks in aircraft industry demand (Stekler 1965: 12–13). Putting less work out to sub-contractors was another method by which large firms could soften the effect of the decline in military spending.

Nevertheless, Boeing faced real difficulties in terms of falling demand for its products, in common with most of its competitors. It had been hoped that increasing peace-time demand for commercial aircraft would compensate for the decline in the military sector. There had indeed been a surge in demand in the civilian sector in the late 1940s, but this had petered out by the start of the 1950s due to market saturation. In any case, Douglas had re-established its domination of this market with its propeller-driven DC-4 and DC-6s. By 1955, of the 1352 aircraft in service with US airlines Douglas had produced 770, its only other major competitors being Convair, Lockheed and Martin (Stekler 1965: 13–14). The Korean war did in fact contribute to a temporary build-up in US military plane production which had peaked in 1953 before beginning a steady decline throughout the rest of the decade (Stekler 1965: 14). Nevertheless, Boeing continued to expand throughout the decade, from 28 000 employees in 1950 to 90 280 in 1960.[12] The traumas of post-war cutbacks were offset by steady corporate expansion over the decade, albeit from a very low base. However, the dependency on military markets meant that Boeing remained highly vulnerable to future cutbacks in military spending.

It was as this point in its history that Boeing management faced critical decisions as to the future direction of the company. Much of the aircraft industry had attempted diversification out of the defence market, usually with poor results. Skills developed in making and selling military machines were not easily transferable to mass-marketed consumer-product sectors. Further, the present threat posed by military market cutbacks was accompanied by the potential technological threat represented by the development of missiles; small tactical missiles had been developed by the early 1950s and six were in service by 1955. By the early 1950s it was also known that large long-range missiles were possible (Stekler 1965: 18). Thus, Boeing faced a possible pincer attack on its business: not only had its market base been threatened by military cutbacks, but there was a danger that the technology (aircraft) with which it operated in this market would be rendered partially or totally obsolete by the new technology (missiles). The actual and potential environmental threats are illustrated in Figure 7.1.[13]

The squeeze on military aircraft due to market and technological threats in the environment meant that Boeing's survival was endangered. The potential escape routes from this dilemma were dictated by resources. Boeing had two major bundles of resource skills and

Figure 7.1 Boeing environmental threats 1952–54

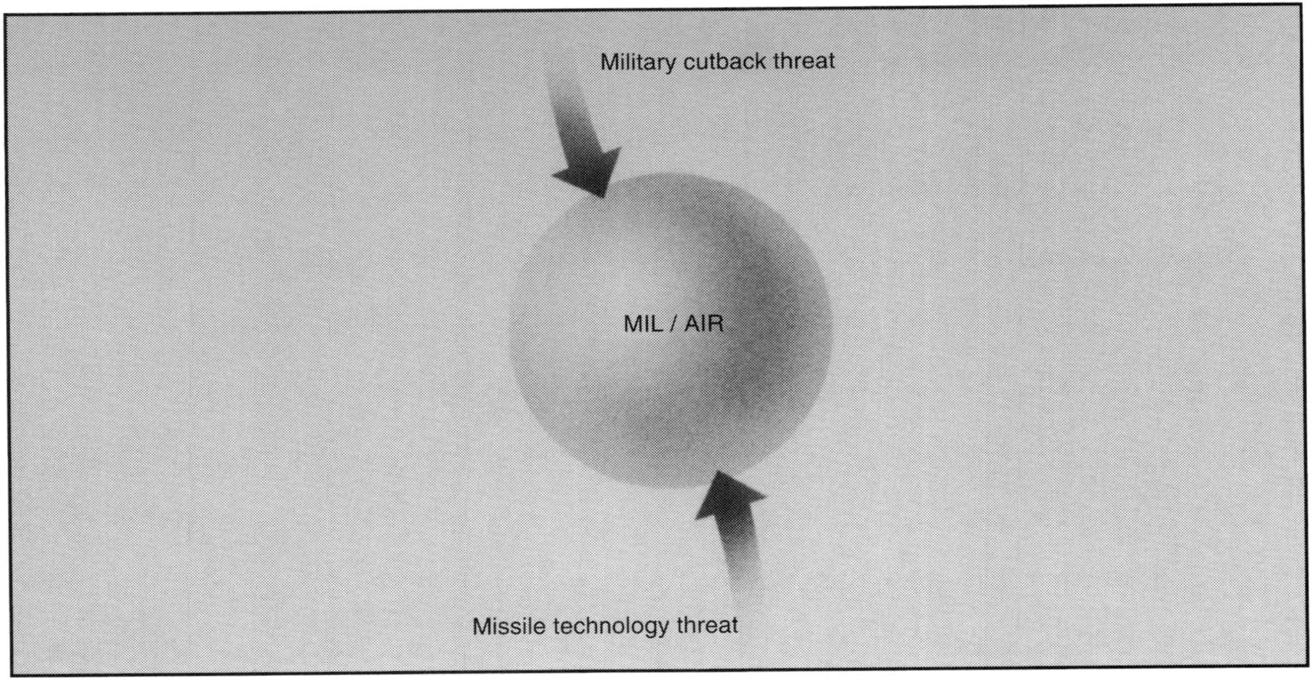

Military cutback threat

MIL / AIR

Missile technology threat

Code:: MIL/AIR, Military aircraft

expertise: in marketing and selling products to the government, and in the technology and construction of aircraft. If these bundles of resources could be separated out from each other, they could provide stepping stones for diversification into other markets and other technologies. To the extent that the area to be diversified into has similar or familiar resource characteristics to existing areas of operation, synergies or economies of scope from operation may be provided, as well as initial entry facilitated.[14]

The resource-based opportunities for Boeing diversification in the early 1950s are illustrated in Figure 7.2. The government marketing element represents one possible direction or signpost for diversification; the aircraft technology element represents another.

Boeing responded to the environmental threat by pursuing a diversification strategy based on *both* resource bundles. The government market link was first exploited by diversifying into missile production, and the aircraft technology link was exploited through entry into the commercial jet field with the 707. The UK-built De Havilland Comet had pioneered this latter market in the early 1950s but had suffered from problems of metal fatigue. Boeing was well placed to enter this market given its experience in developing the first American jet bombers, the B-47 and B-52, and by 1958 had begun producing the 707 (Bluestone *et al* 1981: 38). The 707 design closely followed that of the KC-135, a jet tanker developed by Boeing to service the bombers, permitting a high level of economies to be exploited in design, tooling and production (Mowery and Rosenberg 1982). Also by the end of the 1950s, the new Aerospace Division was working on Bomarc missiles as well as assembling and testing Minutemen ICBMs.

Boeing was therefore able to exploit strong links in its diversification strategy in marketing for missiles diversification and technology for civil aircraft diversification. However, diversification was facilitated by the existence of weaker links in so far as some military marketing skills were transferable into the civil arena, while experience in aircraft technology assisted entry into the missiles market (see Figure 7.3). By the early 1960s, Boeing's corporate strategy had been transformed from specialisation in military aircraft into diversification in missiles/space production and civil aircraft manufacture; diversification into the space market had been a logical extension of missile diversification and Boeing was developing the first-stage booster of the Saturn V rocket by 1961.

In Figure 7.3 we construct the map of Boeing's strategy using the principles discussed in the previous section. It illustrates the dramatic extent

139

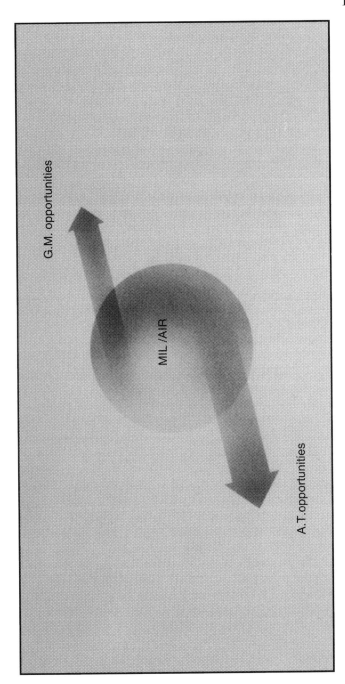

Figure 7.2 Boeing diversification opportunities 1952–54

Code: A.T., Aircraft technology; MIL/AIR, Military aircraft; G.M., Government marketing

Figure 7.3   Boeing 1962–64

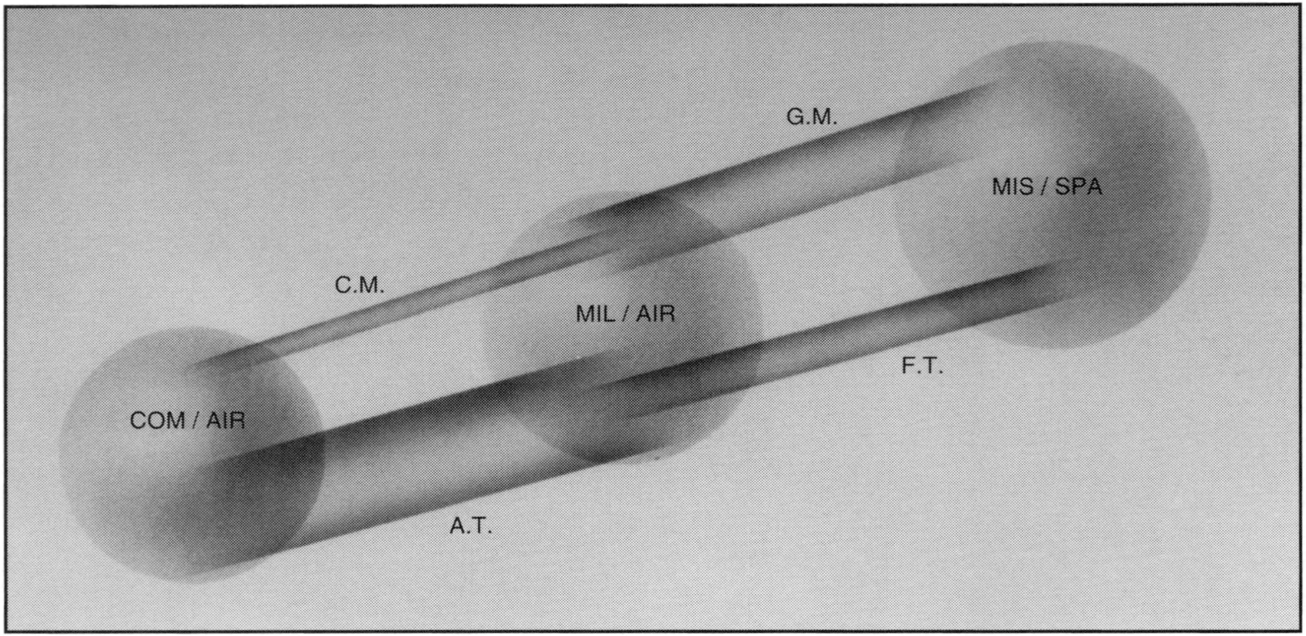

Code: COM/AIR, Commercial aircraft; MIL/AIR, Military aircraft; MIS/SPA, Missiles/Space; A.T., Aircraft technology; F.T., Flight technology; G.M., Government marketing; C.M., Concentrated marketing

to which Boeing had diversified out of its narrow 1950s base in military aircraft. There had been a real decline in military aircraft sales from the early 1950s to the early 1960s[15] which had been more than compensated for by the growth of commercial aircraft and missiles/space businesses. Missile/space was now the major business operated by Boeing.[16]

In order to construct the links between businesses, an exhaustive analysis involving a number of sources was carried out. The major links identified were, as expected, the government market (GM) link between military aircraft and missiles/space, corresponding to GM opportunities in Figure 7.2, and the aircraft technology (AT) link between military aircraft and commercial aircraft, corresponding to AT opportunities in Figure 7.2. The strength of the links is reflected in the relative thickness of AT and GM in Figure 7.3. However, two other minor links were also identified, in marketing skills between all three businesses (CM) and in flight technology, (FT) again between all three businesses. These two relatively thin links are common to all the businesses, CM being a subset of GM and FT a subset of AT. They are discussed in more detail below.

7.5.1   AT link

Boeing's first commercial jet transport, the 707, was an extension of the aerodynamic and structural features of in-house military designs into the commercial sphere. The major risks in this respect were of a market, not of a technological nature since the 707 strategy was based on a dual military-civil design which could be developed in both directions (Phillips 1971: 125–6).

Subsequent developments in military contracting reinforced the tendency to more spillover into the commercial arena from aircraft technology than in any other technically advanced military procurement programmes (Baldwin 1967: 176). The US Air Force developed a policy of deliberately specifying design characteristics in military aircraft so that it would meet military and civilian needs and so provide an emergency airlift capacity. The Department of Defense reinforced this by a policy of placing contracts for the transportation of personnel and cargo transportation with private carriers in cases where it could just as easily have been carried out by military aircraft (Baldwin 1967: 176).

Military and commercial aircraft designs tended to diverge subsequently, since no large military transport appeared, and later military development programmes such as short-range attack missiles and hypersonic aircraft did not have an obvious relationship to commercial needs (Moxon *et al.* 1984). However, in Boeing's case there remain strong technological links between its military and commercial aircraft business. The KC-135 tanker and B-52 bomber programmes were of the heavier and slower military type that facilitated commercial links and spin-offs. The links would be more tenuous if Boeing were heavily involved in supersonic or fighter projects and there do exist strong commonalities between Boeing's commercial and military designs in design, tooling and production after the commercial advent of jets (Mowery and Rosenberg 1982: 131).

However, Boeing's commercial aircraft manufacturing required flexibility to generate derivatives and options in responding to consumer demand; the military market remained more homogenous and standardised (O'Lone 1966). To that extent, manufacturing methods in the commercial sector had to be differentiated from the more rigid and inflexible methods used in the military sphere.

7.5.2   FT link

A feature of defence work that has been remarked upon is the difficulty of extending military technology into non-military areas (Ullman 1965). The absence of major technological links due to the specialised nature of much defence work, combined with inexperience in commercial marketing, has contributed to these problems. However, there is evidence of some significant technological commonalities between missiles/spacecraft production and aircraft production in the design and manufacture of aerial vehicles.

These links are not so strong as in the AT case, but are significant. The FT or flight technology link first of all exploits a basic similarity in the production of aircraft, missiles and spacecraft in that they have three major sub-systems; airframe, guidance system and power plant. A great deal of common production experience and transferable technical skills facilitated airframe manufacturers diversification into missiles (Simonson 1964); there was also similarity in design, manufacture and materials between early missile production and aircraft manufacture (Bright 1979: 126–7). In addition, smaller space vehicles use the larger missile engines as boosters, while the construction of large boosters is like aircraft manufacture; further, spaceships are also built on the principles of advanced aircraft systems (Bright 1979: 129).

There were, however, major differences between missiles/space and aircraft manufacture. Missiles manufacture involves relatively few large parts in contrast to aircraft manufacture, which comprises a large number of small parts, and missiles/spacecraft manufacture involves higher-quality control standards (Stekler 1965: 125). The move into missiles necessitated a far higher commitment of resources to electronics (1965: 97–101), a trend which was reinforced by the move in the 1960s into space vehicle manufacture (Silk 1968). The plant requirements for missile/spacecraft production require air-conditioning and dust-free conditions, further differentiating the resource characteristics of missile/spacecraft and aircraft production (Bright 1979: 129–71; Simonson 1964: 306–7; Stekler 1965: 125).

7.5.3   GM link

The marketing skills and experience built up through operating in defence markets are, to a large extent, transferable between products and services in this market. There is no advertising of any significance in this industry, and most selling is done directly (Gansler 1980: 46–7). There is considerable specialised knowledge required of how government operates in order to sell to the military. Selling in the defence sector requires familiarity with, and acceptance of, a wide range of conventions and regulations relating to such areas as audit and inspection, security restrictions and numerous paperwork requirements (Baldwin 1967: chap. 7). In addition, producer–customer familiarity built up through successive contracts represented a further characteristic transferable across product markets (Simonson 1964: 305). Military marketing experience was readily transferable to a large extent between military aircraft and missiles (Simonson 1964: 305), and, later, between the space market and traditional military markets (Berkowitz 1970: 504).

There were differences between the three armed services in the area of producer–customer relations to the extent that contractors tended to become aligned with particular services (Gansler 1980: 36–7). Thus, Boeing became the Air Force supplier of strategic missiles and Lockheed became the Navy supplier. This specialisation should strengthen the GM links as far as similarity and familiarity of marketing tasks faced by Boeing in this sphere is concerned.

7.5.4   CM link

A fundamental barrier to aerospace firms diversifying out of the military field was marketing barriers to entry into other fields. Specialised defence contractors had a dismal record of failure in non-military diversification attempts in the period following World War II, with the exception of commercial aircraft development (Baldwin 1967: 172). The technology was geared to producing specialised, high-quality goods, not low-cost, high-volume production, and this was reflected in the package of marketing skills possessed by these firms (Baldwin 1967: 173; Gansler 1980: 49). The problems here included a lack of sensitivity to costs (Baldwin 1967: 173; Ullman 1965: 374, 379–80), lack of transferability of sales force skills to non-military applications (Gansler 1980: 49), new problems in mass-marketing techniques and distribution channels (Simonson 1964: 230). Military marketing is geared to customer-supported R&D, customer-designed products and technical specifications, and a clearly delineated market potential (Rydberg 1970). The minimal sales promotion, market research and advertising and high ratio of technical to non-technical personnel contrast with the requirements of mass-marketing, and consequently defence firms are typically badly prepared for diversification moves involving commercial markets (Rydberg 1970). A survey study of non-defence diversifications by firms used to servicing military markets confirmed marketing as the most common problem area for such firms (Berkowitz 1970: 341–8).

By early 1960s, unhappy experiences with non-defence diversification had led many of the major aerospace firms to conclude that non-defence diversification was a strategy full of pitfalls and dangers, and to be approached with extreme caution at the very least (Watkins 1963: 76–7). Thus, for non-defence diversifications into mass markets there was minimal marketing linkage for Boeing, just as for other defence-orientated aerospace firms. However, for diversification into commercial aviation, there was some transferability of experience as far as marketing was concerned. Customer input into design (particularly when a first major purchaser was critical to product services), face-to-face marketing and the high technical content of marketing were all features of both military and civil marketing. Further, lack of cost sensitivity and commercial market experience was less likely to be a major handicap when all competitors in the commercial field came from the same background in defence and were likely to display similar characteristics in this respect.

There were of course significant differences attributable to the differing orientation of military and civil aviation. The military and civil markets differed dramatically in their associated structures and regulations (Bright 1979: 84–5). While performance is a prime objective in military markets, reliability assumes increasing importance in civil markets. A commercial airplane is likely to be in service for 15 years and accumulate 3000 or more hours in flight a year, while most military aircraft accumulate little more than a total of 4000 in total (Newhouse 1982).

Figure 7.3 is constructed using the information contained in the above sections. The strongest area of linkages is in aircraft technology between COM/AIR and MIS/SPA. The FT and CM links are of less significance, as indicated by the relative thickness of the links.

From the base established by Boeing in Figure 7.3, the early 1960s saw the company establishing itself in the areas discussed above, and during the next decade the company maintained its presence in the government market while consolidating and extending its strengths in civil aviation.

The Vietnam war and the space race to get an American on the moon in the 1960s meant that the government market had provided opportunities for further expansion and development by Boeing. Boeing assumed production and mission support for the Lunar Orbiter programme, which was also designed by Boeing (*Interavia* 1967). However, by the late 1960s Boeing faced a number of simultaneous threats to its survival. From 1968 (the peak war year), to 1971 (the Kissinger 'peace') industry sales to the Department of Defense fell 24 per cent in current dollars; space industry sales to NASA fell 30 per cent from 1966 to 1971; and between 1968 and 1971 industry commercial jet sales fell by 68 per cent (Bluestone *et al.* 1981: 44–5). While diversification had insulated Boeing from specific market or technological threats, the coincidence of a series of separate environmental threats hit Boeing severely, as it did most other aerospace firms. It had been traditional for cyclical changes in military and commercial markets to operate in opposite directions; now they were moving together (Bluestone *et al.* 1981: 44–5).

In fact, from 1963 Boeing's involvement in government programmes had been declining while commercial sales had been increasing, at least until 1968. The three-jet 727, which was eventually to become the best-selling jet airliner ever built, had been introduced in the early 1960s, the short-range twin-jet 737 had been introduced in 1965, and the 747 jumbo jet appeared in 1969.[17] However, just as Boeing was introducing its new 747 jumbo jet,[18] the market for commercial aircraft plummeted due to the imminent recession, Boeing's earnings fell from $83 million in 1968 to $10 million in 1969, and the workforce was reduced from 105 000 in 1968 to 38 000 in 1971.[19] The resulting balance of activities is shown in Figure 7.4.

146

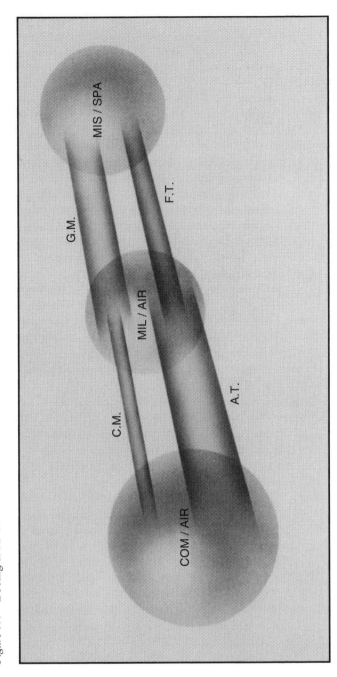

Figure 7.4 Boeing 1972–74

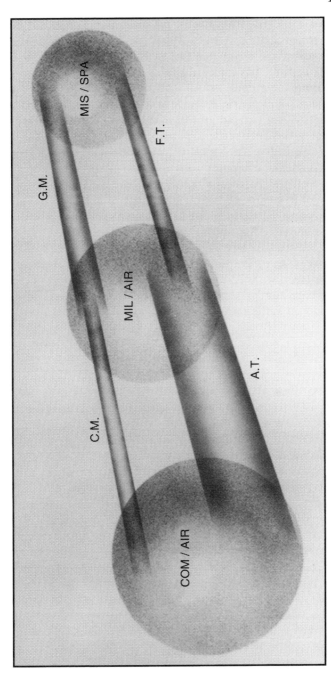

Figure 7.5 Boeing 1982–84

As can be seen from Figure 7.4, government sales had declined in real terms since the early 1960s, while commercial aircraft had emerged as the major business in Boeing's corporate strategy.[20] By this point there has emerged a fairly even balance in terms of the military/commercial split.

The major change in strategic balance associated with the remainder of the 1970s was rapid growth in commercial sales in the late 1970s. Attempts had been made to pursue diversification in the early 1970s in areas like high-technology streetcars, housing developments, hydrofoil development, computer services, irrigation and water plants.[21] However, the 1970s was notable for the consolidation of Boeing's strength in commercial aircraft although 'other' non-traditional areas recorded an increasing presence in Boeing's activities, albeit a relatively minor one (Redding and Yenne 1983: 11).

The 1980s have deepened Boeing's emphasis in the civil sector with now well over half of Boeing's sales attributable to this sphere of operations (see Figure 7.5).[22] The major innovations in the decade to date have been the 757 and 767, two closely related civil developments introduced in the early 1980s.

7.6 ASPECTS OF BOEING'S CORPORATE STRATEGY

The previous section described the evolution of Boeing's strategy over the post-war period by mapping the resource links between business areas. We can now analyse the relevance of the argument stated earlier that a link or commonality between product-markets has two implications: it might (but not necessarily) generate economies or synergies and it might (but not necessarily) provide an area of common vulnerability to environmental threats. The existence of the link itself is necessary but not sufficient to generate specific synergies and vulnerability to individual threats.

A corollary is that the richer or stronger the links between product-markets, the greater the potential for synergies *and* the greater the vulnerability to specific environmental threats. The price of synergy is vulnerability, and a further corollary is that the price of diversification is the sacrifice of economies from specialisation.

The usefulness of the mapping technique applied to Boeing is that it can be combined with these points to provide a systematic basis for analysing Boeing's strategic choices. We shall consider a number of issues in turn using this framework as a basis for discussion. In doing so we shall concentrate on corporate strategy rather than the respective businesses strategies of Boeing's various segments such as commercial, military and space. This is not to diminish the significance of the role of business strategy; for example, there have been major changes within the commercial aircraft sphere in recent years as far as the growing electronic or avionics-related content of aircraft is concerned and evolution in engine technology with turbo-fans or fan-jets replacing early jet technology (Schiff 1967). These changes are obviously important, especially in a company like Boeing in which its commercial business strategy is a major part of its overall activity. Our concentration on corporate strategy here reflects concern with the overall balance of activities. In practice, a fuller analysis would study the interplay between corporate strategy and business strategies.

A first major issue is the curious success of Boeing in diversifying into missiles. Resource linkages described above help explain why Boeing, in common with a number of other aircraft manufacturers, generally competed successfully against electronic companies for the role of prime contractor in the new guided missile market – despite the apparent technological advantages possessed by the electronic companies. The high electronic content of missiles relative to aircraft, and the complex and dynamic nature of that technology, had led many industry observers to suppose that electronic companies would be able to capture a significant share of this market, or even to dominate it. In fact, while electronic companies were able to establish themselves in the market for smaller missiles, aircraft companies dominated in the market for larger missiles.

The factors which led to firms like Boeing diversifying successfully into missiles reflected the *totality* of resource linkages, not just simple technological competition. The aircraft companies had some technological competencies (the FT link) which could be transferred into guided-missile manufacture, but these only partially compensated the electronics companies for mastery of what was widely regarded as the key technology. An additional critical advantage possessed by the aircraft companies was the GM link – skills, experience and contacts built up through selling aircraft to the military were readily exploitable in selling missiles to the military (see the GM link discussion earlier). The electronics companies' experience of military markets tended to be much more limited, and it was the combination of GM and FT links that gave companies like Boeing an advantage in winning prime contractor status in guided missiles. Simonson (1964) confirms that it was the production, R&D *and* government marketing skills that gave aircraft manufacturers the edge in this arena.

A second set of issues that the framework helps illuminate is that the apparent risk-spreading advantages of some types of diversification may conceal risk-sharing characteristics at a deeper level. For example, to the extent that missiles and military aircraft are substitutes, we would expect a negative correlation in their fortunes in a static market situation, one product succeeding at the expense of the other. The existence of the GM and FT links also means that synergies may be exploitable, suggesting that this diversification may exploit economies *and* spread risks. Superficially, this appears to contradict our argument above, that the existence of links means potential vulnerability as well as potential economies.

In fact, the GM and FT links *do* signal possible vulnerability to specific environmental changes that could turn a risk-spreading relationship into a risk-sharing one. For example, if Federal spending on defence was cut back, the GM link means that both missiles and military aircraft may be attacked simultaneously through this shared link. A negative cross-elasticity of demand is thus a dubious basis on which to pursue a risk-spreading strategy; if the market itself is attacked by particular environmental changes, *all* substitute products may be threatened together.

This raises important questions with regard to the strategic implications of making an environmental threat to existing product-markets a corporate opportunity by internalising it. Boeing pre-empted the potential threat posed by missile technology by early entry into the market; it also reacted to the possibility of supersonic commercial travel rendering its existing array of sub-sonic jets partially or totally obsolete by competing intensely with Lockheed for the (eventually abortive) SST contract. If the company can successfully ride from one product life cycle to another, then such strategic moves can be successful. However, to the extent that market and/or technological links exist between these product-markets, it is possible to conceive of specific 'Star Wars' innovations which could render both military aircraft and missiles instantly obsolete; thus the technological link could be attacked by technological change, or even the market link attacked by defence cutbacks. Consequently, apparent risk spreading may be spurious, and analysis of resource links may give a truer picture of both potential synergies and vulnerability to environmental surprises.

This turning-threat-into-opportunity strategy is particularly important in the case of Boeing. Klein (1977) argued that it was central to Boeing's success and cited examples different from the ones discussed above, such as how the company reacted to a disastrous stratoliner crash just before World War II by building a wind tunnel and putting together a capable group of aerodynamicists. This helped develop the company's competence in this area and strengthened its competitive edge.[23] However, the wider implications of such a strategy are revealed by analysis of linkage in respective cases. A third set of issues may be examined by considering the strength and weakness of individual market/technological links; that is, the degree to which businesses exhibit similar resource characteristics. For example, the military market may provide a certain level of synergy and vulnerability. Boeing in military aircraft and missiles became particularly associated with the Air Force; this relative specialisation within defence should further increase potential economies to the extent that the Air Force involves specific skills, issues and problems with respect to the other services. However, this increased specialisation and deeper marketing linkage brings with it increased potential vulnerability; for example, if the Air Force's position or ranking within defence should slip for any reason.

The move into the space business illustrates this process in reverse. The marketing-resource linkages are to some extent reduced – it is still the government market, but NASA as a contractor demonstrated different objectives and characteristics compared to the military services (Holz 1962). To that extent, there were reduced transfer possibilities for marketing resources and skills, but also reduced dependence on the defence market. Nevertheless, to the extent that the GM link existed, economies were still exploitable and vulnerability still existed (for example, to a general cutback in Federal spending).

On the technological side similar patterns hold. The AT link is strengthened by Boeing's emphasis on the sub-sonic technology and larger aircraft rather than fighter aircraft; such specialisation facilitates the exploitation of economies but offers increased vulnerability to external threats by limiting the technological base. An extreme example of this can be observed within the commercial aircraft business with the 757/767 development. Both aircraft were designed to take advantage of a high level of commonality in components and manufacturing techniques (O'Lone 1979a, 1979b). They incorporate similar fuel-efficient high-technology systems, and therefore within this business sector exploit an extremely rich set of market and technological links. However, the 757 and 767 were designed and developed in the 1970s in a period of low interest rates and rising fuel prices when such technological innovations appeared to be guaranteed a secure place in the market. The 1980s has seen a reversal of trends, with aviation fuel prices falling and interest rates rising, making airlines less sensitive to the fuel-efficiency characteristics of the 757 and 767, but more sensitive to the capital costs of purchasing expensive new technological systems (Stuart 1982; Gregory 1982). Thus the shared market and technological characteristics of the 757 and 767 provide high levels of economies *and* environmental vulnerability.[24]

However, if there are surprises within the composition of air travel over the foreseeable future, Boeing's broad commercial aircraft range also gives it the ability to respond flexibly. Boeing estimates of the growth in air traffic from the mid-1960s to late 1970s were about right, but they mistakenly perceived the composition to be more biased towards large aircraft like the 747 than towards smaller aircraft (Kraar 1978). Such mistakes, understandable and indeed inevitable in such a highly uncertain environment, would be more serious for a company which did not have the product scope of Boeing; Boeing's coverage of the market is the widest of any of the manufacturers, permitting widespread exploitation of technological and market economies,[25] as well as the ability to respond to surprises within the commercial aircraft business. In this respect, its diversity within commercial aircraft makes it potentially less vulnerable in this business than its competitors who are all more specialised (in commercial aircraft terms). Joe Sutter, Boeing Commercial Airplan, Executive Vice President, commented that flexibility was a basic necessity in operating in such markets (Birkett 1985).

A fourth set of issues relate to what Boeing does not do rather than what it does do. It is more difficult to establish the logic of actions not taken than the logic of diversification moves actually undertaken and consequently observable. However, the framework does help in formulating questions in this area. One point worth noting is that Boeing's strategy in the past has often demonstrated a strong commitment to a particular area: the military market in the 1950s, the commercial market in the 1980s. Diversification did provide some hedge, especially since the early 1960s, but even so the turbulent military and civil aviation markets are traditionally dangerous territories for specialised corporations, and one might expect a corporation concerned with its long-term survival to attempt to loosen its dependency on either or both markets.

Boeing's objectives here are obviously of central importance. The company may wish to remain only in these areas in which it already operates. However, Boeing has made strenuous efforts to diversify in the past, notably in the late 1940s and early 1970s, but its notable successes have been in areas in which it has strong links (GM and AT) supported by weaker links (FT and CM, respectively). In common with most other aircraft companies which attempted diversification in the late 1940s, tenuous technological links were not sufficient for successful diversification. It is conjectural but arguable that Boeing's continued emphasis on government markets and aircraft technology reflects limited diversification possibilities as far as exploitation of sufficiently rich resources linkages are concerned.

As far as further developments of the model developed here is concerned, there are a number of possibilities. Mapping strategy can provide a starting point for exploring strategy/structure relationships, and previous works (Kay 1982, 1984) have shown how this may be done. Also exploitation of links need not be carried out inhouse; joint ventures, licensing, leasing, consultancy and rental agreements are all market alternatives that may be adopted by the firm in certain circumstances. We have concentrated on diversification here, but a fuller analysis could more fully analyse comparative governance costs[26] to explore strategic alternatives to diversification, such as joint venture. The model could also be useful as a diagnostic tool for analysts to test the corporate strategy in terms of perceived strengths/weaknesses/opportunities/threats. For example, Figure 7.6 replicates the strategic position of Boeing in the early 1980s described in Figure 7.5, and adds certain actual or possible environmental threats. The internal strengths/weaknesses of the firm at corporate strategy level could be analysed by examining the pattern of linkages in conjunction with a resource audit. Diversification opportunities could be analysed in a similar fashion to Figure 7.2.

Figure 7.6 also shows how the sensitivity of the corporate strategy to actual or possible external threats could be explored. For example, Airbus Industrie and NASA cutbacks may represent a threat to individual businesses, or parts of businesses, in Boeing's case. Other threats may have a more general impact; for example, if a competitor makes a technological breakthrough in aircraft technology, it may threaten both COM/AIR and MIL/AIR through the AT link, while a Federal spending cutback may attack both MIL/AIR and MIS/SPA through the GM link.

The framework itself does not provide the answers to the possible questions that could be raised in relationship to Boeing's strengths/weaknesses/opportunities/threats. However, it does provide a systematic basis for examining the questions and exploring the implications of alternative answers.

Figure 7.6 Selected strategic problems

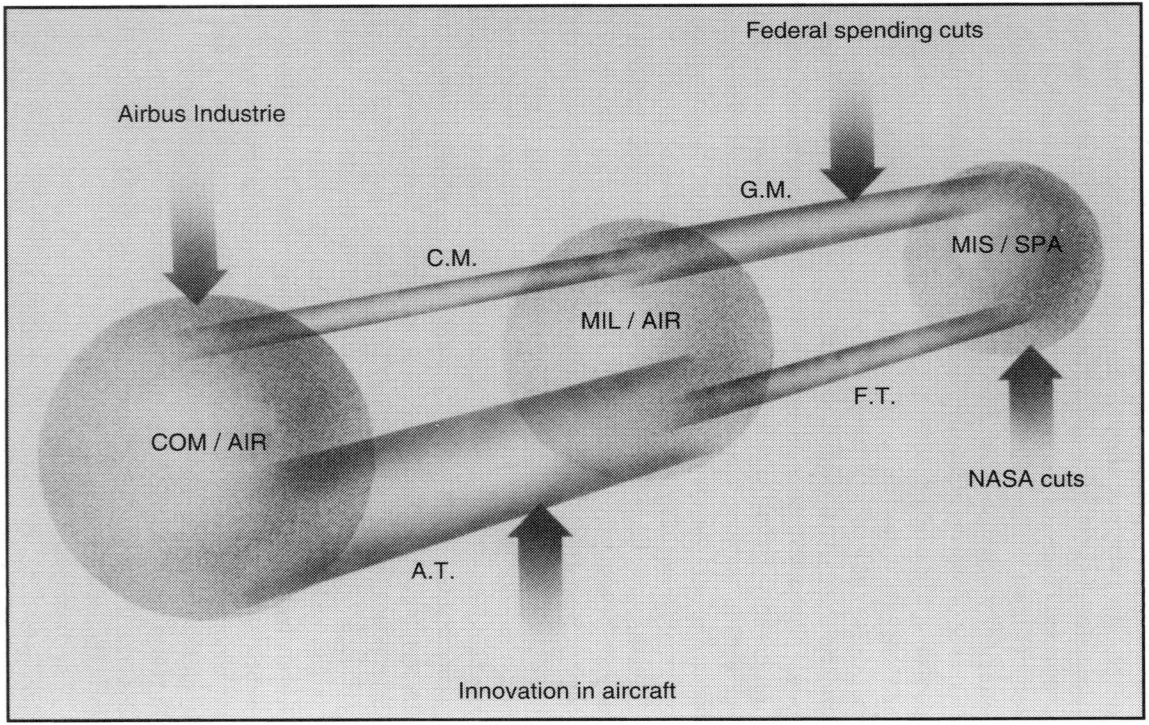

Lastly, it is important to bear in mind that further analysis should desirably extend to business strategy as well as corporate strategy. We have only really looked at business strategy in so far as it also demonstrates principles discussed under corporate strategy; for example, the synergy/vulnerability implications of joint 757/767 development. However, there are many important strategic issues which appear at business strategy level which are not obvious at corporate strategy level. For example, in Boeing's commercial aircraft business strategy, major issues have included financing,[27] especially alleged government subsiding of Airbus in price competition, airline deregulation and the strategic issue of whether Boeing is right to delay launching its competitor to the Airbus 320 in the 150-seats market (Learmount 1985; Birkett 1985). In this latter case, Boeing believes there are significant developments in areas such as propfan engines and materials which will permit it to introduce a technologically and economically superior product in the 1990s (Birkett 1985). There are a number of other strategic issues in this business, including multiple sourcing, subcontracting and joint ventures.

As far as business strategy is concerned, there already exist useful frameworks for analysis at business strategy level, such as Porter (1980). Also there have been useful surveys of the economics (Mowery and Rosenberg 1982) and business strategies (Newhouse 1982) of the commercial aircraft business in which Boeing plays a dominant role. We believe that the corporate strategy approach here complements business strategy approaches such as Porter's, which may be appropriate for the study of competitive financing, marketing and technological issues within each business. The corporate strategy approach naturally concentrates on supply-side resource questions, such as the extent of marketing and technological resource commonalities. Business strategy introduces demand side questions as well; our downplaying the demand side here is merely a reflection of the level at which our analysis takes place, and does not signify anything as far as ranking the importance of supply-side versus demand-side questions is concerned.

7.7 CONCLUSIONS

The purpose of this chapter has been to analyse a particular firm's corporate strategy, using a framework first developed to analyse problems in industrial organisation. It has provided a method of systematically ordering strategic issues that facilitates the strategy analysis. What has only been touched on here is how the framework may provide a vehicle for further developing and integrating analysis and insights provided by other writers in what might be termed alternative traditions in industrial organisation. For example, Schumpeter's gales of creative destruction generated by technological innovation are of obvious relevance to the role of threats and opportunities in this approach. Nelson and Winter's (1982) analysis of technological trajectories and paradigms may be helpful in providing guidelines for strategy formulation in different technological regimes. Penrose (1959) provides an extensive analysis of how resource linkages may facilitate or inhibit the development of corporate strategy. Writers in industrial organisation following on the contributions of H. A. Simon – such as the behavioural theorists Cyert and March (1963) and neo-institutionalists like O. E. Williamson (1975) – provide analysis highlighting the implications of bounded rationality and environmental uncertainty in decision making.

A workable approach to corporate strategy should recognise the central importance of technological change, corporate resources and bounded rationality. Neoclassical theory is an inappropriate starting point for the development of economic analysis of corporate strategy because of its neglect of these issues. However, the development of the framework above suggests that it is possible to develop useful economics-based approaches to corporate strategy and reflects a belief that considerable payoff could be achieved by drawing upon insights and analysis of a number of writers in what has been termed 'alternative' traditions in neoclassical economics.

NOTES

1. Originally produced as 'Boeing: corporate strategy and technical change', Heriot-Watt University Economics Department Working Paper, co-authored with Peter Clarke.
2. See, for example, Freeman (1982) and Ergas (1984).
3. A difficulty in this area is that strategy may be studied from a number of disciplinary perspectives, which in turn may be composed of a number of rival theoretical frameworks. See, for example, articles by Biggadike, Jemison and Porter in the *Academy of Management Review* (1981).
4. Studies of survival strategies do exist in the literature, often in an emergency turnaround context, The point made here is that the literature on the strategy-making process is in general biased towards more immediate time horizons, with quantifiable, easily operational goals such as sales and earnings.

5. See Kay (1984) for further discussion of this point.
6. The question of whether or not Williamson's work really breaks with the neoclassical tradition or is instead 'closet neoclassicism' has been debated in the economics literature. However, the tools he provides certainly offer researchers the opportunity to contribute to the economics of internal organisation in a non-neoclassical fashion.
7. The analysis in Kay (1982, 1984) is to a large extent based on this premise.
8. These points were developed further in Kay (1982, 1984).
9. In the economic analysis of the mapping technique in Kay (1982, 1984), the sales of each business activity was measured by the area of each circle representing the appropriate activity. One reason for using volume above is that it permits more extreme variations in scale of activity to be accommodated on the same diagram (since radius is a cube-root function of volume but only a square-root function of area) while communicating scale visually. It also provides potential scope for analogies with visual models of chemical molecules and the associated bonding relationships between atoms.
10. Derived from company annual reports.
11. The producer price index was used. Sources were US Department of Commerce, *Statistical Abstract of the US* and US Department of Labor, *Monthly Labor Review*, both Washington, DC. Changes in the price index were used from 1950–84 inclusive.
12. Company annual reports
13. Boeing was producing a mean annual sales of $1.01 bn of military aircraft, 1952–54 in 1967 dollars (Producers Price Index and company annual reports).
14. This is a very Penrosian argument in that resource similarities may provide both temporary economies or synergies from operations (Penrose 1959).
15. In 1967 dollars, military aircraft sales had averaged $1.01 bn annually, 1952–54 and now averaged $0.6 bn annually, 1962–64 (company annual reports and Producer Price Index).
16. In 1967 dollars, the annual average sales of each business 1962–64 was $0.49 bn (commercial aircraft), $0.60 bn (military aircraft) and $0.85 bn (missiles/space). Figures derived from company annual reports and Producers Price Index.
17. Company annual reports.
18. Military–commercial technological links are again illustrated in the development of the 747. It was the loss of the C-5A large military transport contract to Lockheed in 1965 that led to the development of the commercial jumbo-jet concept based on the Boeing version of the C-5A transport (Ingells 1970).
19. Company annual reports and Bluestone *et al.* (1981).
20. In 1967 dollars, commercial sales now exceeded $1.24 bn, military aircraft sales had declined to $0.40 bn, and missiles/space had declined to $0.49 bn each in mean annual terms, 1972–74 (company annual reports and Producer Price Index).
21. Various sources in *Aviation Week* and *Space Technology*: 23 November 1979, 29 March 1971, 19 June and 25 September 1972 and 28 April 1975.

22. In 1967 dollars, mean annual commercial sales had increased to
     \$1.93 bn, military aircraft sales to \$0.88 bn, and missiles/space had dec-
     lined to \$0.37 bn, for the period 1982–84 (Company annual reports and
     Producers Price Index).
23. Steiner (1979) agreed with Klein (1977) on the importance of building a
     wind tunnel in-house, describing it as one of the three major decisions
     made by Boeing in the post-war period. The other two he identified
     were the decision to go it alone on the 367–80 prototype, and the deci-
     sion to stay in on the 707 development.
24. The commonality issue is a central preoccupation in Boeing's commer-
     cial aircraft business strategy. Boeing has excelled in producing designs
     that can be stretched or given increased take-off weight (and therefore
     more range) in response to market demand (Kjelgaard 1984). Also
     Regelin (1980) argues that product reliability and product improvement
     through derivatives are probably the most important reasons for the
     success of the Boeing Commercial Aircraft Company.
25. Even for different models there are substantial economies in manufac-
     turing methods and labour skills as well as marketing skills. The family
     relationship between planes of different sizes also permits other
     economies, which may include components (O'Lone 1970). The 757
     and 767 exhibit these shared characteristics very strongly, to the extent
     that many operating sub-systems are common to both aircraft.
26. Such as in Williamson (1975). But see the discussion in Chapter 4 (this
     volume) and in Kay (1997) for problems with the transaction-cost
     framework. See also the analysis of joint ventures in Chapter 9 in this
     volume.
27. A number of sources discussed this issue in the late 1970s to mid-1980s,
     including *Interavia*, 7, 1978, p. 585, and *The Economist*, 3 April, 1982,
     pp. 105–6; 3 October, 1982, pp. 77–8; 17 August 1983, pp. 58–9.

8 Towards a Theory of Multinational Enterprise[1]

8.1 INTRODUCTION

Since the well-documented post-war increase in the number and size of multinational enterprises, economists, marketing and management theorists have paid considerable attention to the determinants of the multinational decision. In general, early studies investigating the multinational phenomenon have concentrated on demand-side factors, such as the present size and anticipated growth rate of an overseas market, and how they impact on a firm's decision to go international. These studies have not been successful in discriminating between the different organisational and strategic options available to the multinational enterprise; this is at least partly due to the standard neoclassical assumptions of aggregation which ignore market and technological interdependencies, and assume perfect knowledge on the part of economic decision makers.

Recent developments in the theory of the firm have attempted to replace the framework of neoclassical theory with a transaction-cost approach based on analysis of corporate strategy. Coase's (1937) work has been interpreted as showing that firms supplant markets because of problems of information. Transaction costs deriving from imperfections of knowledge create firms and determine their boundaries and in the absence of information problems there is no basis for discriminating between firm co-ordination and market exchange in terms of potential efficiency. Williamson (1975), in developing Coase's early work, applied transaction-cost analysis to vertical integration. Subsequent work by Teece (1980, 1982) and Kay (1984) have extended the transaction-cost approach to diversification, merger and takeover, by rejecting the assumptions of separability and independence of individual product-markets, and incorporating economies of market and technology interdependencies into the analysis.

As far as the multinational enterprise itself is concerned, its neglect in industrial organisation has been rectified in recent years, with transaction-cost analysis increasingly serving as a unifying framework. Dunning has made a number of important contributions, beginning with his 1958 work in which he analysed multinationalism in terms of the firm-specific ownership advantages of such firms, and Hymer (1960) extended these ideas by identifying four types of market imperfection that contribute to the formation of multinational enterprise. Subsequently, a number of factors were emphasised as potentially significant in the development of multinational enterprise by different authors. Kindleberger (1969) developed Hymer's earlier approach to build a model of foreign direct investment in which market imperfections, economies of scale and government intervention were important elements. Later studies emphasised the ability of the firm to utilise technological advantages, while Aliber (1970) analysed the possible role of foreign exchange risk in multinationalism. Vernon (1971) perceived product life cycles as being important in determining the incidence and timing of the decision to go multinational.

More recently, Buckley and Casson (1976) articulated the role of transaction-cost analysis in determining whether or not markets will be internalised in the form of multinational enterprise, while Dunning (1981) developed his 'eclectic theory' in which net ownership advantages are crossed with consideration of external markets versus internalisation. The process of internationalisation, a variant of the transaction-cost approach, is contained in Caves (1982), Rugman (1981, 1982) and Gilman (1981).[2] In this chapter we shall continue in this tradition by developing the implications of firm-specific advantages in the context of costs associated with operating in external markets.

8.2 CORPORATE STRATEGY AND TRANSACTION COSTS

The application of transaction-cost analysis to corporate strategy is based on two basic principles derived from the concept of bounded rationality associated with Simon (1965). Simon defines bounded rationality as referring to human behaviour that is 'intendedly rational but only limitedly so' (p. xxiv). In the face of complex and uncertain environments the decision maker naturally displays limited mental and analytical capacity – in contrast to the omniscient entrepreneur of neoclassical theory. The effect of combining the notion of bounded rationality for organisations with transaction-costs leads to the first principle of corporate strategic behaviour.

> *Principle 1*: Bounded rationality in the face of transaction-costs encourages corporate specialisation.

The second principle of corporate diversification combines the notion of bounded rationality with environmental dynamics:

Principle 2: Bounded rationality in the face of technological change encourages corporate diversification.

Simply stated, corporate-level strategy is a consequence of trading off the gains from specialisation against the gains from diversifications. We can demonstrate these two principles by introducing a simple example. Consider a football manufacturer, Football, Inc, which produces, markets and distributes leather footballs. This firm can enjoy potential gains from co-ordinating its activities with the activities of two other producers, one a manufacturer of leather volleyballs, and the other a manufacturer of inflatable air mattresses. The interacting relationships between the football, volleyball and air mattress product-markets is illustrated by the links shown in Figure 8.1.

For the purpose of this chapter, the potential links between respective product-markets parallel the sources of synergy initially discussed by Ansoff (1965), and later in the economies of scope or 'contestable markets' literature.[3] The possibility of obtaining gains from synergy depends on two conditions: firstly, the existence of common, joint or shared elements between product-markets; and secondly, the potential for exploiting indivisibilities or increased specialisation and division of labour around the shared elements (Willig 1979). In this context, Figure 8.1 identifies market (M) links and technological (T) links for the football/volleyball/air mattress example. Each of these links may provide

Figure 8.1 Potential synergy for Football Inc.

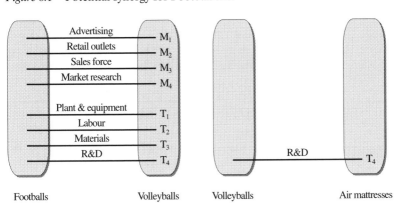

Advertising	M_1		
Retail outlets	M_2		
Sales force	M_3		
Market research	M_4		
Plant & equipment	T_1		
Labour	T_2		
Materials	T_3		
R&D	T_4	R&D	T_4

Footballs   Volleyballs   Volleyballs   Air mattresses economies in the form of synergy. For example, an advertising campaign in sports magazines (M_1) can be shared by footballs and volleyballs; shared retail outlets mean that indivisibilities in trucks may be better utilised if both footballs and volleyballs are transported (M_2), while the shared distribution system means that the productivity of the sales force can be increased (M_3). The results of sports-related market research (M_4) can also be shared between footballs and volleyballs.

Economies are also realised from technological links. To the extent that the same physical facilities and machinery can be used in both football and volleyball production, indivisibilities in plant and equipment can be exploited (T_1). Labour skills in producing leather goods can be transferred to the work place (T_2), while materials and the results of R&D into leather goods may be shared between both product-markets (T_3, T_4).

By way of contrast, we assume that inflatable air mattresses have a different consumer base, are distributed through different outlets and are produced with dissimilar material inputs; only a single shared element, R&D of valves, exists as a common link. Apart from this single shared element, there are no other technology or market links providing potential synergy.

Two important points need to be emphasised regarding the concept of synergy at this juncture. Firstly, synergy results from the same sources that provide economies of scale; that is, gains from indivisibilities and increased specialisation of labour. Economies of scale, however, should be interpreted as a limit case of perfect or complete links between product-markets – for example, at least partially achievable through markets. While Ansoff's 1965 work concentrated on articulating the potential gains from synergy through corporate diversification strategies, market alternatives always exist to in-house corporate exploitation of synergy, including such mechanisms as tie-in sales, leasing, commissioning, consultancy and sub-contracting. In all cases, the distribution of gains between the two parties involved in the market trading of synergy is an outcome of the bargaining process.

8.3   TRANSACTION COSTS AND SYNERGY

In order to compare the respective merits of market exchange versus corporate systems of exploiting synergy, issues of bounded rationality must be made explicit. Bounded rationality is reflected in the costs of transacting or achieving organisational economies which must be set against the potential gains from market and technological synergy links. While the potential gains from product-market synergy links can be exploited through management co-ordination, there will always be corresponding costs of organising associated with the expanded scope of new product-markets. These costs are likely to be different in the respective cases. In general, markets and technologies that are richly linked facilitate transferring managerial experience and knowledge, thus providing lower costs of achieving the respective economies.

In contrast, diversification into loosely linked product-markets is likely to result in high organisation costs associated with unfamiliar market conditions and technological characteristics. Not only will the absence of common market and technological links inhibit the transferability of managerial experience and knowledge, but they may also give rise to diseconomies to the extent of creating what Ansoff (1965) aptly describes as 'negative synergy', or what Loasby (1967) calls 'allergy'. In short, there is an inverse relationship between the richness of market and technological synergy links between the different product-markets associated with a diversification move and the organisation costs involved in achieving these economies.

An interesting contrast is observed if market exchanges (versus diversification) are used to exploit the potential economies in our example. In the football/inflatable mattress linkage, for example, a single market contract securing a supply of the common R&D element would be sufficient to ensure a trade to the mutual benefit of both parties. In the case of football/volleyball, though, the exploitation of potential economies by market exchange involves a significant information problem. Each link could require a detailed specification of the service to the transacting parties, and involve lengthy economic/technological/legal analysis. In addition, uncertainty about the future would typically restrict the market transactions to short-term agreements (Coase 1937). Further, each party to a market transaction is vulnerable to potential opportunism by the other parties (Williamson 1975).

In practice, the actual organisational arrangement will depend on the contractor's attitude to potential opportunism. For example, if the parties take a relaxed attitude to possible opportunism, then the contract may be loosely specified, economising on resource costs of contract formation. However, there still may be transaction-costs impeding or inhibiting contract efficiency in the form of residual opportunism which loose specification of contracts may entail. Reducing costs of opportunism may necessitate increasing resource costs of contract formation; in the face of bounded rationality and future uncertainty, alternative contracting arrangements may simply trade off one form of transaction-costs for another, in this case resource costs of contract formation for potential opportunism. Whether 'tight' or 'loose' contracting is chosen will depend on such factors as the respective parties' attitudes towards contract formation, contracting experience, familiarity with each other, mutual trust or distrust, and the degree of complexity of the transaction. Williamson (1979) provides useful analysis of circumstances dictating alternative contractual arrangements.

In the present analysis the nature of contractual alternatives need not be pursued too far. It is sufficient to argue that transaction-costs of market exchange are directly related to the number of links and potential economies to be exploited, *ceteris paribus*. These transaction-costs may be incurred in the form of potential opportunism, or in the resource costs of contract formation, depending on whether the contract is loosely or closely specified.

In general, then, transaction-costs of market exploitation of synergy through diversification are directly related to the richness and number of links between product-markets that need co-ordinating. *Ceteris paribus*, the greater the number of potential market and technological synergy links between two product-markets, the lower the cost of corporate organisation associated with exploitation of potential synergy through diversification, and the greater the transaction-costs of achieving a market exchange solution. Combining the gains from synergy links with the costs of organising the economies of different product-markets leads to the first principle of bounded rationality discussed earlier – bounded rationality in the face of transaction-costs encourages firms to specialise rather than diversify. The comparative advantages of corporate diversification strategy in relation to market exchange agreements lies in exploiting the economies associated with richly linked product-markets. Conversely, the comparative advantage of market exchange systems lies in the relatively inexpensive exploitation of synergy between weakly linked product-markets.

8.4 SYNERGY AND THE 'MUGGING' EFFECT

The transaction-cost analysis of the preceding section explains corporate specialisation but not diversification. A more general theory of corporate strategy which accounts for complex diversified strategies as well as single-product or highly synergistic strategies can be explained in terms of the vulnerability to external technological change associated with synergy links. Market and technological links may not only provide synergy but may also create common points of vulnerability to technological threat. Market links may be ultimately traceable to a common consumer, while technological links are dependent on shared technological characteristics. The shared element in each case creates a common point of potential weakness to external technological change; thus cable television may threaten not only movie theatres but also popcorn sales through the market link, while skills in mechanical assembly may be attacked along the technological links by developments in electronic technology (as the Singer company discovered in sewing and calculating machines).

The extent to which exploitation of links creates serious corporate vulnerability depends crucially on the nature of the corporate environment. If corporate management has the opportunity and time to anticipate or respond to external technological developments, then there should be few problems associated with the unqualified pursuit of synergy, providing management remains flexible once innovation pushes their products into the decline phase of the product life cycle. The managerial baton could then be passed on to new runners in the technological race. Unfortunately, in this respect the innovative process is Schumpeterian; it is less like a relay race, more like a mugging. As with a mugging, it may be difficult or impossible to anticipate how, where, and when an attack may take place; all that can be reasonably expected of decision makers is to rank environments in terms of mugging potential.[4]

Since the link is the source of potential vulnerability, the avoidance of links is the obvious method of dealing with this potential threat. Diversification, as a hedging strategy of deliberately avoiding links, will localise mugging to the extent that any link being attacked has limited scope in the firm's corporate strategy.

The extent to which a firm will pursue hedging strategies will depend on the mugging potential of the environment. If industrial environments are slow changing with long product life cycles, synergy has little potential cost or penalty attached to it. On the other hand, exploiting synergy is liable to create shared vulnerability to environmental change in dynamic environments with rapidly changing product characteristics; in those circumstances, diversification away from shared links as a hedge against possible mugging by external innovation is likely to be a preferred strategy. If environments suddenly switch from placid, low technology to rapidly changing high technology, we might expect specialised synergy-exploiting firms to be caught flat-footed, as in the case of the Swiss watch industry. Thus we would expect that corporate strategy would move from specialisation (synergy-rich) to diversification (synergy-poor) as the level of environmental technological change increases.

The objective of hedging would therefore tend to result in either related-linked diversification involving a chain of market and technological links (Rumelt 1974), or conglomerate diversification involving a series of unrelated product-markets or product-market groupings – both being attractive strategies for technologically dynamic industries. These strategies permit hedging by localising the impact of specific technological threats around individual product-markets or short-range market and technological links. As expected, among large firms, specialised strategies tend to be restricted to more stable low-technology industries (Kay 1984).[5]

Hedging in this context is fundamentally different from portfolio diversification as analysed by Markowitz (1952, 1959), Adelman (1961), Smith and Shreiner (1969) and Weston (1970). In fact, portfolio theory is based on very restrictive assumptions which are not generally applicable in this context. Firstly, in portfolio theory the decision maker has to be able to estimate precisely the expected variance of future profit levels associated with specific activities, and secondly, risk is symmetric in that positive variations are as likely as negative. We need not invoke such strong assumptions here. The decision maker merely has to order environments conceptually in terms of mugging potential (rather than cardinally estimate risk). Also, the threat of product-market decline and obsolescence is emphasised here in contrast to the symmetrical treatment of variance in portfolio theory. Consequently, in this context hedging is not interpretable in portfolio theory terms. A more detailed discussion of this issue is found in Kay (1982: 79–84 and 109–12).

It should be noted that 'mugging' hazards have sources other than technological innovation. Some firms have pursued multiple sourcing or country diversification on a multinational basis to guard against country-specific 'surprises' such as political coups, unionisation and so on. However, Schumpeterian-type technological change is still liable to be the most important category of threat facing the firm.

8.5 THE RATIONALE FOR MULTINATIONAL ENTERPRISE

In the preceding sections it was suggested that corporate strategy is determined by trading off the gains from specialisation against the gains from diversification. The ultimate choice among strategic alternatives is determined by the level of environmental technological change, and the resulting 'mugging' effect on synergy links.

Consequently, multinational enterprise should also exploit gains from either hedging or synergy. Multinational hedging, however, is unlikely because the objective of hedging can generally be better satisfied by domestic, related-linked or conglomerate strategies without the additional costs of going multinational. Domestic, related-link strategies and conglomerate hedging, for example, take place in the context of shared knowledge for each product-market within the confines of a country, whereas multinational enterprise typically involves additional information problems associated with a new set of legal, social, economic and political systems.

If economic justification is to be found for multinational enterprise, it must be sought in the notion of potential economies. For a multinational enterprise, however, economies are likely to be particularly elusive. Multinational enterprise is unlikely to provide exploitable synergies from increased specialisation, division of labour or improved utilisation of physical indivisibilities. Even if there are similar market and technological developments between parent and foreign subsidiary, spatial separation and distinctive markets will generally inhibit exploitation of synergy across national borders.

On the market side, economies will be very difficult, if not impossible, to realise. In principle, economies of marketing information and knowledge are effectively the only market synergies that are achievable from multinational expansion, and only then to the extent that similarities in consumer behaviour exist across national boundaries.

On the technological side, multinational expansion faces similar difficulties. Only informational links, such as R&D, can provide significant economies to the extent that appropriate information and knowledge can be transferred and shared between parent and foreign subsidiary, spreading the cost of individual projects. We expect gains of technological research to be more easily transferred than other possible forms of synergy, which tend to be country-specific.

Seen from this perspective, the rationale for multinational strategy must be sought in terms of potential economies of information; yet potential *dis*economies of information are also likely due to the bundles of country-specific information that must be assimilated by the firm to produce and market in a foreign country. Thus, the expansion of multinational enterprise is facilitated by firm-specific information, such as R&D, and inhibited by country-specific information, such as marketing know-how. It follows that multinational enterprise typically represents a potentially expensive strategic alternative in terms of synergy sacrifices. To the extent that there are limits on the firm's access to capital, multinational enterprise fails to exploit non-informational market and technological synergies that may generally be expected from alternative options of domestic expansion or diversification. In addition, it may create significant diseconomies of information to set against the specific economies of information that multinational operations can exploit.

Consequently, in practice there are real barriers and significant costs attached to multinational expansion strategies. In such circumstances, it appears that, contrary to the opinion given by some authors, the logic of multinational enterprise is neither natural nor inexorable but must rely heavily on informational economies. Only a limited class of firms are thus likely to be attracted to multinational activity. Such firms are likely to have two important characteristics; firstly a relatively high level of spending on firm-specific informational resources (especially R&D).[6] Further evidence is provided by Wolf (1977) who found that the proportion of industry sales accounted for by foreign subsidiaries was related to a technical skills indicator (employment of qualified scientists and engineers) for 95 US industries. Mansfield et al (1979) found that about one third of returns from R&D was obtained from foreign subsidiaries for a group of US multinationals. – potential informational economies increase as the firm-specific information resource level increases; secondly, there must be product-specific informational content that is transferable internationally. If the latter condition were not satisfied, domestic diversification strategies could take advantage of the non-product-specific informational economies without the costs attached to multinational operation.

These are likely to be necessary, but not sufficient conditions, for multinational strategies. In regard to the first condition relating to informational economies, Buckley and Casson (1976), Hymer (1960), and Rugman (1980a, b) contribute relevant analysis. Each developed Coase's (1937) analysis to conduct transaction-cost analyses of international business. A generally accepted inference arising from this body of work is that imperfections in international markets may result in a decision to find an overseas production location, and that multinational operation may be preferred if there are high transaction-costs of granting technological licences to overseas firms. This is liable to be the case if any licensee is opportunistically inclined to exploit the technical knowledge contained in the R&D package without compensating the licenser. Therefore multinational enterprise results from the incentive to internalise firm-specific informational advantages. We can extend this argument by examining the role of product-specificity in technical information in creating multinationalism.

8.6   MULTINATIONAL STRATEGY OPTIONS

The role of product-specificity in R&D knowledge can be demonstrated by considering alternative options for servicing overseas markets: (1) exporting, (2) multinational enterprise and (3) licensing specific technology. For convenience of exposition, the following discussion is limited to transfer of technical know-how, though it may also be applicable to market information in certain circumstances. If free trade exists, exporting would be preferred to foreign production (whether in the form of licensing or multinationalism) since exporting could increase exploitation of technological economies (such as T_1, T_2 and T_3 in Figure 1) through country specialisation and consolidation of production. Neither option exploits possible market links. Overseas location is only able to take advantage of shared R&D on the technological side. However, barriers to free trade such as tariffs, taxes, quotas, offsets or transportation costs may encourage foreign location, whether through multinational operation or overseas licensing, by creating impediments to exporting.

We have already suggested that multinational enterprise must exploit high levels of firm-specific informational economies and that these economies must be product-specific, otherwise a firm could follow domestic diversification as a line of least resistance. However, the degree to which these information economies are product-specific will determine whether a licensing or multinational strategy is the preferred option within the foreign location decision. If the technical information is entirely product-specific, there is liable to be minimal transaction-cost associated with using an overseas licensee, since patents and copyrights may adequately protect property rights in the licenser's firm-specific advantage. The patent or brand is supported by the totally product-specific nature of the technical information, which limits the ability of licensees to opportunistically exploit parts of the overall package. Further, the licensees are most likely to possess the country- and market-specific information necessary to complement the actual knowledge of the licensor.

The transaction-costs for licensing will rapidly increase as the degree of product-specificity declines since securing property rights for non-product-specific information may be costly or impracticable. Typically, technology transfer on a licensing basis involves a package or bundle of R&D know-how, some of whose elements are product-specific and some non-product-specific. If the licensee can acquire, then apply the component of non-specific, or extensible, information to other products without appropriate compensation, then the licenser may be naturally reluctant to adopt a licensing strategy.

For example, instant cameras utilise advanced technology in which R&D constitutes a high proportion of costs. If impediments to free trade exist, then an instant camera manufacturer may decide not to export, but to locate production abroad instead. If product-specificity of R&D existed, then property rights in camera R&D could be safeguarded legalistically through the terms of the licence agreement, and essentially combine the product-specific technical know-how of the developer with the country-specific knowledge of the licensee.

However, in reality instant cameras are based on extensible technologies, containing a number of product non-specific technological relationships that diversification out of instant cameras might exploit. The potential exists for technology transfer into electronic components, miniature batteries, chemicals, sensing and measurement devices, and precision machine tools. An opportunistically inclined licensee might be able to unpack the technological bundle and use the knowledge gained to further its own diversification. The possessor of the firm-specific advantage might therefore decide on the multinational option to internalise and protect potential diversification advantages that may be difficult to anticipate and specify within a licensing contract.[7]

We therefore expect that, as the level of product-specificity of R&D information diminishes, the multinational option is more likely to be preferred over the licensing option. However, as the level of product-specificity decreases, domestic diversification will become an increasingly attractive option with respect to foreign location. Since foreign location must be justified by reference to informational economies, if these same economies can be exploited by domestic diversification then the other potential economies sacrificed by going multinational make this latter strategy appear increasingly expensive, a point made by Wolf (1977).

Product-specificity in R&D encourages foreign location to exploit effectively informational economies that domestic diversification cannot utilise, while a high level of product-specificity would tend to favour licensing over multinationalism within the foreign location decision; the polar extremes of non-product-specificity and product-specificity tend to favour domestic diversification and licensing strategies respectively, with multinational enterprise being restricted to intermediate cases in which R&D information is partially product-specific. The R&D package will usually have some product-specific and some non-product-specific elements; the former favours foreign location, while the latter swings the balance towards multinationalism and away from licensing within the foreign location decision.

Three additional points are relevant to this discussion. Firstly, examining the types of R&D activity that the firm may conduct, the informational content tends to become more product-specific as we move away from basic research towards applied research and development. R&D with a high basic research content should contain a significant proportion of non-product-specific information. In such circumstances, policing the international transfer of technology becomes highly complicated, as recent US government action to stem leakage of strategic information to foreign countries has indicated. Thus, the likelihood of transaction-costs in the form of potential opportunism on the part of a licensee depends largely on the nature of the research content, whether low or high in basic research.

Secondly, the ability of a licensee to operate opportunistically depends on the level of technical sophistication of the licensee and/or the host country. The host firm or country is more able to appropriate benefits from non-product-specific information if they are also technically advanced. With respect to a given R&D package, potential transaction-costs of licensing may be higher for a technically developed host country or firm compared to a less developed country (LDC) or firm. As a result, multinationalism could be the preferred strategy in advanced countries, licensing in LDCs. However, a limiting factor on the ability of LDCs to handle licence agreements is that they may lack sufficient skills and experience to handle the salient production and marketing responsibilities associated with licensing. Further, even if a licensee is not advanced enough to exploit non-product-specific information, residual opportunism still exists if know-how can be leaked to more advanced agencies.

Thirdly, multinationalism and domestic diversification are not mutually exclusive strategies, despite the heuristic assumptions made earlier. In fact, empirical evidence indicates that the multinational also tends to be a highly diversified company (Vernon 1971). Rather than substituting diversification with foreign expansion, multinationals tend to operate both strategies jointly. A partial explanation of this phenomenon is provided in the respective strategies to exploit different aspects of partially non-product-specific information – diversification exploits non-product-specific information, while multinationalism directly exploits the product-specific aspect of the R&D package, and so both may utilise different aspects of the same technical bundle. This, however, does not fully explain why there is apparently a strong relationship between multinationalism and diversification, merely that the two strategies may not be mutually repellent.

A more fundamental explanation is found in the role played by technological change. In the context of the previous discussion, firms in technically dynamic industries are likely to be more diversified than firms in technologically placid environments in order to guard against the possibility of technological 'mugging'. Also, firms in high-technology industries are by nature R&D-intensive and thus able to extract a high level of information economies by sharing R&D costs across international boundaries. Therefore multinationalism and diversification are associated by the common feature of technologically dynamic industries; the former because of high levels of internal R&D, the latter because of high levels of external technological change.

8.7 CONCLUSIONS

With the above analysis in mind, we can now summarise the rationale for multinational enterprise. First, organising for scope economies, or gains from potential synergy, is likely to be the preferred strategy for multinationals since a hedging motive can usually be better satisfied with domestically orientated strategies (except when the hedging motive derives from country-specific surprises). Multinational enterprise is expected to pursue product-market links.

Secondly, firm-specific information and knowledge, especially in R&D, are the most likely sources of economies for the multinational. In order for a multinational strategy to exist, the gains from these economies must overcome the inherent costs and potential vulnerabilities to technological 'mugging' a multinational enterprise faces. Other market or technological links, while exposing the multinational to threats, do not provide benefits from synergy.

Thirdly, if free trade exists, then exporting is the preferred strategy for international expansion. This allows for economies based on the consolidation of research, development and production to be realised. If market imperfections exclude exporting as a viable strategic option, the exploitation of these firm-specific informational economies will depend on the extent to which these informational advantages are product-specific. If the informational content is completely product-specific, licensing technology is the preferred solution. If the information content is non-product-specific, and easily transferred to other types of products and processes, exploitation of R&D economies can be most effectively realised by a domestic strategy of technological diversification without the need to allocate capital to multinational enterprise. It is the intermediate case of firm-specific/partially product-specific information that provides the rationale for multinational enterprise. Foreign location is necessary to exploit product-specific economies, while the multinational option internalises and guards the non-product-specific informational content of overseas investment.

NOTES

1. This chapter was co-authored with Craig Galbraith, and is reprinted from *The Journal of Economic Behavior and Organization*, 7, 'Towards a theory of multinational enterprise', 1986 1–19, with kind permission of Elsevier Science, NL Sara Burgerhartstraat 25, 1055 KV Amsterdam, The Netherlands.

2. A review of these and other major recent books in the field, as well as an assessment of the state of play in transaction-cost analysis of multinational enterprise, is found in Kay (1983).

3. Although the term 'synergy' was used more or less casually in the business literature before Ansoff's 1965 work, Ansoff produced the first rigorous examination of the concept and its implication for corporate diversification. In the last several years, a number of papers have appeared on the topic of economies of scope. As defined by Willig (1979: 346), 'economies of scope arise from inputs that are shared or utilized jointly without complete congestion', while Baumol (1977: 807) comments that for economies of scope 'the initial concept is ... strict subadditivity of the cost function, meaning that the cost of the sum of any output vector is less than the sum of costs of producing them separately'. Baumol, Bailey and Willig (1977), Baumol and Braunstein (1977), and Baumol and Fischer (1978) explore the concept further and

analyse its implication for multiproduct operations with respect to market structure and natural monopoly though no insights are provided regarding the logic of corporate diversification. It is interesting to note that, although none of these papers refers to synergy, there is no effective formal distinction between the earlier concept as employed by Ansoff and economies of scope.

4. Research has indicated that although technological substitution is generally a gradual process where the new technology tends progressively to capture a series of different market segments, organisations tend to be slow in responding to technological threat, and in most cases, are ineffective if opting to participate in the threatening technology (Cooper and Schendel 1976). Thus we get the 'mugging' effect of environmental technological change. The mugging effect is not only descriptive in content, but also illuminates the type of attack technological change inflicts on most modern business firms.

5. A dominant hypothesis in the industrial organisation literature is that the degree of diversification (usually measured by the percentage of the firm net output or employment outside the primary industry of firm) is determined by the level of technical skills available within the firm (usually measured by the percentage of total employees represented by qualified scientists and engineers, or QSE). Thus, in this interpretation, diversification is primarily a consequence of inventive activity *internal* to the firm's technical skills. This contrasts with the interpretation above that diversification is primarily caused by inventive activity *external* to the firm – environmental technological change.

Studies examining the relationship between inventive activity and diversification fall into two camps. Five studies – Gort (1962), Amey (1964), Hassid (1975), Gorecki (1975) and Wolf (1977) – each found significant relationships between the degree of diversification and the level of inventive activity when these variables were measured at the *industry* level; each study utilised a sample of UK or US industries. Three studies – Scherer (1965), Grabowski (1968) and Comanor (1965) – found little evidence of a link between diversification and inventive activity when these variables were studied at *firm* level; only Grabowski found evidence of a positive relationship for two of the three industries he studied.

If the technological skills hypothesis holds (and each of the authors of industry-level studies argues that it does), the second set of studies is difficult to explain. The inconsistencies can be resolved if we interpret the QSE ratio at industry level as an indicator of environmental technological change rather than aggregate technical skills. This would explain why relationships appear between inventive activity and diversification when both are measured at industry level, but not when they are measured at firm level.

Rumelt (1974) suggests a related hypothesis to the internal skills hypothesis; he suggests that 'extensible technologies' in the science-based/research-intensive industries lead to a higher level of diversification in those industries. However, this does not explain why he found the unrelated strategy to be the most commonly associated with the science-based industries, whereas the environmental technological change argument does. Also it ignores the possibility that low-technology diversification may proceed around 'extensible markets', e.g., Rank and AMF in leisure. Extensible markets may provide market synergy just as extensible technologies may provide technological synergy. We suggest the specific *form* diversification takes is determined by potential synergy, but its *extent* is determined by the environment.

6.   There is empirical evidence of a relationship between propensity to go multinational and the technological dynamism of an industry. Caves (1974) found a significant relationship between foreign firms' share of Canadian and UK industry, and industry R&D expenditure as a percentage of sales. The likelihood of going multinational was related to industry R&D intensity in Horst's (1972) study. In this latter study, however, within industries the development of multinationalism was more closely related to firm size, this latter measure being interpreted by Horst as an indicator of a firm's managerial professionalism.

Horst's two findings may both be consistent with the hypothesis that multinationalism is determined by R&D activity. We have argued earlier that locating overseas exploits R&D informational economies at the cost of informational diseconomies associated with operating abroad. Firm size is likely to be a crude proxy for absolute size of R&D effort *within* industries and so provides a measure of the potential informational economies from research effort, while industry R&D intensity is likely to be a more appropriate indicator of potential informational economies *between* industries. Further evidence is provided by Wolf (1977), who found that the proportion of industry sales accounted for by foreign subsidiaries was related to a technical skills indicator (employment of qualified scientists and engineers) for 95 US industries. Mansfield *et al.* (1979) found that about one-third of returns from R&D was obtained from foreign subsidiaries for a group of US multinationals.

7.   Highly product-specific information is likely to be associated with informational packages of recipes that cannot be profitably broken down into exploitable opportunities, e.g., by 'reverse engineering'. Food and drink provide some examples of this, for instance, in licenses to produce beer overseas or fast food franchises.

9 Collaborative Strategies of Firms
Theory and Evidence[1]

9.1 INTRODUCTION

In recent years the proliferation of collaborative arrangements between firms has stimulated much academic interest in the phenomenon. The evolution of joint venture activity has attracted a great deal of interest, with research joint ventures receiving particular attention. There are now a number of databases providing evidence as to patterns of corporate activity in this area.

In this chapter we shall provide a broad survey of the literature in this area before looking at evidence from studies and databases. Firstly, we shall look at general issues and problems relating to collaborative arrangements and joint venture activity, with special reference to high-technology industry. Secondly, we shall consider the special problem of co-operative R&D and research joint venture. In addition, patterns of collaborative behaviour will be analysed with reference to a number of existing databases. We shall also consider empirical questions relating to this analysis, in particular what transactional and organisational issues influence current patterns of joint venture activity in high-technology industries.

The nature of collaborative activity between firms has recently received much attention in both the economics and managerial literature. While the managerial literature has noted and analysed co-operation between firms for some time, it is an area which has been relatively neglected in economics until very recently.

We argue below that there is generally a remarkable difference in emphasis between the two literatures as far as the efficiency implications of collaborative activity between firms is concerned. The economic literature tends to focus on the ability of collaborative activity such as joint venture to avoid wasteful duplication of activity, encourage spread of knowledge at low cost, facilitate appropriability, provide devices to deal with free riders, and spread risks. When compared with the alternative of independent competing firms, the ability of co-operative ventures to internalise and synchronise control over economic activity appears to offer significant opportunities for dealing with traditional market failure problems in this literature. The major efficiency problems in the economics literature are the anti-competitive implications of co-operation and collusion. By way of contrast, the managerial literature is characterised by persistent concern with contractual and administrative costs of collaboration, as well as the appropriability problems created by such arrangements. Rather than solving efficiency problems, this literature generally views them as high-cost options and basically to be treated as devices of last resort. In the following sections we argue that the economics literature must recognise and deal with the efficiency implications of the managerial literature's general treatment of collaborative arrangements as problematic and costly devices to be used only when there is no reasonable alternative.

There are immediately a number of qualifying statements to be made about the above generalisations. Firstly, to some extent the differences may reflect differences in perspective rather than belief; for example, the managerial literature's concern with the *promotion* (as opposed to the control) of competitive (in practice, monopoly) advantage may be 'wrong-side economics' from the point of view of the economics literature. Secondly, some economists do explicitly recognise issues raised by the managerial literature and incorporate discussion of them in their writings (e.g., Jacquemin 1988; Teece 1986). Thirdly, in developing economic explanations of collaborative activity consistent with their being treated as devices of last resort as in the managerial literature, we have found that the most likely explanations have actually been anticipated in the economic literature (e.g., Berg and Friedman 1977 and 1978: Mariti and Smiley 1983). Fourthly, collaborative arrangements are typically a much more varied and heterogenous bunch than the strategic alternatives of mergers and arm's length transactions. For example, US R&D consortia and technology-marketing alliances between Japanese and US firms may both be classified as collaborative activity. There is obviously a danger of comparing fish with fowl, a problem that exists even within the literatures.

However, even allowing for these qualifications, there remain strong differences between the respective literatures which invite comment and speculation. Therefore in Section 9.2 we shall first of all summarise the economic literature's approach to the problem of collaborative activity (in particular joint ventures) before contrasting this with the managerial literature's perspective in Section 9.3. In Section 9.4 we first consider joint venture (henceforth JV) as a form of economic organisation, before considering possible motives for JV activity in Section 9.5. In this section we take the managerial literature as our starting point. In Section 9.6 we consider empirical evidence in the light of arguments developed in Section 9.5 concerning the nature of JVs.

The conclusion of the chapter is that conventional economic explanations based on mainstream economic foundations (including neoclassical, decision- and game-theoretic sources) tend to neglect important features and behavioural characteristics of collaborative activity. In one sense at least we make a plea for a step backward; there is little point in building normative and policy-orientated analysis of JV activity until we can explain such basic issues as the apparent rapid escalation of collaborative activity in recent years, the apparently high failure rate of JVs and the short-lived nature of most agreements.

We also suggest that alternative perspectives and frameworks are consistent with the explanations developed here. However, for ease of exposition we do not refer to these throughout the chapter, not least because of the variety of approaches that may contribute to understanding in this area. Issues (and implied approaches) discussed below include contracting and exchange problems (transaction-cost approach) structuring of hierarchies (organisation theory), the firm as decomposable system (system theory), appropriability problems (property-rights literature) and the development and growth of firms (evolutionary theory). As we shall see, each of these five concepts will be of relevance in our analysis of collaborative activity. That so many issues may be of significance should not be regarded as surprising in dealing with a complex phenomenon which encompasses so many aspects of competition and co-operation, firm and market, organisation and exchange. Our objective here is not to try to provide clear-cut answers drawing upon these sources, but merely to signpost interesting opportunities for future research.

9.2 ECONOMIC ANALYSIS OF COLLABORATIVE ACTIVITY

Collaborative and co-operative activity are generally used as generic terms to describe a wide variety of firm and market relations, including minority shareholding, licensing, certain buyer–supplier relationships, consortia, franchising and JVs. Some of these terms may themselves be used in a variety of ways. In this chapter we shall focus on the particular phenomenon of JV, a particular form of collaborative activity which has aroused a great deal of interest in recent years. JVs are usually defined as involving:

> The creation of either a separate legal undertaking or at least some recognisable joint committee or association clearly identifiable and separate from the founders; the transfer by the founders of personnel and assets (often including intellectual property rights) to the new undertaking; and the allocation to the new undertaking of responsibility for carrying out a particular function or functions decided upon by its founders.
>
> (Goyder 1988: 174)

The subsequent discussion here relates most strongly to JV, though some of it may also be of relevance to collaborative activity in general.

When compared to arm's-length transactions between two firms (e.g., a licensing agreement), a JV has obvious advantages in certain circumstances. These advantages parallel the internalisation advantages that may be provided by in-house operation (such as through merger) and have been extensively discussed in the transaction-cost and multinational-enterprise literature (e.g., Williamson 1985; Caves 1982). Benefits include opportunities to improve monitoring and control of ventures, adaptability of decision making and avoidance of duplication of activity.

However, it is important to bear in mind during the following discussion that JVs are not only an alternative to arm's-length agreements, but also to single-ownership options such as green-field start-ups, mergers, and single-parent venture buy-outs. It is not sufficient to compare JVs to arm's-length alternatives; it has to be shown why they are also superior to single-ownership alternatives, especially since single-ownership alternatives such as merger are the traditional (and indeed obvious) way to internalise control over co-operative opportunity between two firms.

First, however, in Sections 9.2.1 to 9.2.4 we shall summarise some general perspectives in the economics literature on this phenomenon.

9.2.1   Joint venture may be a low-cost form of economic organisation

In one sense this is implicitly assumed by many studies of JVs and R&D JVs in so far as analysis of costs tend to emphasise R&D. In this respect management and organisation of JVs is effectively treated as a free good. Some economic analyses of JVs that discuss organisation costs concentrate on features that may mitigate organisational problems. For example, Casson (1987: 134) argues that it is easy to overstate the risk of conflict in the case of JVs. He suggests that JVs may benefit from a co-operative 'mystique' that may beneficially influence managerial behaviour. Abstinence from day-to-day interference will be observed by sensible parents and they should encourage the joint subsidiary's managers to develop loyalty to the venture itself. Thus, in Casson's view, the avoidance of managerial conflict may only marginally influence the choice between JV and do-it-yourself strategies.

Similarly, Buckley (1988: 139–41) argues that it is possible to analyse some ventures using conventional economic analysis in certain circumstances as devices by which parties can demonstrate mutual forbearance (that is, refrain from cheating each other) and build up trust. Beamish and Banks (1987) also argue that forbearance in JVs may reduce transaction costs associated with opportunistic behaviour, small numbers bargaining problems are also reduced if forbearance is practised, and pooling of information reduces uncertainty. Thus, transaction-cost problems associated with opportunism, small numbers and uncertainty (Williamson 1975) may be handled in a JV in Beamish and Banks's view. Some writers (e.g., Reynolds and Snapp 1986) also argue the related point that free riding can be dealt with more easily when transactions are internalised within a JV.

Slightly anticipating later discussion, I have to admit to some reservations regarding the above argument. In some respects such discussion sails close to tautology by suggesting that the transaction costs of a JV will not be a problem if transaction costs are not a problem. One manifestation of opportunism could be that partners convincingly communicate forbearance and trustworthiness while practising the reverse. In a variant of Arrow's paradox of the demand for information, it should be generally difficult or impossible to ascertain potential partners' intent *ex ante*, or indeed in some cases *ex post*.[2]

9.2.2 Joint ventures may encourage dissemination of knowledge without threatening its appropriability

Katz (1986: 528) argues that 'a co-operative R&D agreement may serve as a mechanism that internalises the externalities created by spillovers while continuing the efficient sharing of information. This … is accomplished by having firms commit to payments before the R&D is conducted and, hence, before any spillovers can occur.'

The literature on research JVs generally emphasises this possibility (e.g., Dasgupta 1988(b): 11; Bozeman *et al.* 1986: 264–5; Ordover and Baumol 1988: 27; Stoneman and Vickers 1988: x; Scott 1988; Reynolds and Snapp 1986: 141; Ouchi and Boulton 1988). In principle, the argument could be extended to cover knowledge spillovers in JVs generally.

However, whether a JV contract is generally an effective method for ensuring appropriability is questionable. Again, by their very nature, spillovers may be difficult or impossible to anticipate *ex ante*, and even *ex post* it may be impossible to evaluate what level or type of spillovers partners may have obtained from a specific venture. There may be no market price for such externalities even in a JV. In the case of tacit or uncodified knowledge embodied in human skills and experience, appropriability problems may even be increased through demonstration effects associated with a JV; 'tacit knowledge by definition is difficult to articulate, and so transfer is hard unless those who possess the know-how in question can demonstrate it to others' (Teece 1986: 287). We shall discuss these possibilities further in subsequent sections.

9.2.3   Joint ventures may spread risks and provide access to capital

'Co-operative R&D ... may allow risk sharing among firms, which can be important to managers and, thus, to stockholders ... [and also] an agreement may provide means by which firms can pool their resources to obtain sufficient capital to finance large R&D projects if capital markets are imperfect' (Katz 1986: 529). Reynolds and Snapp (1986) support this as a possible objective of co-operative R&D.

However, it is not immediately clear why these financial functions could not be better supported by dedicated financial institutions with a competitive advantage in risk bearing and capital-market functions. Such solutions would also reduce appropriability problems and difficulties associated with co-operative arrangements involving competitors. It may be true that technological closeness of JV partners may improve the ability to monitor each other's contribution and performance, but it seems unlikely that financial motives alone could provide a central justification for JVs.

9.2.4   Joint ventures can reduce duplication of R&D activity

Avoidance of wasteful duplication of R&D projects by adopting a co-operative solution is a frequently cited advantage of research JVs

(Dasgupta 1988(b): 10; Ordover and Baumol 1988: 27; Ordover and Willig 1985: 316; Stoneman and Vickers 1988: x; Reynolds and Snapp 1986: 141). Again the argument can be extended naturally to provide an explanation for JV activity in general.

It is true that JVs may provide a superior solution to wasteful duplication in certain cases. However, this still does not explain why JVs should be preferred to single-ownership alternatives. For example, rather than haggle over the JV contract, and have to cope with a dual-control managerial system and associated appropriability problems, a more obvious and efficient solution might be for one partner to buy out the other as soon as the JV subsidiary is set up. Since this frequently happens anyway, an immediate single-ownership solution could economise on transaction cost and organisation costs associated with JV control.

9.2.5   Joint ventures may have anti-competitive implications

To set against the gains in efficiency identified in the points above, there may be anti-competitive implications (Ordover and Willig 1985: 317; Katz 1986: 529, 541; Martin 1988; Stoneman and Vickers 1988: x; Bresnahan and Salop 1986; Reynolds and Snapp 1986; Vickers 1985). Most obviously, collaboration in the JV can lead to collusion in the subsequent product-market.

There is no doubt that such collusion is a possibility. More recently there have also been suggestions that management may pursue JVs as part of a strategy of making their companies bid-proof; an omelette of JVs may be difficult for an acquirer to unscramble. Without denying such possibilities, it will be argued in the next section that JVs are more costly that is generally allowed for in the economics literature. If collusion is an objective of a JV, it is a very expensive, blunt instrument for this purpose. It might seem reasonable to expect that thoughtful and creative managements could develop more subtle methods to collude if they wished.

9.3   MANAGERIAL LITERATURE ON JOINT VENTURES

Not surprisingly, the managerial literature tends to disregard the anti-competitive implications of JVs discussed above. Since the creation of competitive advantage may be interpreted as the establishment of monopoly power in some contexts, the managerial

Figure 9.1 Single ownership and joint venture alternatives

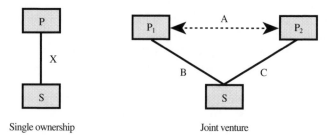

perspective provides recipes for the generation of monopoly, in contradistinction to the economics literature's concern with control of monopoly effects. These perspectives are not necessarily irreconcilable, especially if the managerial literature is viewed from a Schumpeterian perspective. However, they clearly take a different approach to these problems.

While the difference of emphasis is understandable in the case of anti-competitive implications, there is also a considerable difference between the two literatures in terms of their respective implications of the efficiency implications of JV as a form of economic organisation. The economic literature is generally sanguine as regards the ability of JVs to deal with transaction and organisational problems, while the managerial literature consistently reports severe difficulties in this context. Their analyses may be divided into two main categories, contractual and administrative problems. We illustrate these points with the help of Figure 9.1.

9.3.1 Contractual problems of JV

There are a number of transaction costs typically associated with setting up and maintaining a JV, as indicated by the dotted relationship A between the two parents (P_1 and P_2) of subsidiary S in Figure 9.1. Firstly, search for a satisfactory partner may be a non-trivial task, especially if there are cultural and attitudinal differences between potential collaborators (Renard 1985: 42–3). Secondly, negotiation of the JV can be a costly and time-consuming business. Renard (1985: 44–5) identifies 12 rules for effective negotiation; sample rules include step-by-step negotiation and testing the water with trial collaboration. Collectively, systematic application of these rules would ensure that JV negotiation is costly. While firms do economise on the application of the rules, Renard points out that such skimping increases the likelihood of JV failure. Thirdly, appropriability problems are still identified as severe problems in this literature as far as intangible assets are concerned. Two *Harvard Business Review* articles – Reich and Mankin (1986) and Hamel *et al.* (1989) – are typical of this literature, in that they look at recent collaborative arrangements and argue that appropriating partners' intangible assets, such as technological and organisational knowledge, may be an objective of collaboration. Such externalities have no effective market price (Roehl and Truitt 1987) and may impair the effectiveness of JVs, inhibit their formation or result in costly defences to limit leakage of such competitive advantage through JV (Hamel *et al.* 1989). As Roehl and Truitt (1987: 87) point out, relationships bear little resemblance to the 'calm ordered environments often envisaged by the academic ideal based on total trust and shared objectives'. The analysis of Hamel *et al.* (1989) is based on the fact that partners will selfishly try to get as much as possible out of the venture – hoping not to sacrifice their own competitive advantage in the process.

9.3.2 Administrative costs of JV dual control

This is represented in Figure 9.1 by the dual line of control, B from P_1 and C from P_2 controlling subsidiary S. In a sense, the organisational complications of this system of control relative to outright single ownership are self-evident: if it is preferable generally to be the servant of two masters, why are most hierarchies organised on the inverted-V principle? In fact, ambiguity, confusion and conflict is reasonably expected from dual control of a JV. This is confirmed in the managerial literature (e.g., Renard 1985: 46; Lyles 1987: 79; Perlmutter and Keenan 1986; Killing 1982; Schaan 1988). It would be surprising if it were otherwise. For our purposes it is sufficient to note that administrative costs arising from JV dual control are likely to be greater than for the single-ownership option in Figure 9.1.

A point that merits emphasis in this context is that JVs are an extremely complex form of hierarchy. As Figure 9.1 indicates, it is not appropriate to regard it as a partial or compromise structure located on some intermediate point on some market-hierarchy spectrum. Compared to the outright control or single-ownership option, it is a more sophisticated and complex administrative structure. We discuss the implications of this further in Section 9.3.3.

9.3.3   Costs of JV versus single-ownership options

In addition to the above references, useful analyses are also contained in a variety of articles in special issues of *The Columbia Journal of World Business* (Summers of 1986 and 1987), devoted to JVs and collaborative activity. A difficulty is that this literature is more dependent on informal evidence, anecdotes and case studies than is the economic literature. However, many of the issues analysed are difficult to analyse in formal terms, and such studies are often making the best of a difficult job.

It is sufficient for our purposes if this analysis helps to demonstrate a simple point: JVs are typically contractually and administratively more expensive than single-ownership alternatives. Either feature should be sufficient to give single ownership a cost advantage over a JV; together they raise the fundamental question as to why such costly forms of economic organisation should evolve at all. Mergers, green-field start-ups or JV partner buy-outs would all appear to be simpler and cheaper alternatives in general. In a sense, the economic literature has gone too far too quickly; rather than focus on the efficiency gains and competitive losses inherent in JVs, we need to develop explanations as to why they develop in the first place. We develop this theme in the next section.

9.4   JOINT VENTURES AS ECONOMIC ORGANISATION

The previous section has raised an interesting puzzle that has tended to be glossed over in economic analyses of JVs: if JVs are relatively expensive forms of economic organisation, why do single-firm ownership alternatives such as merger, green-field start-up or single-parent buy-out not evolve instead? In fact, many JVs are reported as having failed to achieve their objectives or eventually convert into some form of single ownership; contractual and administrative problems of JVs are frequently cited as the reasons for failure or conversion to single ownership.[3] However, we need to develop explanations as to why management would rationally choose a JV option, unless we are willing to entertain theories based on irrational managerial behaviour.

In Kay *et al.* (1987) we suggested how it may be possible to analyse JVs in this respect.[4] Firstly, if we analyse JVs in contractual and administrative terms as above, it becomes clear that it is generally misleading to see them as a hybrid or compromise form of economic organisation, lying on some hypothetical spectrum between market exchange at one end and full-scale internalisation or hierarchy at the other. It is true that JVs contain both market-exchange and hierarchical elements (relations A and B/C respectively in Figure 9.1). However, it is a simple step from suggesting that JV is a compromise intermediate or hybrid form of economic organisation in markets and hierarchies terms to arguing that JVs may trade off some features of market exchange for hierarchical features (or vice versa, depending on which end of the spectrum one starts at). For example, Jacquemin and Spinoit (1985) argue that

> co-operative agreements are an alternative to either arm's-length markets or integration within the firm under a single administrative structure. Its choice could, therefore, indicate that it is perceived as a less costly or more effective way than the alternatives of either in-house development, merger or normal market transactions.

> (1985: 10)

Jacquemin and Spinoit then argue that the contractual aspects of JVs give flexibility that may or may not be obtainable through full-scale, in-house developments or mergers, while binding together competitors within a JV facilitates appropriability of R&D and overcomes problems of free riding associated with a pure market solution (1985: 10–11).

We believe that it is misleading to regard JVs as a potentially less costly form of economic organisation integrating advantages from the market and hierarchy elements of its structure. As Figure 9.1 indicates, JVs are a more complex form of hierarchy than single-ownership. Relative to the single-ownership option, JVs do not trade off hierarchy for market elements: they generally *exacerbate* hierarchical problems rather than reduce them, as is confirmed by the managerial literature discussed above. In fairness to Jacquemin and Spinoit it should be pointed out that they also recognise such problems of co-operative arrangements in the case of R&D agreements, citing complex hierarchy, contractual and appropriability problems in particular (1985: 12–14; see also Jacquemin 1988). In short, JVs generally add market *and* organisation costs relative to single-ownership alternatives; it is not an intermediate form of economic organisation regarded in market and hierarchic terms.

Consistent with this, JVs are generally treated as a device of last resort as evidenced by the managerial literature. It appears that choice of economic organisation in this context is lexicographic; JVs are adopted when there is no reasonable alternative. In fact, this is a circumstance which is generally recognised in the case of compulsory partnerships; e.g., Third World countries erecting barriers to greenfield start-ups or takeover by foreign firms, and encouraging JVs with local firms. However in Kay *et al.* (1987) we argued that once JVs are regarded as more costly than alternatives, analysing them as devices of last resort is the natural perspective to adopt.

This prompts an obvious question; if JVs are generally more costly than alternatives, surely they would only be adopted in special (and potentially inefficient) circumstances, such as forced partnerships by foreign governments? In the next section we shall in fact argue that they may be a rational response by firms even in the absence of forced partnerships.

9.5   MOTIVES FOR JOINT VENTURES

In a series of papers, David Teece (1986, 1987,[5] 1989) has argued that collaborative arrangements to exploit technological innovation may be based around exploitation of complementary assets supplied by the respective parents. This is consistent with observed patterns of resource provision by parents: for example, one parent may supply technology and the other marketing expertise, or parents may augment each other's technological skills with their own technological expertise. Complementarity is a recurrent theme in the managerial literature, and is also recognised in the economics literature – e.g., Ordover and Willig (1985: 316). However, this raises a further question as far as the choice of JV rather than single-ownership alternatives like merger are concerned. While mergers are devices by which complementary assets can be integrated, they may also be utilised to integrate substitute assets (horizontal merger) and unrelated assets (conglomerate). Why should JVs be limited to cases involving complementary assets?

Conglomerate JVs are ruled out by definition; after all, if JVs' parents are presumed to be providing real technical and marketing resources as well as simply financial backing, parents will be inevitably related to the subsidiary. More interestingly, our analysis above suggests why purely horizontal JVs are unlikely; if all a partnership offers are substitute assets, then firms could more easily and cheaply go it alone. Teece's emphasis on the role of complementary assets appears justified in the context of JVs. We can therefore refine the question at the end of the last section into: why should JVs be utilised to exploit complementary assets if they are generally more expensive than single-ownership alternatives? We suggest some circumstances consistent with such choices.

9.5.1   Joint ventures involving complex systems

Understandably, the basic unit of analysis in the economic literature has been the JV itself. The establishment and operation of the JV is treated as the basic building block of analysis in analogous fashion to the focus on product-markets in traditional neoclassical theory.

In Kay (1979, 1982) it was argued that focusing on the systemic properties of firms could help generate analysis and insights not possible with the traditional reductionist perspective of neoclassical theory. Such a perspective may also be helpful in the case of JVs. Rather than look at the implications of JVs in isolation, it may be helpful to place them in the context of the corporate system.

Figure 9.2 is adapted from Kay *et al.* (1987). P_1 and P_2 are presumed to be large diversified firms, operating four divisions each with intra-firm marketing (M) or technological (T) links with other divisions. Now suppose P_1 could contribute technological resources and P_2 marketing resources to a venture that could commercially exploit these complementary assets; what alternative forms of economic organisation exist to integrate these assets?

Figure 9.2   Joint venture involving two diversified firms

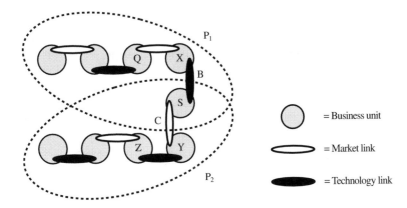

B may be taken as P_1's technological and C as P_2's marketing resources in Figure 9.1. As implied in the discussions of Figure 9.1, a joint venture between X and Y in Figure 9.2 would be a complex and cumbersome choice, contractually and organisationally.

However, consider the choices facing the respective firms in the above case. The assets are complements, not substitutes, and so the firms may require each other's co-operation to pursue the venture: green-field start-ups may not be feasible if complementary assets are difficult or costly to replicate (e.g., in the case of such assets as innovation, reputation, established distribution channels and so on).

Single-ownership could be achieved if one parent was to buy out the other; e.g., if P_1 was to purchase the necessary marketing resources from P_2. Sale of X to P_2 or Y to P_1 is the most obvious solution. However, such trades could have substantial externalities in the form of sacrificed synergies or economies of scale that both divisions at present contribute to within their firms, as indicated by the respective C and B links. Consequently, single-parent buy-outs may be precluded because of these negative externalities.

Outright merger of the two firms may also be impractical. In this case there may be further substantial negative external effects (relative to the JV) in the form of considerably enlarged and complex organisation, $P_1 + P_2$. In the context of the limited co-operation gains represented by X and Y's potential venture, outright merger could be described as akin to using a sledgehammer to crack a nut (Kay *et al.* 1987). Again the gains from single ownership and control of S must be set against the diseconomies of co-ordinating the significantly larger and more complex system. This point is recognised by Mariti and Smiley (1983):

> Mergers involve the combination of whole firms with numerous uncertainties about the ability of the parts to function smoothly together, and the resulting difficulties of the merger may overwhelm the cost reducing benefits of larger volume in one or several individual products. Co-operative agreements, on the other hand [reduce costs] without the uncertainties and difficulties of full scale mergers.
>
> (1983: 444–5)

Berg and Friedman (1977: 1332) also point out that full-scale merger may be inefficient or too costly to arrange 'due to inappropriate meshing of product lines'. As a consequence, JV may be turned to as the form of economic organisation that internalises control (albeit expensively) without incurring the negative effects external to the JV associated with single-parent buy-out or outright merger. In other words, even though JV may be the most expensive form of economic organisation considered at the local level of the venture itself, once system-wide effects are recognised it may be a relatively cheap way of pursuing the venture, looked at from the level of the firm itself.

Two important points can be made regarding the implications of this argument. Firstly, it opens up the prospect of linking the evidence of the managerial literature to a theory of rational choice as far as JV activity is concerned. As long as system-wide effects are ignored, it is necessary to presume that JVs are relatively low-cost forms of economic organisation at the level of the venture itself, and so characterised by such features as forbearance, mutual trust, and success in dealing with appropriability problems – features which may certainly be present in some JV's but which are not generally observed in the managerial literature on this phenomenon. Once system-wide firm-level effects are recognised, the existence of severe contractual and administrative problems within the JV itself can still be reconciled with its being chosen over single-ownership alternatives.

Secondly, it allows for a rational answer to Mariti and Smiley's question: 'if co-operative agreements do allow reduction in costs, why were they not in use as much 15 years ago as they are today?' (1983: 447).[6] They suggest that either increased competition (resulting from decreases in market growth) has forced firms to adopt cost minimisation, or previous conditions of market growth had diverted attention to management of the demand-side at the expense of cost-side considerations.

While both of these considerations may contribute to the formation of collaborative agreements, there is a further explanation consistent with choice of least-cost option over the whole period and not just the latter part. Consider divisions X and Y in Figure 9.2 above. Suppose some years previously they had been independent firms in their own right and that a process of internal growth and/or acquisition had later created P_1 and P_2. How would venture opportunity S have been treated in those early days?

The most obvious solution is the single-ownership solution – say, through X and Y merging or one acquiring the other. The absence of adverse system-wide effects associated with ventures involving large diversified firms (e.g., P_1 and P_2) clears the way for the simple, traditional single-ownership solution. It is only when firms grow in size and diversity (e.g., to P_1 and P_2) that system-wide effects result in collaborative agreements such as JVs evolving as the least-cost solution, at the level of the firm if not the venture.

What is attractive about this explanation is that it sees JVs as a natural consequence of the evolution of firms and industries. System-wide effects from single-ownership solutions to the integration of complementary assets are likely to increase as firms grow in scale and diversity. Scale of firm relative to size of venture opportunity is itself sufficient to generate the adverse system-wide effects discussed above, but the effects are likely to be exacerbated if the growth strategy involves diversification. Thus the growth of firms naturally leads to the evolution of JVs, and may be consistent with profit-orientated strategies throughout.

9.5.2   Other possible motives for JVs as devices of last resort

We have argued that explanations for the evolution of JVs should accommodate the general observation in the managerial literature that JVs are generally more costly than alternative forms of economic organisation, at least over the region of the venture itself. System-wide effects discussed in Section 9.5.1 above help provide one explanation consistent with this observation. Others are discussed in Kay *et al.* (1987), and we briefly summarise them here.

Firstly, *concentrated markets*: single-ownership alternatives may attract the attention of antitrust authorities if monopoly power is a consequence. Further, even if the venture itself does not have direct anti-competitive implications, merger could have other system-wide anti-competitive effects, e.g., in Figure 9.2, Q and Z may be direct competitors. JV may be the only way to integrate complementary assets of X and Y without compromising competition and attracting the attention of the antitrust authorities. Berg and Friedman (1978) argue that JVs between firms in the same industry are generally safer than merger in this respect. It is worth noting that this stimulus to JV would be a natural consequence of growth and evolution at firm level, just as in 9.5.1 above. In this case, however, the effect of growth on incentives to conduct a JV is through the intermediate effect on market concentration.

Secondly, *disincentive effects*: single-ownership options such as a buy-out of the other partner or a merger may have undesirable outcomes from the perspective of either or both parents.[7] For example, independence may itself be an objective (Berg and Friedman 1977: 1332), or merger may deaden innovativeness by incorporating creative systems within larger bureaucracies unfamiliar with their needs and characteristics.[8] Again, these effects may be strengthened by growth effects at firm level in so far as they may be related to the degree of scale and diversity of an innovator's potential partner. In short, even though JVs may be expensive, it may be the only way to achieve the desired outcome. This contrasts with much of the economics litera- ture, which fixes the desired outcome and then considers alternative means of achieving it, such as in races to be first to patent. Forms of economic organisation may affect outcome as well as cost.

Thirdly, *forced partnership*: this is a widely discussed reason for adopting JVs, and little needs to be added here.[9] Again, it is consistent with JVs being a high-cost alternative to single ownership; if JV is the only option permitted, then the potential cost of alternative forms is irrelevant.

It is worth emphasising that all the above possible explanations are consistent with JVs being the highest-cost form of economic organisa- tion over the region of the venture itself. The complex system, concen- trated markets, and disincentive effects explanations all point out that single-ownership alternatives may have undesirable system- or firm- wide effects, while JV may be the only game in town in the case of forced partnership. Apart from the forced partnership, each explana- tion is strengthened by systemic effects arising from growth and diversification on the part of at least one of the potential partners. They are entirely consistent with the managerial literature's emphasis on JV as a costly device of last resort. There is no need to follow the common route adopted in the economics literature and to presume that JVs may be lower-cost alternatives over the region of the venture itself, if free riding and appropriability problems can be dealt with, and partners co-operate in a spirit of trust, forbearance and mutual harmony. In a sense it is a relief to know that the old, familiar, self- seeking economic man can still be found in collaborative arrange- ments, even though it may be disappointing that the existence of such arrangements does not necessarily imply the existence of a nobler form of *Homo sapiens*.

It is also noteworthy that each of these explanations has been previ- ously alluded to in the economics literature (e.g., Berg and Friedman 1977, 1978; and Mariti and Smiley 1983). Yet there has been no real evidence of attempts to develop them into anything other than casual *ad hoc* explanations, and their potential relevance has not been recog- nised by most current analyses in the economics literature. Indeed, as long as the evidence of the managerial literature is ignored, there is little pressure to invoke such explanations. It is only when the increasing use of JVs has to be reconciled with their observed costliness that the potential significance of such explanations becomes apparent.

In Sections 9.6 and 9.7 we shall consider empirical evidence on JVs and the extent to which it is generally consistent with this perspective of JV as a costly device of last resort.

9.6   PATTERNS OF JV ACTIVITY

From our preceding discussion, potential determinants of JV activity of direct interest to us include size, diversification of firms and degree of market concentration. We consider here available evidence in this respect and the implications of other empirical findings of relevance.

Berg and Friedman in their 1978 survey of JVs in American industry confirm that if any co-operation between two firms in the same industry attracts antitrust attention, 'there is evidence that horizontal JVs are viewed as safer than full horizontal mergers'. They argue that this helps to explain why 62 per cent of the JVs by basic chemical firms from 1966 to 1973 were horizontal, while only 38 per cent of the mergers were horizontal (Berg and Friedman 1978: 30). This tends to be consistent both with arguments that concentration will tend to encourage JV activity, as well as exploitation of complementary assets between firms in the same industry. In a 1976 article, Pfeffer and Nowak had contested that JV should receive a less stringent treatment than mergers on the part of antitrust authorities. Finding the proportion of horizontal parent-pairings to be positively correlated with the concentration of the child industry, they concluded that corporate JVs in concentrated markets provided evidence of their use to secure monopoly advantages. In fact, Berg and Friedman (1980: 164) argue that it is firm size rather than concentration which determines the extent and incidence of JV activity, the concentration measures providing a positive correlation with JV activity only because of a link through the size of firms in an industry.[10] Predominance of JVs in concentrated markets should not allow for an interpretation of JV as being mainly used to enhance market power, an interpretation frequently given, but rejected by Berg and Friedman after a rate-of-return analysis of JV.

That size is the most important single factor for JV creation is also claimed by Boyle, whose early study of JVs having at least one parent among the 'Fortune 500' showed that joint subsidiary participation increases as the size of firm increases. For example, firms classified among the 100 largest manufacturing corporations were identified as parent corporations in 42 per cent of the cases (Boyle 1968: 85). Also, 'the larger the company, the more likely it is to be involved in many joint subsidiaries' (1968: 92), a result which is consistent with our size argument, but also with the diversification one; the larger the firm, the more likely it is to be diversified. More empirical studies are needed here, especially from the point of view of separating out effects of size and diversification, and also with respect to the role of the M-form in stimulating JV activity.

That JVs tend not to be used as transitional, intermediary structures preceding merger is evidenced by Berg and Friedman's (1978) study of the termination of chemical JVs between 1924 and 1969. In 50 cases of termination studied, only 2 were due to a parent merging into the other. In the 48 remaining cases, those which were not due to financial failure (20 cases) or an antitrust settlement (4 cases) were the result of a purchase by one parent (22 cases), by a third party (4 cases) or result of a merger of the JV into another JV by the same parents. So there seems to be a tendency for JVs to be transformed into some other organisational form after a few years of operation, but *not* to be a step towards *merger* of the parents.

Simultaneously, Berg and Friedman (1979a and b) notice the relatively short lives of JVs, but stress the fact that the absorption of the JV by one parent does not necessarily mean that the JV failed (1979a: 10). If JVs are not without risks, 'some terminations reflect not the "financial failure" of the JV but rather the advent of new areas of investment of higher potential returns for at least one of the parents' (1979b: 30).

Therefore, it does seem that the evidence is consistent with JVs evolving as firms grow and diversify (as we would expect from our earlier analysis), though the relationship in concentrated markets appears more complex. The last two sets of empirical results discussed above are also of relevance as far as our interpretation of JVs as a device of last resort is concerned. Firstly, it is natural to think of JV as a stepping stone to merger as long as it is thought of as an intermediate form between market and hierarchy. That it is not a stepping stone is consistent with its being a device of last resort. Secondly, with respect to the short life of ventures, this is a natural corollary to the earlier argument that increase in the size of firms may generate significant system-wide effects relative to the venture itself; diminishing the scale of the venture itself relative to a given size of firm might reduce the incentive to merge to exploit limited venture opportunities. Consequently, JV may appear as the natural solution to short-lived minor opportunities; while short life may reflect failure, it may also reflect a bias towards choosing JV in these cases.

9.7   CONCLUDING COMMENTS

In this chapter we have not attempted to match the degree of formalisation and rigour of the standard economics literature on collaborative activity. We have traded off rigour and precision for a broad-based approach in an attempt to explain general patterns of collaborative behaviour, such as the relatively recent proliferation of JV activity.

Therefore, the chapter should not be analysed or tested against a precise model-building standard, but, it is hoped, should be seen as signposting promising areas of analysis. However, it should be acknowledged that the chapter does have a subversive intent in so far as the signposts tend to point away from mainstream economic theorising. For example, once contactual problems are recognised, the transaction-cost literature[11] is of obvious relevance. Appropriability problems suggest we should draw upon the property-rights literature.[12] The role of organisation and hierarchy suggests that research into organisational decision making may be of relevance.[13] Our emphasis on the growth and development of corporations draws upon insights offered by the evolutionary theorists,[14] while the concept of the firm as a non-decomposable system is a development of system-theoretic concepts.[15] The role of systems concepts and problems of decision making under uncertainty are recurring themes in this chapter, and these literatures have directed, suggested or influenced their use here.

Collaborative strategies of firms have been a useful test-bed for comparing the mainstream perspectives of conventional theory with some alternative interpretations and frameworks. As well as pursuing further theory development and empirical testing, it could be useful to conduct dialogues between researchers in this area to explore the extent to which differences in analysis are a reflection more of emphasis than belief; for example, while we have argued that Buckley and Casson's concepts of forbearance, altruism and mutual trust are unlikely to describe collaborative activity in general, nonetheless there may be special cases where such attitudes are rational (e.g., mutual dependence of partners having made JV specific commitments, or cases involving repetitive transactions). Also, both these authors recognise the role of obstacles to mergers in encouraging collaborative activity.[16] To what extent there actually exist irreconcilable differences is unclear, and should be one avenue for further consideration.

However, our major conclusion is quite simple. Looking at the firm as an integrated system in which participants may be faced with severe and intractable information problems is a helpful and potentially productive perspective. It helps account for the managerial literature's treatment of JVs as measures of last resort only, while indicating a variety of theoretical frameworks that could be drawn on for future analysis in this area.

NOTES

1. Originally published in A. Del Monte (ed.) *Recent Developments in the Theory of Industrial Organisation*, London: Macmillan 1992, pp. 201–31; reprinted by kind permission of the publishers.
2. The process of internalisation itself may not eliminate problems of monitoring of opportunistic behaviour, especially if firms are trying to appropriate such intangible assets as tacit knowledge and organisational methods of their partners.
3. Analyses that indicate that JVs are characterised by high failure rates include Killing (1982: 120) and Gomes-Cassieres (1987: 97). It should be pointed out, however, that many of these studies implicitly assume that failure is indicated by short life or absence of accounting profits. However, if JVs are characterised by objectives other than profit or high levels of externalities, this may be too simplistic a view of failure.
4. The discussion here and in Section 9.5 draws on this paper.
5. With G. Pisano.
6. However, Mariti and Smiley caution that it is difficult to identify trends in this case, the absence of reliable data being a complicating factor.
7. Michael Dietrich (1991) has pointed out that transactions may involve demand-side effects as well as supply- or cost-side implications.
8. Size mismatch is cited as a common problem in merger and integration studies in the managerial literature. For an early study of this problem, see Kitching (1967).
9. Much of the literature on JV activity in the Third World reports forced partnerships.
10. See Berg and Friedman (1980: 164). Although Berg and Friedman's empirical findings concerning the size-of-firm effect are consistent with JVs being adopted as a device of last resort, their explanation for the relationship is quite different. Device-of-last-resort explanations here depend on size of firm increasing barriers to merger alternatives. Berg and Friedman instead argue that size of firm generates capital

economies to fund JVs and enables the larger firm to engage in multiple JVs.

However, the device-of-last-resort explanation developed here is preferred in so far as it is simpler, parsimonious and consistent with a wider range of observed phenomena.

11. For example, see Williamson (1975 and 1985). However, for problems with the transaction-cost approach, see Chapter 4 in this volume.
12. For example, see Alchian (1977).
13. See March and Shapira (1982) for a stimulating coverage of some recent work in this area.
14. See especially Nelson and Winter (1982).
15. For work in this vein, see Kay (1979 and 1982).
16. For example, see Buckley (1988: 140).

Part III Policies

INTRODUCTION

Part III is made up of three related articles, each dealing with European policies on corporate strategy. Just as the earlier work on diversification strategies (represented here by Chapter 7) begat the work on joint ventures in Chapter 9, so work on Chapter 9 begat Chapter 10, and in turn Chapter 10 begat Chapters 11 and 12. As our introductory chapter explains, the European Commission's view of corporate strategy was founded on a misleading view of the issues.

The three chapters forming Part III together paint a very different of picture of the economics of corporate strategies at European level from that portrayed by the European Commission. Collectively they suggest that European policies are being based on flawed interpretations of the nature and efficiency implications of corporate strategies. In turn, these policies are likely to lead to the misallocation of considerable amounts of public and private resources. However, as yet there appears to be no real recognition of these points at policy-making level in the European Community.

10 Industrial Collaborative Activity and the Completion of the Internal Market[1]

10.1 INTRODUCTION

In this chapter we consider an issue that will be of major significance in the context of the completion of European market (or the 1992 programme); what happens to industrial collaboration if a market is completed? This is in fact a key question in investigating the effect of 1992 on corporate strategies, while also having implications for trade liberalisation within a common European space and with the Eastern European countries. The major focus for our study is how 1992 will affect joint venture activity within the Community. Joint venture is selected in full knowledge that it is only one of a range of collaborative strategies, but in fact tends to be the archetypal collaborative strategy identified by the Commission.[2] It is therefore convenient to focus on joint ventures, not only because of the growing importance of this corporate strategy in recent years, but because we can contrast our arguments with the Commission's own analysis of this form of industrial collaboration using Commission data.

We argue below that there is a consistent theme running through the Commission's analysis of the effects of 1992, but that it is disturbingly misplaced. The Commission claims that market fragmentation has impeded industrial co-operation within the Community, that EC cross-border collaborative strategies such as joint ventures will be encouraged by 1992, and that the evidence of the Commission's own survey supports these arguments. We argue the opposite point of view on each of these counts: fragmentation has encouraged collaborative strategies; market completion will encourage firms to substitute other strategies for joint ventures; and the Commission's own evidence does not support its arguments, despite its claims to the contrary.

It will be suggested that the problem with the Commission's analysis of collaborative strategies is that it is reducible to a basic flawed

201

premise: that collaboration is intrinsically desirable and worthwhile, and that many firms have been prevented from collaborating by the existence of barriers and impediments within the Community that 1992 will help to remove. We argue instead that collaboration is typically the last thing that firms wish to do, and that it is usually treated as a final option to be resorted to when all other options have been discounted.

Before we go any further it is worth noting that these differences from the Commission viewpoint are not simply matters of academic debate. Apart from the general significance of what will happen to corporate strategies after market completion, considerable amounts of public money invested in science and technology programmes like ESPRIT are riding on the Commission's bet that 1992 will facilitate cross-frontier industrial collaboration which these programmes will help to cement. If the Commission is wrong, we may encounter instead a deterioration in the cost or performance aspects of such programmes, especially if 1992 discourages rather than encourages collaboration in high-technology industries.

In the next section we examine critically the Commission's arguments on the effects of 1992 on EC joint ventures, before looking at actual evidence on the effects of market completion on industrial collaboration.

10.2   THE 1992 PROGRAMME AND INDUSTRIAL CO-OPERATION

The White Paper 'Completing the Internal Market' makes industrial co-operation within the EC a major objective of the 1992 programme:

> The removal of internal boundaries and the establishment of free movement of goods and capital and the freedom to provide services are clearly fundamental to the creation of the internal market. Nevertheless, Community action must go further and create an environment or conditions likely to favour the development of co-operation between undertakings.
>
> (CEC 1985: 34)

It argues that the barriers to industrial co-operation will be reduced by the 1992 programme, and that industrial co-operation will consequently increase:

In spite of the progress made in creating such an environment, co-operation between undertakings of different Member States is still hampered by excessive legal, fiscal and administrative problems, to which are added occasional obstacles which are more a reflection of different mental attitudes and habits. The absence of a Community legal framework for cross-border activities by enterprises and for co-operation between enterprises of different Member States has led – if only for psychological reasons – to numerous potential joint projects failing to get off the ground. As and when the internal market is developed further, enterprises incorporated in the form of companies or firms will become more and more involved in all manner of intra-Community operations, resulting in an ever-increasing number of links with associated enterprises, creditors and other parties outside the country in which the registered office is located.

(CEC 1985: 34–6)

The White Paper also promises to deploy competition, technology and regional policies towards the objective of encouraging cross-border co-operation between firms in different Member States:

The Commission will also continue to apply competition rules by authorizing co-operation between undertakings which can promote technical or economic progress within the framework of a unified market. The Commission will also seek to ensure that Community budgetary and financial facilities make their full contribution to the development of greater co-operation between firms in different Member States. It will seek to guide future research programmes in this direction, both at the pre-competitive research stage and at the stage of pilot or demonstration projects. The ESPRIT and BRITE programmes now under way have already had a very positive impact on European firms in terms of the opportunities for co-operation which they represent. The Regional Fund must also be enabled to contribute to greater co-operation between firms.

(CEC 1985: 34–5)

The conclusion of the research work sponsored by the Commission to investigate the economics of 1992 are consistent with the White Paper in these respects. Cecchini also sees increasing business co-operation in R&D as a major consequence of the 1992 programme:

Europe-wide standards ... are an essential lever both for prising open national markets and then welding them together through technological alliances. Of greater importance to such alliances are EC-sponsored R&D programmes like ESPRIT which, way beyond their monetary significance, are a crucial focus for fusing cross-frontier innovation and business.

(Cecchini *et al.* 1988: 89)

Market integration brings with it a number of factors giving European firms the chance to regain technological leadership ... [including] the rapid development of cross-frontier business co-operation for R&D.

(Cecchini *et al.* 1988: 75)

Emerson *et al.* (1988), endorse this view, identifying a number of regulatory and political obstacles to co-operation in Europe, many of which would be removed or reduced by the 1992 programme (1988: 174). Both Cecchini *et al.* (1988: 87–8) and Emerson *et al.* (1988) identify what they call a 'paradox' in the existing patterns of co-operative behaviour on the part of EC firms:

The paradox which emerges is that co-operation with Community partners has so far been less frequent than co-operation with partners in non-member countries. The total number of joint ventures set up has remained very stable; in 1985–6, Community operations still lagged behind (24.7% of the total) by comparison with domestic operations (42%) and international operations (33%) ... . But European co-operation could grow substantially as a result of the removal of some of these barriers.

(Emerson *et al.* 1988: 175)

We note in passing that if you believe removal of trade barriers should encourage collaborative behaviour, it does indeed appear paradoxical that the EC does not already have a higher level of joint venture activity, given the already lower level of EC trade barriers relative to the rest of the world. The study by Emerson *et al.* concludes that the claim that collaborative activity such as joint ventures will increase after 1992 is supported by the empirical evidence of the business survey conducted under the auspices of the 1992 research programme into strategies envisaged by firms to prepare for 1992. Emerson *et al.* conclude that co-operation agreements will be facilitated by 1992:

Hitherto there have been many obstacles in the way of cooperative agreements, and the failure rate has been high. In addition to the difficulties of finding a partner able to make balanced contribution, setting up a management structure to minimize the running costs of cooperation, and ensuring full and fair use of the proceeds, there is also a set of regulatory and political obstacles to cooperation in Europe.

(Emerson et al. 1988: 174)

Before considering the likely actual patterns of future collaborative behaviour at industry level, it is essential to realise how this theme of co-operation has infused the packaging of the whole 1992 programme, from the White Paper onwards. The White Paper sees co-operation as a natural feature of the programme at all levels, including technological and industrial at national level. The Cecchini Report and Emerson *et al.* reinforce this general perspective. We shall argue in the next section that these perspectives are misplaced, and indeed misleading.

10.3   COMPETITION, CO-OPERATION AND 1992

In analysing industrial co-operative behaviour it is essential to understand that for firms joint ventures are typically a device of last resort (Kay *et al.* 1987; and Chapter 10 here). They are turned to when projects are too big or expensive for one firm, when other firms have assets that the firm does not have, and when merger is excluded as a strategic option for some reason (such as antitrust policy or the large scale and diversity of firm relative to venture opportunity). If firms can easily perform a particular venture on their own, they will generally prefer to do so. Open markets facilitate trade and exporting strategies, while barriers to trade may encourage multinational locations. Exporting and multinational options help the firm to retain control over the technology and profit streams accruing from specific developments. By way of contrast, co-operative arrangements such as joint ventures are often costly and cumbersome to set up and administer, dissipate profit streams and, most crucially, may erode the firm's competitive advantage by giving potential rivals access to valuable technological knowledge.[3]

In the high-technology industries especially, this last point is a major consideration influencing and inhibiting collaborative activity. The post-war evolution of the Japanese economy provides useful evidence of the dangers intrinsic in technological collaboration. Technological agreements with overseas partners, especially US firms, gave Japanese firms invaluable access to Western technologies after World War II. In the absence of the effective barriers to imports and inward direct investment created by Japan, it is likely that many of the Western firms would have preferred to have obtained access to the Japanese market through exporting or direct investment rather than through collaborative arrangements.

For our purposes, the important question is how the 1992 programme will affect collaborative behaviour between firms. There are two relevant points here. Firstly, the more open a market, the more likely it is that firms will be able to compete satisfactorily on their own without the need for local partners; the general lowering of fences and the process of harmonisation and mutual recognition make exporting and unilateral control (through in-house expansion or mergers and acquisitions) increasingly attractive options. Secondly, the more open a market, the greater the possibility that potential collaborators are also potential competitors. Consequently, firms may be increasingly reluctant to enter into co-operative agreements that give away their technological knowledge. Thus, completing the Internal Market should enhance intra-EC trade and/or mergers and acquisitions, but inhibit joint venture activity. In short, both the need and the willingness to conduct co-operative agreements with other EC partners should diminish as a direct consequence of the completion of the Internal Market.

This is a radically different pattern from that predicted by the White Paper and the Cecchini Report. We look now at empirical evidence on various aspects of corporate behaviour from this alternative perspective. In the studies below, co-operative agreements usually cover joint product development, marketing and/or production elements, while the description 'joint venture' is typically reserved for an agreement involving a 'child' with distinctive legal identity and decision-making capacity relative to the parents, and continuing resource contribution from the respective parents. Joint ventures, especially in the high-technology industries, are frequently associated with the development of new, leading-edge technology.

However, before we analyse evidence from existing studies and databases on the likely effect of 1992 on industrial collaboration, it is necessary to consider the Commission's own evidence on this point. The 'Cost of Non-Europe' research programmes organised by the Commission surveyed firms in all Member States regarding their perceptions of 1992 and possible associated strategies.[4] According to Emerson *et al.*:

The survey ... provides some information regarding the strategies envisaged by firms to prepare for 1992. Two main responses emerge: measures to improve productivity, and increases in the number of international co-operation agreements. It should be noted that the intention to increase the number of agreements is by far the dominant one, with partners located in other Community countries being preferred to partners in non-member countries. Firms of all sizes display a similar desire for co-operation.

(1988: 170)

Such statements have been widely reproduced in Commission literature when they are in fact unjustified. The evidence referred to by Emerson *et al.* is contained in replies to a single question asked of managers in various firms.[5] The question was 'What changes to your company strategy would be needed within the next years in order to meet the requirements of a completely open Common Market in the European Community?'[6] Co-operation agreements were suggested as one of the various options.

Careful analysis of the question and the survey itself suggest that the Commission's interpretation is unwarranted. The question is a hypothetical one which refers to what ought to happen, and does not relate to actual plans despite reference in the Commission's view to company 'intentions'. The report of the survey does not clarify what is meant by 'co-operation agreements', so it is unclear what managers are actually agreeing to. Also, in the actual survey itself, interviewers were instructed to interview product-line managers and seek answers with respect to this product line only, not for the establishment as a whole (CEC 1987: 273); merger and acquisition was not one of the strategic options offered as a possible answer. It is therefore unconvincing as a supposed survey of 'the strategies envisaged by firms to prepare for 1992' (Emerson *et al.* 1988: 170). A properly designed survey would have interviewed chief executives (not product line managers), and explicitly included merger as a strategic option. It is perhaps not surprising that the Commission's interpretation of the survey supports its views on 1992-induced collaboration, but this should be disregarded as a misleading interpretation of a very limited survey.

In the next section we shall consider actual evidence on the effect of market completion on industrial collaboration, in the light of the Commission's and alternative views discussed in this section.

10.4 THE EFFECT OF MARKET COMPLETION ON INDUSTRIAL COLLABORATION

It is argued here that 1992 will have the opposite effect on EC cross-frontier collaboration to that predicted by the Commission. It will be recalled that we agreed that the more open a market, the more likely it is that firms will be able to compete satisfactorily on their own without the need for local partners; the general lowering of fences and the processes of harmonisation and mutual recognition make exporting and unilateral control (through in-house expansion, merger and acquisition) increasingly possible. Also, the more open a market, the greater the possibility that potential collaborators are also potential competitors. Consequently, firms may be increasingly reluctant to enter into co-operative agreements that could give away their technology and other knowledge to neighbouring rivals, especially in high-technology sectors. Thus, completing the Internal Market should enhance intra-EC trade and/or merger and acquisitions relative to joint venture activity. In this section we consider the effects of market completion on collaborative activity in the light of available evidence.

The INSEAD database[7] on trends in international collaborative agreement provides invaluable information in this respect. The analysis by Morris and Hergert (1987) of this database confirmed Cecchini's 'paradox' that EC firms were more likely to choose non-EC than EC partners. However, what is particularly striking is that, while 47 per cent of collaborative agreements reported in the INSEAD database involved at least one US partner, only 8 per cent of agreements involved solely US partners. Thus, Cecchini's 'paradox' holds even more strongly from the perspective of the US despite – or rather because of – its status as a completed market; US firms tend not to seek other US collaborative partners. It is notable that there were marginally more US–Japanese collaborative agreements than solely US ones despite geography, culture and other barriers to US–Japanese co-operation.

These are extremely significant patterns considering the Commission's view of the US as a classic completed market, to be taken as an example for Europeans. One of the 'Cost-of-Non-Europe' research volumes is even devoted to looking at the US as a role model for 1992.

Turning to the Commission's own data on collaborative activity, the latest Competition Policy Report (CEC 1989a) argues that 'the significant switchover during 1987/88 from international to national as well as Community operations, which were motivated primarily by R&D marketing and production, might indicate a trend by EEC companies to reinforce their intra-Community co-operation in view of the 1992 single market' (p. 241). The evidence for the apparent switchover is contained in Table 10.1. As can be seen, Community cross-frontier joint venture activity almost doubled in numbers from 1986–87 to 1987–88, while the frequency of joint ventures with non-EC partners actually declined over the same period. On the face of it, the Competition Policy Report comments appear legitimate and are consistent with the Commission's views on 1992 and collaboration described earlier.

The problem with such interpretations is that they treat collaboration in isolation and do not analyse it as a strategic option. If we are correct in regarding merger and joint venture as substitute strategies rather than complements, a more appropriate treatment would be to consider how the relative frequency of merger and joint venture varies according to degree of market completion. We would expect that the more open the market, the more frequent will be go-it-alone strategies such as merger, acquisition and intra-EC trade. Conversely, joint venture should increase in frequency relative to go-it-alone strategies for economic activities spanning domains with low degrees of market completion. As one measure of this aspect of strategic choice, we describe the ratio of mergers to joint venture creation for a given market for a particular year as the 'aversion ratio'[8] (meaning aversion to collaborative activity). For completed markets, the aversion ratio should be high, while for market domains over which there is a low degree of market completion, the propensity to collaborate should be relatively strong, implying a low aversion ratio.

Table 10.2 reproduces aversion ratios for national, Community and international markets (that is, EC/non-EC) for 1983–88. Degree of market completion increases as we move from international through Community to national domains, with the EC having the intermediate status of a partially completed market. We can see immediately that the aversion ratio increases in the predicted direction for each of the five time periods, being highest for national markets and lowest for ventures involving EC and non-EC partners. There were 4.5 times as many mergers as joint ventures within national markets over the five-year period, while there were actually more joint ventures than mergers for international ventures over the same period. The Community aversion ratio is consistently higher than the international aversion ratio, but lower than the national aversion ratio for any given

Table 10.1 Joint ventures in the Community in 1983–84, 1984–85, 1985–86, 1986–87 and 1987–88

Sector	National					Community					International					Total				
	1983–84	1984–85	1985–86	1986–87	1987–88	1983–84	1984–85	1985–86	1986–87	1987–88	1983–84	1984–85	1985–86	1986–87	1987–88	1983–84	1984–85	1985–86	1986–87	1987–88
1 Food	2	1	2	0	6	1	0	1	1	3	–	1	1	4	1	3	2	4	5	10
2 Chem.	4	5	7	3	7	2	0	7	1	5	5	7	9	10	12	11	12	23	14	24
3 Elec.	8	3	10	4	8	1	3	4	3	5	10	7	5	14	7	19	13	19	21	20
4 Mech.	5	8	5	9	4	1	3	1	0	0	3	5	4	8	3	9	16	10	17	7
5 Comp.*	–	3	0	1	2	–	0	1	1	1	–	0	1	3	2	–	3	2	5	5
6 Meta.	6	8	5	1	2	3	1	1	1	6	1	1	4	1	2	10	10	10	3	10
7 Trans.	3	3	0	3	1	1	1	3	3	4	3	2	1	0	1	7	6	4	4	6
8 Pap.	–	4	0	0	7	1	4	0	1	1	3	2	0	2	1	4	10	0	6	9
9 Extra.	2	3	2	0	3	–	1	0	1	1	–	1	0	0	1	2	5	2	1	5
10 Text.	0	0	0	0	–	1	0	0	2	–	0	0	0	1	–	1	0	0	3	
11 Cons.	2	2	3	3	1	1	1	2	2	2	–	1	0	0	3	3	4	5	5	6
12 Other	–	0	0	4	4	–	0	0	2	1	1	0	2	3	1	1	0	2	9	6
Total	32	40	34	29	45	11	15	20	16	31	26	27	27	45	35	69	82	81	90	111

For definitions and sources, see Table 10.5

* In 1983–84 included under mechanical engineering (mech.)

Table 10.2   Community aversion ratios for industry, 1983–88

Degree of market completion	Domain/ year	1983–84	1984–85	1985–86	1986–87	1987–88	Whole period 1983–88
High	National	3.2	3.7	4.3	7.3	4.8	4.5
Medium	Community	2.6	2.9	2.6	4.7	3.6	3.3
Low	International	1.0	0.7	1.1	0.4	1.7	1.0

Note: aversion ration = $\dfrac{\text{mergers}}{\text{joint venture}}$

Source: Commission data on mergers and joint mergers, Tables 10.1 and 10.5.
See Table 10.5 for fuller definitions of national, Community and international domains

year. It is also worth noting that the Community aversion ratio has increased over the last two time periods (4.7 in 1966–67 and 3.6 for 1987–88) and now approaches the five-year average for national markets (4.5) – ironically, consistent with what we would predict if the EC's 1992 programme was expected to convert the Community market into one with similar degrees of openness as national markets. Thus the apparent 'switchover' to cross-frontier collaboration described by the Commission disappears once aversion ratios are examined. The frequency of cross-frontier joint ventures has actually diminished relative to merger activity since the publication of the White Paper in 1985.

One other study provides invaluable insight into the probable effects of market completion. PROGNOS (CEC 1988: vol. 7) surveyed the motives for co-operation of 114 French and German firms (aerospace and defence co-operation excluded). The results of the study are shown in Table 10.3. The consultants compared their results with other studies, including one by Bayliss and collaborators at the University of Bath on British-led joint ventures and subsidiaries in Europe. The conclusions of the authors are:

The striking results of the PROGNOS study is that market access forms the main or a very important motive in 2/3 of all co-operation cases [motives (1), (2), (7) of the table]. R&D co-operation – one of the major thrusts of the Community's 'promotional' policies – hardly figures at all. On the other hand, gaining access to technology, embodied or otherwise, does play a respectable role in motivating co-operation. Another conclusion to draw from this table … is the fact that a great proportion of the motivation for co-operation would disappear if the rest of the White Paper agenda would be successfully implemented. This finding, incidentally, causes serious methodological difficulties when we try to measure the Cost of Non-Europe in relationship to a better 'anti-monde', a completed national market where, with reduced obstacles to co-operation, many of the reasons for co-operation must be assumed to be reduced as well.

(1988: 53–4)[9]

What is particularly remarkable about this study and its interpretation is not just that it is consistent with the alternative view developed here, but that it is produced by the Commission's own consultants for the 'obstacles to trans-border activity' section of the 'Cost of Non-Europe' project and detailed in Volume 7 of that report. The 'methodological difficulties' reported by the consultants are understandable, in view of the specific remit given to them which involved finding how 1992 would *stimulate* collaboration. However in the 27-page 'executive summary' of this part of the project in 'Cost of Non-Europe', Volume 1, joint venture is subsumed along with subsidiaries under trans-border activity (TBA); and not referred to separately. The official report by Cecchini *et al.* and Emerson *et al.* makes no reference to these findings.

Table 10.3 Motives for co-operation between French and German companies (frequency of motive in percentage of co-operation cases)

	Motive	F-initiated	D-initiated
1	Securing sources of supply	4	2
2	Improving market access	70	60
3	Securing market access, including to third markets (LDCs)	10	35
4	Overcoming NIBs, of which standards, customs	4	6
	procurement, local constant	10	20
5	Completing product range, system solutions	18	25
6	Cost/efficiency criteria: economies of scale exploit	4	10
	production costs differentials	–	5
7	Access to new production technology	20	15
8	Joint R&D	2	2

Source: PROGNOS, CEC: 1988: vol. 7: p. 46 (translated and re-arranged by ERA)

One further area of particular concern is the likely effect of 1992 on collaboration in the critical high-technology industries. The Commission places particular importance on the role of collaboration in these industries as devices for restoring or retaining technological competitiveness with respect to the US and Japan, as the development of programmes like ESPRIT, RACE and BRITE testify. Pre-1985, when the 1992 White Paper was published, the portents for collaboration in the knowledge-intensive industries were not encouraging. A LAREA/CEREM study of 497 collaborative agreements in the aerospace, biotechnology, information technology and material industries 1982–85 found that only one-quarter of agreements involving EC firms were with other EC firms, while a FOR study of 468 agreements involving EC firms in the aerospace, information technology, scientific instrumentation and pharmaceutical industries 1982–85 found that only 29 per cent of agreements were with other EC firms (Mytelka and Delapierre 1987). While the Commission would see this as evidence of an unfulfilled potential for EC collaboration that 1992 will help to develop, it is in fact consistent with the alternative view developed here reflecting aversion to collaboration in a partially completed market. It would be obviously relevant to look at recent collaborative activity for the high-technology sector in the Commission's analysis of merger and joint venture activity, and so Table 10.4 reproduces aversion ratios for the high-technology electrical, mechanical, chemical and computer sectors only.

The table contains some very interesting information. As we would expect, the aversion ratios are much higher in individual years for national and Community domains than for international ventures. Also consistent with our expectations (but contrary to the Commission's), aversion has not diminished for cross-frontier, high-technology collaboration since the publication of the White

Table 10.4 Community aversion ratios for high technology industry, 1983–88

Year Domain	1983–84	1984–85	1985–86	1986–87	1987–88	Whole period 1983–88
National	2.7	3.4	2.4	5.5	4.0	3.5
Community	4.5	5.3	2.4	8.2	4.4	4.4
International	0.9	0.7	0.8	0.3	1.3	0.8

Sources: Tables 10.1 and 10.5

Table 10.5 National, Community and international mergers (including acquisitions of majority holdings) in the Community in 1983–84, 1984–85, 1985–86, 1986–87 and 1987–88

	Industry																			
	National[b]					Community[c]					International[d]					Total				
Sector[a]	1983–84	1984–85	1985–86	1986–87	1987–88	1983–84	1984–85	1985–86	1986–87	1987–88	1983–84	1984–85	1985–86	1986–87	1987–88	1983–84	1984–85	1985–86	1986–87	1987–88
1 Food	7	20	25	39	25	2	1	7	11	18	2	1	2	2	8	11	22	34	52	51
2 Chem.	21	25	23	38	32	13	23	28	27	38	7	5	6	6	15	41	53	57	71	85
3 Elec.	9	13	10	33	25	2	5	2	6	4	2	4	1	2	7	13	22	13	41	36
4 Mech.	16	24	19	21	24	3	4	3	8	5	4	3	7	2	9	23	31	29	31	38
5 Comp.	0	2	1	2	2	0	0	0	0	1	0	1	0	0	0	0	3	1	2	3
6 Meta.	9	13	14	15	28	3	3	1	4	9	3	1	2	0	3	15	17	17	19	40
7 Trans.	5	8	6	15	3	1	2	0	6	9	3	0	4	0	3	9	10	10	21	15
8 Pap.	11	10	18	17	24	2	5	3	7	6	1	3	6	1	4	14	18	27	25	34
9 Extra.	4	7	7	8	9	0	0	1	1	2	2	0	2	0	1	6	7	10	9	12
10 Text	5	7	7	4	11	3	0	2	2	2	0	0	0	0	1	8	7	9	6	14
11 Cons.	13	14	12	13	21	0	1	2	3	12	1	0	0	3	0	14	15	14	19	33
12 Other	1	3	3	6	10	0	0	3	0	5	0	0	0	1	7	1	3	6	7	22
Total	101	146	145	211	214	29	44	52	75	111	25	18	30	17	58	155	208	227	303	383

[a] Key:
Food: Food and drink
Chem.: Chemicals, fibres, glass, ceramic wares, rubber
Elec.: Electrical & electronic engineering, office machinery
Mech.: Mechanical & instrument engineering, machine tools
Comp.: Computers & data-processing equipment (in 1983–84 included under mechanical engineering)
Meta.: Production & preliminary processing of metals, metal goods
Trans.: Vehicles & transport equipment
Pap.: Wood, furniture & paper
Extra.: Extractive industries
Text.: Textiles, clothing, leather & footwear
Cons.: Construction
Other: Other manufacturing industry

Notes:
[b] Involving firms from the same Member State
[c] Involving firms from different Member States
[d] Involving firms from Member States and third countries with effects on the community market

Source: Data gathered by the Commission from the specialist areas

Paper in 1985 and indeed appears to have increased (8.2 for 1986–87 and 4.4 for 1987–88, compared to an average of 3.5 for the three preceding years 1983–86). This should be particularly worrying for the Commission in view of the importance placed on collaboration in these industries, as well as the considerable financial and regulatory efforts being made to foster such collaboration with 1992 in mind.

One other pattern is particularly noteworthy. As before, we would have expected aversion ratios for national markets to be the highest for each year. Yet the cross-frontier Community measures record the higher levels of aversion in each year (tying with the national ratio in 1985–86). Why should aversion be typically lower for *national* level collaboration than for European-wide collaboration in the high-technology sectors? On the face of it, this reversal of the expected ordering is puzzling in the light of our earlier arguments.

Table 10.5 provides some clues. As can be seen from this table, mergers in the chemical industry dominate Community mergers 1984–88, accounting for 41 per cent of mergers in this category over this five-year period. There has been a massive European-level merger wave in this industry during the 1980s that has been closely monitored by the Commission's competition policy reports in the mid-1980s.

> A large proportion of the acquisitions in the chemicals industry, especially those involving other European firms, appear to be induced by a need for reorganization and rationalization among large firms in the industry. This is not surprising as some parts of the industry have overcapacity problems and some large chemical groups have been making losses in some activities.
>
> (CEC 1984: 216)

> The significant increase in mergers and majority acquisitions during 1986–87 is simply an additional step in the restructuring process following the industry's severe recession in 1982–83.
>
> (CEC 1988: 232)

It may be that the severe problems facing this sector during the 1980s and the rescue strategies adopted could have significantly influenced and distorted merger and joint venture activity, with the flurry of merger activity in chemicals inflating aversion ratios relative to what normally might be expected in the steady state. To check this possibility, aversion ratios for the high-technology sectors were recalculated with chemicals excluded. The results are shown in Table 10.6.

Table 10.6 Community aversion ratios for high-technology industry, excluding chemicals, 1983–88

Degree of market completion	Year Domain	1983–84	1984–85	1985–86	1986–87	1987–88	Whole period 1983–88
High	National	1.9	2.8	2.0	4.0	3.6	2.9
Medium	Community	2.5	1.5	0.5	3.5	1.7	1.7
Low	International	0.5	0.7	1.0	0.2	1.3	0.6

Sources: Tables 10.1 and 10.5

The rank ordering of aversion ratios in each year is generally consistent with increasing aversion to collaboration as degree of market completion increases, although in 1983–84 the Community ratio is lower than the national aversion ratio, while in 1985–86 the Community aversion ratio was lower than the international ratio. In view of the relatively low numbers of Community mergers and joint ventures in those sectors, occasional reversal of orderings from those expected is not surprising.

10.5 CONCLUDING REMARKS

Our conclusions differ markedly from Cecchini in important respects. The direct effects of 1992 will be to diminish collaborative activity between Community firms as the elimination of non-tariff barriers sharpens intra-EC competition and facilitates market access within the Community. These effects would also be expected to hold in the high-technology areas identified by the Commission as being critical for Europe.

It should also be emphasised that, while the direct effects of 1992 will be to diminish the level of collaborative arrangements between Community firms, other factors contribute to their formation. These include globalisation of corporate strategies; increasing cost and complexity of technology in certain sectors; residual market insulation by national government (for example, possibly in some defence industries); entrenched firm-customer networks and linkages impeding market access (for example, possibly in certain sectors of banking); and direct Community support for collaboration (for example,

ESPRIT, BRITE). Each of these may facilitate or necessitate collaboration, but it is essential to recognise that these effects are despite 1992, not because of it. Where EC policies in industry, competition, science and technology, and regional areas are designed to facilitate the expected increase in collaboration and joint ventures by Community enterprises following 1992, they will be successful only to the extent they work against the grain of 1992.

EC, national and regional policies should be reassessed in the light of the actual evaluation of corporate strategies contingent on 1992, otherwise there is likely to be much by way of misplaced effort and missed opportunities. The appropriateness of specific policies lies outside the scope of this chapter, but what we can say is that we expect the direct impact of 1992 would be to raise the price of collaborative activity in general, and that this may be reflected in phenomena such as the level of subsidy necessary to effect collaboration, market sharing in co-operative behaviour or simple avoidance of collaboration.

NOTES

1. Originally published in the *Journal of Common Market Studies*, 29, 1991, pp. 247–62, and reprinted here by kind permission of the publishers, Blackwell.
2. Henceforth we refer to the Commission of the European Communities simply as 'The Commission'.
3. There is now a considerable literature on joint venture activity. The *Columbia Journal of World Business* is a valuable source and has devoted issues to the topic (summers of 1984 and 1987). See also Teece (1986); Teece and Pisano (1987).
4. The survey itself was organised by Commission departments in all Member States and elicited 11 000 replies. The evidence for co-operation plans is based on an optional question.
5. Replies were obtained only from Greece, Spain, Luxembourg, Ireland, the Netherlands and the United Kingdom.
6. For the full details of the survey and the responses, see CEC (1987b).
7. The database is completed from public announcement of collaborative agreements reported in *The Economist* and the *Financial Times*.
8. The aversion ratio is obviously a limited measure of strategic choice since it considers only mergers and joint venture activity.
9. The authors also point out that the findings of the Bayliss study referred to in their report were consistent with theirs; 'the more "difficult" the market the more the choice tended towards JVs rather than subsidiaries; having a [more independent] local partner was indispensable. Thus one third of all British JVs were in Italy, but only one twentieth of the subsidiaries!' (CEC 1987a: 56).

11 Mergers, Acquisitions and the Completion of the Internal Market[1]

11.1 INTRODUCTION

The completion of the European Internal Market has stimulated considerable interest in the corporate strategies that will be developed by corporations to cope with the demands and opportunities presented by the emerging European economy. Since the publication of the White Paper on completing the Internal Market (Commission of the European Communities [CEC] 1985), the Commission[2] has been enthusiastic about the role of external strategies such as joint venture and merger in stimulating and reinforcing the effective operation of the completed market. Elsewhere (Chapter 10 of this volume) we have argued that the Commission's view that 1992 will directly stimulate industrial activity such as joint venture is misplaced. In this chapter we consider the parallel question of merger in the context of 1992, and conclude that there is serious cause for concern that the acceleration of the rate of cross-frontier merger activity may be to the detriment of the completed market and may reduce both competition and efficiency.

In this chapter we shall argue that the Commission has adopted too permissive an attitude towards European merger and acquisition activity, and that there is a real danger that the emerging Europe-wide merger wave may sacrifice some of the gains in productive efficiency and consumer welfare that 1992 is intended to generate. The Commission's policy proposals are dependent on an obsolete theoretical framework, and it recognises, but then neglects, clear and consistent evidence on merger failure.

We shall first consider the foundations of the Commission's approach to merger control and then critically examine this in the light of the available empirical evidence. The relevance of the benchmarks and indicators nominated for merger control purposes will be discussed before consideration is given to the broader context of the development of European competition and the conflicting agendas in which it is set.

11.2 THEORY AND EVIDENCE IN MERGER ACTIVITY – THE COMMISSION'S PERSPECTIVE

The Directorate-General for Economic and Financial Affairs (DGII) produced a systematic analysis of the effect of horizontal mergers and the implications for competition policy in 1989 (CEC 1989a). The analysis builds on the idea of an efficiency/monopoly-power trade-off as developed in an early model of Williamson (1968).[3] The basic model identifies three possible effects resulting from merger: cost savings obtainable from increases in the scale of production (economies of scale),[4] the creation of monopoly power (CEC 1989a: 17), or some combination of the two:

> Those who give precedence to the efficiency effects believe that the increased concentration resulting from mergers leads to cost reductions which, other things being equal, allow increases in margins.
>
> Those, on the other hand, who focus more on the dangers of monopolization see the causality as working mainly in the opposite direction: mergers tend to induce price rises, as a result both of increased concentration and the expectation of more collusive behaviour....
>
> In fact, it is probable that in many cases mergers simultaneously produce some efficiency gains, notably in the form of cost reductions, and some increase in monopoly power which may manifest itself in higher prices. There is thus the question of a trade-off between the two types of effect.
>
> (CEC 1989a: 18)

Consistent with this, the later section on 'analysis for the purposes of merger control' is introduced with the statement, 'The impact of a merger can be of three basic types: it can improve efficiency without any reduction of competition; reduce competition without any gain in efficiency; or have effects at once conducive to efficiency and harmful to competition' (CEC 1989a: 45).

The Williamson trade-off has implications for profitability which can be illustrated with the help of Table 11.1. The three basic types of merger effects associated with the Williamson trade-off can be analysed in terms of effect on corporate profitability. If efficiency improves without any reduction in competition (Case 3 in Table 11.1), then profitability increases due to the decrease in costs. On the other

Table 11.1 Impact of merger on corporate profitability

| | | Efficiency | |
	No effect	Costs decrease	Costs increase
Competition:			
No effect	0 (Case 2)	+ (Case 3)	– (Case 5)
Decrease	+ (Case 1)	+ (Case 4)	? (Case 6)

Notes: +: profits increase: –: profits decrease: 0: no effect on profits:
?: net effect on profits uncertain

hand, if merger reduces competition without any effect on efficiency, then profitability increases, this time due to monopoly power and the raising of price-cost margins (Case 1 in Table 11.1). Finally, if merger results in efficiency gains *and* increased monopoly power, *both* effects will contribute to increased profitability (Case 4).

The three possible outcomes associated with the Williamson trade-off differ in their welfare implications. Outcomes in which efficiency gains are more than compensated for in terms of losses due to mono-polisation represent a diminution of welfare, while those in which efficiency gains predominate are more likely to be treated as benign and not a problem. Consequently, much attention has been given to the likelihood of one or other of the effects dominating, and CEC (1989a) is consistent in this respect:

[A]t the present time, judgements as to whether a merger presents a danger of monopolization, potential efficiency gains or a combination of the two must be based on general indicators.

As far as monopoly power is concerned the indicators favouring its emergence are well-known; high market share with a scattered competitive fringe, low import penetration and high entry barriers, demand that is inelastic and also static or only slowly increasing, and a differentiated product, etc.

Among the factors that point to the likelihood of efficiency gains are large-scale economies and learning effects, substantial excess capacity and high capital intensity and technology content. It is cri-teria such as these that will be used to examine the present situation in the EC in part B of this paper.

(CEC 1989a: 19)

This appears entirely reasonable in the light of the Williamson trade-off model; the Commission's study then goes on in Part B to use indicators of the factors mentioned above to make a preliminary classification of industries into those in which mergers – and thus concentration – are likely to have on balance beneficial effects and those in which the overall effect is likely to be negative (1989a: 23). The analysis is carried out at three-digit level and results in three major categories of industries classified by likely prospects for merger: (1) those offering little or no prospect of efficiency gains, whether or not competition is reduced; (2) those in which merger activity is prima facie beneficial due to potential efficiency gains and little danger of reduction in competition; and (3) those likely to produce both efficiency gains and dangers of reduction in competition.

For our purposes, one of the most significant features of this analysis is the assignment of most of the high-tech industries (including chemicals, pharmaceuticals, computers, telecommunications, electronics, the motor and aerospace industries, and precision instruments) to the second category of industries, 'in which there is less danger of a reduction of competition and mergers offer real prospects of efficiency gains' (CEC 1989a: 29).

We therefore have what appears to be a reasonable and well-balanced perspective on probable effects of mergers, devised from a simple and convincing theoretical framework. The report discusses the proposal for a merger control regulation in the light of this classificatory approach, concluding, for example, that mergers in the high-tech sector may enhance and help European industry catch up with American or Japanese rivals.

Unfortunately, this approach is simply not supported by the empirical evidence which the report itself cites (1989a: 21–2). The problem is that the approach builds on Williamson's simple trade-off model, which is itself inconsistent with the body of knowledge on merger effects that has been built up over recent years. We can summarise the problem by emphasising that the three basic merger effects of 'danger of monopolisation, potential efficiency gains or a combination of the two' (CEC 1989a: 19) are represented by Cases 1, 3 and 4 in Table 11.1. As can be seen, *all* three cases lead to increased profitability due to merger effects on demand and/or costs. Case 2 (no effect on efficiency or competition) is neglected in the simple trade-off model since it would be of no interest to a rational profit-maximising firm. The simple trade-off model does not recognise Cases 5 and 6, in which merger may have an adverse effect on efficiency and costs.

Thus, increased profitability is a concomitant of merger *whatever* the balance of efficiency versus monopoly power in the Williamson trade-off model. This directly contradicts the empirical evidence cited by CEC (1989a):

> A comparative study, directed by Mueller (1980), of results from various EEC countries concerning full legal mergers concluded that ... the tests of post-merger profitability suggested that the mergers had little or no effect on the profitability of the merging firm in the three to five years following the merger; nor was there any significant difference in the return per share three years after the merger. This confirms the results obtained in many American studies (see Scherer 1980a: 138–9).

Further, a comprehensive recent survey of research into the impact of mergers in the UK concludes that most studies looking at their effect on profitability lead to 'the clear impression of a small, variable but negative impact' (Hughes 1989: 79). Another recent survey paper, by Mueller, studies the impact of mergers on profitability in a variety of countries and time periods and concludes that 'a ... consistent and dramatic positive effect of mergers on profitability has not been observed' (1988: 54). Indeed, many studies report neutral or even negative effects on performance, and Thompson (1988) interprets Mueller's survey as indicating that 'mergers actually reduce profitability' (p. 78).

The evidence on mergers' effects on efficiency cited in CEC (1989a) is consistent with this depressing performance:

> Detailed studies of the success of mergers in the UK (Meeks 1977; Cowling *et al* 1980) confirm that efficiency is rarely increased by merger, and sometimes reduced. Studies by management consultants come to similar disappointing conclusions. Coley and Reinton (1980) looked at US and British companies in the *Fortune* 250 list and the *Financial Times* 500 which in the past had made acquisitions to enter new markets ... only 23% of the 116 firms analysed were able to recover the cost of their capital or better still the funds invested in the acquisition programme. It also appears that the higher the degree of diversification, the smaller is the likelihood of success. For horizontal mergers in which the acquired firm is not large, however, the success rate is high (45%).
>
> (CEC 1989a: 21)

Since outcomes in this last study were classified as either success or failure, the last line could be rewritten as 'the failure rate is still high (55%)'. It is a remarkable comment on a consistently dismal message from the empirical literature that the Commission report can take comfort from a 'high' success rate in a small sub-sample in which the majority of outcomes are still failures.

Dennis Mueller makes a crucial point on one set of studies in which no increases in profitability were reported on average: 'It is difficult to believe that some of these mergers did not result in sufficient increases in market power to generate extra profits. However, the reduction in profits, due to losses in efficiency among the other mergers, were apparently sufficiently great to offset these gains' (Mueller 1988: 54).

This point is an extremely important one which is worth spelling out in some detail. Since mergers increase concentration and reduce actual or potential competition, they will typically have, at best, a neutral effect on monopoly power, and, at worst, an adverse effect on monopoly power. The net effect from this factor would typically be to increase profitability for any group of mergers. Therefore, if any group of mergers report neutral effects on profitability overall, it is natural to conclude that the gains in profitability due to increased monopoly power have been offset by efficiency losses such as those reported in the Coley and Reinton study referred to in CEC (1989a).

This has major implications for merger control and competition policy. It implies a rejection of the simple version of the Williamson trade-off model used by the Commission. In that framework only outcomes in which profitability increases are recognised, that is Cases 1, 3 and 4 in Table 11.1. Ironically, it means that the three cases *not* recognised by the Commission (2, 5 and 6) are on balance more likely in practice than are the three officially recognised cases. If there is a trade-off, it more commonly appears to involve increased monopoly power and *decreased* efficiency. It also implies a rejection of the comment in CEC (1989a): 'the only conclusion to be drawn from the empirical evidence is that a general presumption in favour of [horizontal] mergers is not justified' (p. 22). This is incorrect. A more accurate interpretation would be 'The only conclusion to be drawn from the empirical evidence is that a general presumption *against* (horizontal) mergers is justified'. Even if mergers had no net effect on profitability, the tendency of some mergers to increase concentration and facilitate collusion suggests that on average they would diminish efficiency. The fact that some studies report negative effects on profitability suggests that losses in efficiency in these cases are more than sufficient to compensate for any increases in monopoly power, signalling the probable existence of the twin hazards of increased monopoly power and diminished efficiency.

One obvious question which is raised by these studies is *why* merger should still be pursued by corporations in view of its consistently disappointing performance measured in terms of profitability. The studies were not generally designed to answer such a question. However, it can be pointed out that the results are easier to reconcile with managerial theories of firms in which growth and size are managerial objectives, than with traditional neoclassical profit-maximising perspectives.

However, there is a further consideration of particular relevance to the issue as to whether or not merger activity will tend to diminish efficiency in the context of 1992. The studies that have been carried out so far have been predominantly concerned with single-country merger and acquisition activity. If it is so difficult to extract efficiency gains from two US firms merging, or a UK firm taking over another UK firm, there is liable to be less hope for European cross-frontier merger, with Italian firms taking over Dutch, and German firms merging with Spanish. It is difficult enough to marry together two different firms in the same country, without the added complications of different cultures, language, legal systems and political conventions. While the evidence at the moment is mostly anecdotal, there is every reason to suppose that the emerging wave of cross-frontier mergers identified in Table 11.2 are likely to be even more problematic than are single-nationality amalgamations.

There is one other efficiency defence that can be put forward in favour of a liberal attitude towards mergers, and that concerns the market for corporate control. CEC argues that the threat of takeover may discipline management and encourage them to pursue profit-orientated behaviour (1989a: 20). However CEC (1989a) also recognises that against this must be set the dangers of short-termism and a concern with financial transactions at the expense of productivity and competitiveness.

In addition, it should be pointed out that the market for corporate control is fairly weak or even non-existent in many EC countries, with hostile takeovers being frequently difficult or practically impossible to mount. The relatively well-developed markets for corporate control in the UK and the USA are not typical of the EC situation and therefore the takeover threat argument is of diminished

Table 11.2 National, Community and international industrial mergers (including acquisitions of majority holdings) in the Community in 1983–84, 1984–85, 1985–86, 1986–87 and 1987–88

	National[a]					Community[b]					International[c]					Total				
	83/4	84/5	85/6	86/7	87/8	83/4	84/5	85/6	86/7	87/8	83/4	84/5	85/6	86/7	87/8	83/4	84/5	85/6	86/7	87/8
	101	146	145	211	214	29	44	52	75	111	25	18	30	17	58	155	208	227	303	383

Note: Data gathered by the Commission from the specialist areas: [a] involving firms from the same Member State; [b] involving firms from different Member States; [c] involving firms from Member States and third countries with effects on the Common Market relevance in this context. It is also ironic that this argument is raised in the context of 1992; if the Community does approach market completion, then 1992 should generate increased competitive pressure in product and factor markets, encouraging profit-orientated behaviour and increased efficiency. Since competition in these markets is more direct and focused than the vague possibility of takeover even in economies where the market for corporate control is well developed, focusing on the efficiency implications of threat of takeover in the EC context seems at best redundant. There appears little need to look to the market for corporate control to stimulate efficiency in a 1992 context if the liberalised product and factor markets post-1992 are achieving the objective more precisely and effectively. If anything, the evidence suggests that an active market for corporate control at European level could seriously detract from the very objectives of competition and efficiency embodied in the 1992 programme itself.

In the next section we shall consider how the Commission's enthusiasm for pan-European co-operation may have led to the construction of a misguided typology of industries for merger control purposes.

11.3 SECTORAL ANALYSIS AND MERGER CONTROL

The CEC (1989a) report analyses merger activity in EC industries over the period 1982–87, comparing growth industries with other EC industries. Growth industries were classified as those in which domestic EC demand growth averaged at least 5 per cent a year over the period, and was heavily characterised by high-technology industries including computers, electronics, telecommunications, chemicals and pharmaceuticals (1989e: 41).

According to CEC (1989a);

> The number of mergers and acquisitions of majority holdings involving firms in the top 1000 has risen significantly less quickly in growth sectors than in the rest of industry ... this is at first sight surprising in that in these industries mergers often produce substantial efficiency gains. A comparison of the size of European firms with that of their American and Japanese competitors ... reveals that the European market leaders are smaller.

> (1989a: 41–2)

There are a number of problems with this line of argument. Firstly, no evidence is provided for the 'substantial efficiency gains' claimed for mergers in growth sectors. Indeed, the evidence already cited by CEC (1989a) above, and the evidence generally available, tends to conflict with this claim. Secondly, there appears to be a implicit assumption that American and Japanese firms are often better performing than their European competitors because they are larger. A more reasonable claim would be that they are larger because they are better performing: – success breeds size rather than vice versa. Thirdly, even if size was a contributory factor in strong industrial performance in these sectors, it certainly does not automatically follow that growth by merger is the route by which scale should be achieve. For example, internal expansion may be slower but is more likely to be a guarantor of success in the long run.

Despite this, CEC (1989a) analyses industries by four main groups based on the assumption that merger activity should be encouraged in growth sectors: industries were assigned to the groups on the basis of whether or not merger was likely to lead to a reduction in competition and/or efficiency gains in a particular industry. The results are shown in Table 11.3.

The four groups identified above can be related to the corresponding four cases identified in Table 11.1, Group 1 being interpretable as Case 1, and so on. In order to measure danger of reduction of competition, two indicators were used: demand growth[5] and the import penetration ratio.[6] The CEC (1989a) report argued that *prima facie* there is less danger of reduction of competition if there is either strong demand growth *or* above-average import penetration for a given industry.

The prospect of efficiency gains was assessed on the basis of two indicators intended to measure economies of scale and technology content on an industry-by-industry basis. Potential economies of scale were measured by estimates of cost gradients operating in a particular industry; that is, the additional unit costs borne by firms operating at below 50 per cent of the optimal scale.[7] Technology content was measured by the ratio of R&D expenditure to output for each industry. Since the evidence discussed earlier suggested that mergers typically do not provide efficiency gains, the status of both these indicators merits closer examination.

The earlier CEC report on the economies of 1992 (CEC 1988) carried out an assessment of the prevalence of economies of scale drawing upon the same study by Pratten (1988) cited by CEC (1989a).

Table 11.3 Illustration of classification of industries for merger control purposes

Group	Industry	Characteristics	Implications
1	Building materials Metal goods Paints & varnishes Furniture Paper goods Tobacco	• Declining or mature industries • Markets closed to international trade • Not technology-intensive or only slowly changing technologically • Economies of scale limited or acting as entry barriers	In these industries mergers offer little prospect of efficiency gains and present a danger of a reduction of competition
2	Steel Industrial & agricultural machinery Leather & leather goods Fur Clothing & textiles Sawn & processed wood and related products Pulp, paper & board Jewellery, toys, musical instruments	• Declining or mature industries • Fairly open to imports from inside and outside EC • In some industries, strong competition from low-wage countries • Economies of scale limited or already exploited • Not technology-intensive or with technology known throughout the world • Some industries highly fragmented (toys, furs)	Less danger of reduction of competition because of high import penetration and the fragmentation of some industries. But growth by merger is no longer an appropriate strategy for European firms. Instead, they should set out to specialise in top-of-the-range products, requiring modern and flexible production facilities

Table 11.3   (Cont'd)

Group	Industry	Characteristics	Implications
3	Advanced materials Chemicals/pharmaceutical Computers/office automation Telecommunications Electronics Motor vehicles Aerospace Instruments	• Growth industries • Open to international trade • Strong competition from American and Japanese products • Large economies of scale • R&D very important, fast-changing technology	Less danger of monopolisation and prospects of substantial efficiency gains from mergers. In these industries, link-ups between European firms would allow them to internationalise their operations from a solid European base
4	Boilermaking Cables & heavy electrical plant Railway equipment Shipbuilding Some food industries (confectionery, chocolate, flour & pasta) Beer	• Mature industries • Little intra-Community trade & competition restricted by segmentation of public procurement markets or differences in standards & regulations • Not technology-intensive (food & drink industries) or only moderately so • Large economies of scale	In these industries the removal of barriers with the single market programme will lead to rationalisation and European-scale mergers. These may produce efficiency gains but there is also a danger of reduction of competition

Source: CEC (1989a) 32.

In fact, Pratten's study indicates that economies of scale are not a major issue in the substantial majority of industries in the Community. In 73 per cent of the cases studied, there was room in the EC for at least 20 plants all operating at minimum efficient technical size (METS). In these cases that would still leave room for at least two or three plants exploiting METS *within* larger EC national economics such as the UK, France and Germany. This hardly constitutes convincing grounds for arguing the case for cross-frontier mergers to promote efficiency, even if mergers were the preferred route to effective attainment of economies of scale.

However, CEC (1989a) further muddies the waters by adopting a curious and limited interpretation of economies of scale as measured by cost gradients (CEC, 1988). But identifying industries as being characterised by economies of scale on the basis of cost gradients alone can give bizarre results. CEC (1988, p. 112) provided a list of industries for which the cost gradient is at least 10 per cent.

The highest cost gradients in this list were for books and bricks, neither of which are sectors known for massive economies of scale. There is in fact room for 100 brick manufacturers in the UK alone all exploiting METS. The median METS for the highest cost-gradient industries in CEC (1998) was only 11 per cent of UK production and 1.4 per cent of EC (Kraft paper). When METS is looked at in these cases, the idea that cost gradient alone is a reliable indicator of economies of scale in European industry is simply untenable. Consequently, CEC's claims (1989a): 29 and 64) that mergers could lead to potential efficiency gains in industries characterised by at least modest cost gradients (that is about 5 per cent) should be set aside as being unreliable and unjustified.

As to the second indicator, technological content, CEC (1989a: 25) claims:

> There is an arguable case for saying that mergers can also be beneficial in high-technology industries. These industries are highly R&D intensive and because of indivisibilities in R&D up to certain thresholds firms require a sufficient scale of operation in order to undertake research programmes.[8]

However, the earlier (1988) CEC report did survey the empirical evidence in this area, and it is worth quoting their conclusions in some detail as an accurate summary of current research findings:

Many empirical studies conclude that there are no economies of scale in the innovation process. The function of transforming research inputs into innovation outputs seems to be characterised by constant or even decreasing returns to scale ... [also] according to empirical studies the elasticity of R&D activities with respect to size of firms is less than unity ... it seems that research activities increase proportionately more than size, up to a certain threshold (which varies with the industry), but that large firms spend relatively less on research than small and medium-sized enterprises.

The above two results (constant or decreasing returns to scale and elasticity of R&D with respect to size less than unity) mean that the efficiency with which research inputs are transformed into innovation output does not increase with size of firm. ... Most of the empirical studies confirm this finding and show that, apart from the chemical industry, large size does not favour innovation.

(1988: 113)

Therefore the 'arguable case' in CEC (1989a) that scale economies in R&D mean that mergers can be beneficial in the high-technology industries is simply not supported by the available evidence cited in DGII's own research.

The CEC report (1988: 113) goes on to cite a study undertaken by Geroski for that report which found that in the UK firms with fewer than 10 000 employees generated 56.1 per cent of innovations in the period 1945–83. Further, small firms seem to be playing a growing role in the innovation process with 43.2 per cent of innovations coming from firms with fewer than 1000 employees in 1983 compared with 29.6 per cent in 1945. Small firms also contributed more in terms of innovation than large firms in the most innovative sectors – machinery, mechanical and electronic equipment, chemicals, electrical equipment and instruments (Geroski 1987).

Even if mergers had no integration problems relative to internal expansion, there appears to be an arguable case for de-merger rather than merger in the EC high-technology industries when considerations based on technology content are brought into play. Once it is recognised that evidence consistently points to merger being a clumsy, costly and inefficient route to increased size, there remains no reason to encourage merger activity on technology content grounds, despite CEC's (1989a) arguments to the contrary.

In short, CEC's (1989a) claims that there are industries in which merger activity may be at first sight beneficial (see p. 29 especially) are unjustified on the basis of evidence cited by both CEC reports. Instead, there is no obvious case for encouraging merger activity on the grounds argued in the report. The report should be set aside as a largely unhelpful contribution to the policy debate on European merger policy. In the next section we shall consider the context in which the Commission's policy on European merger control has been developing in recent years, and argue that CEC (1989a) is representative of a Commission perspective that may have adverse implications for European competitiveness post-1992.

11.4 THE CIM AND CEM OF EUROPEAN COMPETITIVENESS

The CEC (1989a) study was developed in the context of the basic question identified in the foreword, 'should European competition policy be strengthened or loosened in the context of achieving the internal market?' (p. 9).

Unfortunately, the subsequent analysis continues a confusion of themes that was introduced in the White Paper on the completion of the internal market (CEC 1985). The very first sentence of the White Paper embodies the tensions and conflicting agendas that have characterised the subsequent development of the programme and related economic analyses:

unifying this market [of 320 million] presupposes that Member States will agree on the abolition of barriers of all kinds, harmonisation of rules, approximation of legislation and tax structures, strengthening of monetary co-operation and the necessary flanking measures to encourage European firms to work together'.

(CEC 1985: para 1)

The sentence starts with the concept of a market (and by implication, competition and trade) and finishes with the picture of European firms finding ways to work together. Working together and co-operation is interpreted loosely and widely in the White Paper, but does include joint projects, minority shareholdings and mergers (paras 133–144). The White Paper argues that co-operation between firms will 'strengthen the industrial and commercial fabric of the internal market' (para 133).

In principle, there may be no conflict between improving and reinforcing the working of the Internal Market through competition and trade, and encouraging mechanisms to help firms 'work together' (for example, joint ventures and mergers). In practice, merger and joint ventures reduce the domain over which competition and trade operate and reduce the number of competitors in specific industries and/or product-markets. The inclusion of measures that *reduce* competition in a programme designed to eliminate non-tariff barriers and so *increase* competition appears inconsistent and even perverse on closer examination. In fact, the treatment of co-operative measures in the White Paper is symptomatic of the existence of two separate agendas that have underlain the White Paper and subsequent economic analysis undertaken by the Commission in this area. The first agenda is represented by the explicit objectives of the White Paper concerning the *Internal* Market and the elimination of non-tariff barriers to trade. The second and more general agenda is focused on improving Community productivity and trade performance with respect to the rest of the world – that is, competing in the *external* market.

While the two agendas may be mutually supportive in some cases, there are also circumstances in which they will be inconsistent. The problem is that the different agendas are never recognised as such, let alone reconciled; for example, CEC's (1988) opening section is titled 'Dimensions and structure of the *internal* market' (italics added), but in fact most of this section is concerned with external trade and the EC's relations with the USA and Japan.

This ambiguity in agenda setting has permeated the published work of the Commission's Economic Directorate (DGII) since the publication of the White Paper, including CEC (1988). There is a genuine conflict between the explicit agenda set out in the White Paper of completing the *internal* market (CIM) and the parallel agenda of competing in the *external* market (CEM). The CIM agenda is really a device for attainment of the CEM objective in the Commission's view as its informal discussion in various publications since the 1985 White Paper makes clear.

The fusion of agendas is used to legitimate a loose approach to merger control that bodes ill for a balanced and reasonable treatment of European mergers in a post-1992 context. For example, the empirical evidence that tends to find direct relationships between concentration and both price-cost margins and X-inefficiency is recognised by CEC (1988), but when this study looks at the possible relationship between competitive pressure and 'restructuring' (which includes mergers, joint ventures and bankruptcies), it recognises the direct effect of increased competitive pressure on restructuring, but ignores the possibility of a feedback effect in the opposite direction (p. 106). Since 'restructuring' tends to involve reduction in actual or potential competitors and a general softening of competitive pressure, such neglect is unjustified. In a similar vein CEC (1989a) argues that, for the majority of industries which do not pose efficiency opportunities for merger, this should 'not lead to the rejection of mergers which do not reduce competition, competition policy and industrial policy should be kept separate' (p. 29). This is consistent with Emerson *et al*'s (1988) promotion of 'mergers and takeovers ... [which] create truly European companies which have no special links to a particular country and are thus able to escape from the "national champion" mentality' (pp. 173–4). In these cases the CEM agenda appears in the guise of industrial policy and the promotion of 'European champions'.

These arguments explicitly indicate a willingness to subvert CIM objectives to CEM objectives. Ironically, however, if the Commission's enthusiasm for stimulating cross-frontier mergers post-1992 is allowed full rein, all the evidence cited above suggests it could have profoundly deleterious consequences, not only for competition within the Internal Market, but also for Community competitiveness *vis-à-vis* the rest of the world. Compromising CIM will in turn impede CEM.

Similar problems appear in the Commission's treatment of joint ventures and other collaborative activity. As discussed in more detail in the previous chapter, the CIM/CEM dyad is also to be found in the Commission's treatment of industrial collaborative activity, and suffers from the same problems of interpretation. The White Paper sees 1992 as creating an environment favouring industrial co-operation (p. 34) and the formation of collaborative arrangements such as joint ventures (pp. 34–6), and a major section of the White Paper is devoted to this issue.

In fact, the previous chapter here surveyed a number of studies and databases and as we have seen, draws the opposite conclusion: the direct effect of moving towards market completion is typically to *diminish* the frequency of industrial collaborative activity in general, and joint venture arrangements in particular. Joint venture activity tends to be a bureaucratic and costly form of economic organisation compared with fully internalised alternatives such as internal expansion and multinational enterprise. In high-technology sectors particularly, joint ventures may be characterised by severe appropriability problems in so far as intangible assets such as intellectual property may be appropriated by partners.

Evidence suggests that firms tend to resort to joint ventures only when simpler or cheaper avenues of exploiting venture opportunities have been exhausted – for example, multinationals being forced into joint ventures with local firms by Third World governments as the price of market access.[9] Therefore joint venture activities as strategies of last resort tend to be stimulated by trade barriers, and these same barriers may also help to provide insulating barriers with respect to appropriability problems – losing intellectual competitive advantage to a partner is likely to be more problematic if they are potential future competitors and very close rivals within a completed market.

Thus, where 1992 is successful, its direct effect should be to switch the emphasis in corporate strategies from co-operation to competition. Yet there is no acknowledgement in the Commission's reports on 1992 and corporate strategies that there is likely to be a 1992/industrial collaborative trade-off. The official perspective instead appears to be dictated by the White Paper's arguments (pp. 34–61) that non-tariff barriers to trade have typically *impeded* industrial collaborative activity that would otherwise have been undertaken. For example, CEC (1988) argues for industrial R&D co-operation within the completed market without recognising that their public good benefits of knowledge spillovers are also the innovating firms' appropriability problems and possible strategic own goals.

Industrial technological collaboration programmes like ESPRIT and BRITE are discussed in the White Paper as programmes supporting the development of the Internal Market, while CEC (1988: 112–14) argues that market integration helps create the conditions for the rapid development of cross-frontier co-operation for R&D. The reality that 1992 will *raise* the price of technological cross-frontier collaboration within the EC is not recognised, a serious omission considering the political and economic significance of the EC technology co-operation programmes. However, as with mergers and acquisitions, the CEM objective underlies the Commission's strategy in this area; in discussing high-technology industry, CEC (1988), 'argues 'concentration and co-operation at European level are ... often necessary (but not sufficient) conditions for the recovery of lost global market share' (p.135). Again, in a report on the implications of CIM, CEM objectives subvert the analysis at the expense of a realistic appraisal of the likely effects of 1992 and its policy implications.

11.5   THE EC'S 1990 MERGER REGULATION

The growth in importance of European merger and acquisition was not adequately anticipated in the Treaty of Rome, and its Articles 85 and 86 provided an incomplete and unsatisfactory basis for dealing with this phenomenon. The 1990 Merger Regulation was designed to give the European Commission the direct authority to control or prevent EC mergers that threaten competition.

A merger is now deemed to fall within the competence of the EC authorities if the combined world-wide turnover of the combined companies is ECU 5 billion or more, and the EC turnover of each of at least two of the companies is ECU 250 million or more, though a merger will be exempt from Brussels jurisdiction if each company has more than two-thirds of its EC turnover in one country. It was expected that this would result in 50–100 mergers a year for the EC authorities to vet.

The question which the Commission has to decide is whether the merger is 'compatible with the Common Market'. It must decide whether the merger creates or strengthens a dominant position in the EC. The question and criteria to help judge it are all related to the question of *competition*. The idea of an 'efficiency defence' to trade off against any anti-competitive effects of mergers was not written into the regulation, despite hard lobbying from some quarters. Although the regulation does recognise that account should be taken of technical and economic progress, this is not allowed to detract from the principle of competition as the yardstick by which the merger should be judged.

The mergers falling within the competence of the Merger Regulation are a sub-set of all EC-related merger and acquisition activity in the EC and amounted to 54 deals in the first year of operation from September 1990. Of these, virtually all were approved without change, except three which were approved after modification of the terms and one (France's Aerospatiale and Italy's Aleria's plans to share in the acquisition of De Havilland) which was blocked. The Commission ruled that the new company would have achieved combination of 67 per cent of the EC market for commuter aircraft.

It is ironic that EC competition policy has been attacked by lobbyists for not entertaining an 'efficiency defence'. As CEC's own survey (1989a) of the empirical evidence indicates, there are stronger grounds in general for putting forward an efficiency *objection* to mergers. The fact that only one European merger was blocked in the first year of the new merger policy suggests that competition policy in this area is too permissive and tolerant.

11.6 CONCLUSIONS

The European Commission's analysis of trends towards industrial concentration as represented by the report of the Economics Directorate are highly problematic. Contrary to these arguments, there is no sound, *prima facie* case for encouraging cross-frontier mergers in a wide range of industrial sectors. The resulting analysis of the efficiency implications of merger is unsound, and leads to policy conclusions that may be to the detriment of European competition and competitiveness.

If there is a root cause for these problems it appears to be the argument that consolidation and amalgamation, whether through merger or joint venture, may be necessary to achieve European competitiveness in a global context. There is no general case for such arguments. A further problem is that 1992 policy development has been characterised by a fusion of agendas on the part of the Commission in which completion of the internal market is frequently analysed in terms more appropriate to competing with other trading blocs in the external market. The result has been detrimental to the analysis of the roots of European competitiveness and the policy proposals on which this builds.

NOTES

1. Originally published in K. S. Hughes (ed.) *European Competitiveness,* 1993, pp. 161–80. Reprinted here by kind permission of the publisher, Cambridge University Press.
2. Henceforth 'CEC' and 'Commission' will be used to represent the Commission of the European Communities.
3. The CEC (1989a) study concentrates on horizontal mergers, while some of the empirical evidence cited here covers mergers in general. Horizontal mergers tend to bring policy issues into sharper focus because of the general expectation that they may generate stronger efficiency *and* monopoly effects compared with mergers between less closely related partners.
4. Learning curve effects and scope economies (economies from products sharing resources) may reinforce scale economies in this basic model (CEC 1989a: 17).

5. Domestic demand is calculated for EUR 9 (D + DK + F + I + IRL + NL + B/L + UK) as production plus imports minus exports in real terms over the period 1980–85.
6. Import penetration was defined as the proportion of domestic demand supplied by imports for EUR 9.
7. The data were mainly drawn from a survey of research by Pratten (1988).
8. From Scherer (1980) and Kamien and Schwartz (1982).
9. As discussed in the previous chapter.

12 Industrial Collaboration and the European Internal Market[1]

12.1 INTRODUCTION

This chapter is an update and further development of an earlier paper by Kay (1991b) (Chapter 10 here) concerning the likely effects of European market integration on co-operative or collaborative activity by European firms. Each of us has separately monitored subsequent trends in collaborative activity – e.g., see Ramsay (1995) – and in this chapter we pool our efforts and comment on recent developments using the concept of aversion ratios introduced in the earlier chapter. Changes in the sources and nature of the databases used by the Commission add a further reason for this exercise, since it will be argued that the changes made will greatly inhibit the ability of researchers to comment on patterns of activity and Commission policy in this area in the future.

The initial analysis (Kay 1991b) was prompted by evidence that there was a contradictory theme running through the Commission's policies on market completion and collaborative activity, most notably those associated with DGII, the Directorate-General for Economic and Financial Affairs. In particular, fundamental problems exist with the claims made by DGII that market fragmentation has traditionally impeded industrial co-operation within the Community and that EU cross-border collaborative strategies such as joint ventures will be encouraged by the completion of the internal market. Following the publication of the White Paper 'Completing the Internal Market' (CEC 1985), subsequent studies by DGII have tended to reinforce the line taken in the White Paper that market completion will tend to support and encourage co-operative activity cross-frontier within the EU (see especially Emerson *et al.* 1988: Cecchini *et al.* 1988). While co-operative activity of all kinds is seen as being potentially reinforced by market completion, joint ventures are seen as the archetypical form of co-operative activity whose development has been stunted by previous failures to move quickly enough to market completion:

241

The paradox which emerges is that co-operation with Community partners has so far been less frequent than co-operation with partners in non-member countries. The total number of joint ventures set up has remained very stable. ... But European co-operation could grow substantially as a result of the removal of some of these barriers.

(Emerson *et al.* 1988: 175)

The barriers to be removed that Emerson *et al.* refer to are non-tariff barriers targeted by the Internal Market programme. The 'paradox' identified by Emerson *et al.* only exists if it is believed that co-operative activity such as joint ventures are stimulated by moves towards market completion.

In fact, Kay (1991b) argued that the opposite was typically the case since joint venture activity tends to be a device of last resort for firms – see also Hennart (1988) and Kay *et al.* (1987). Firstly, joint ventures facilitate the pooling of complementary capabilities, and hence they are useful to enter markets where high barriers to entry by foreigners make it necessary to have a local partner. As these barriers are being reduced by the Europe 1992 process, we would expect that firms would decide to go it alone through mergers, and feel less need to joint venture. Secondly, the more open a market, the greater the possibility that potential partners are also potential competitors. Consequently, firms may shy away from co-operative agreements within completed markets for fear of sacrificing competitive advantage to a close neighbour and potential rival. Such co-operation may be easier to foster if firms continue to be buttressed and protected by trade barriers that would inhibit present partners from becoming future rivals. In short, the direct effects of the EU moving successfully in the direction of market completion would be to *diminish* the formation of co-operative strategies such as joint venture cross-frontier within the EU.

Kay (1991b) reviewed previous studies, including evidence produced by DGII's own consultants, and found that patterns of co-operative activity were generally consistent with their being discouraged by market completion. To explore this further in the specific context of the completion of the EU market, Kay (1991b) used data provided by the annual competition policy reports published by DGIV. As an indicator of relative incidence of co-operative activity, a measure termed 'aversion ratio' was developed ('aversion' meaning aversion to co-operative activity). The aversion ratio represented the ratio of merger to joint venture activity in a given year for a particular domain. Most usefully, DGIV provided measures on an annual basis gathered from the specialist press on the incidence of mergers and joint ventures involving the largest firms in the Community for three domains: *national* level within the EU (e.g., UK/UK, or NL/NL operations), *Community* level cross-frontier within the EU (e.g., UK/NL operations), and *international* level, involving EU and non-EU partners but with effect on the EU market (e.g., US/UK operations).

If firms did become more averse to joint venture activity as markets moved towards completion through the abolition of barriers to trade, then it should be reflected in a higher aversion ratio as firms replace joint ventures by go-it-alone strategies such as merger. While this would raise aversion ratios, so would a unilateral increase in the avoidance of joint ventures. The DGIV database neatly arranged domains in terms of degree of market completion; *national* domains represent the ideal type or limit case of completed markets, *international* domains are characterised by relatively low degrees of market completion (as evidenced by the existence of formal barriers to market access such as tariffs and quotas between the EU and its trading partners), while the *Community* domain represent an intermediate case of a partially completed market in which formal barriers to trade between firms in different Member States have been abolished, but many non-tariff barriers to trade remain. It is, of course this latter category of trade barrier that the EU Internal Market programme was designed to eliminate or reduce, with the target of moving the EU towards the ideal type of completed markets represented by national domains.

If aversion to co-operative activity did tend to increase along with degree of market completion, this should be reflected in aversion ratios: they should be the lowest for the international domain, the highest for the national domains, and somewhere in between for the Community domain. Figure 12.1 shows industry aversion ratios reported in Kay (1991b) for the five-year period 1983–88 (to the left of the vertical dotted line in Figure 12.1). The predicted patterns of aversion ratios hold, with national domain aversion being highest in each of the three years, international lowest, and Community exhibiting intermediate values in each case. Because we would expect joint ventures to be chosen over mergers to enter partially closed markets, Kay (1991b) concluded that the relative incidence of joint venture activity observed at Community level was quite consistent with a partially completed market. It also warned that to the extent that the Commission's Internal Market programme was successful, it would increase aversion to Community-level co-operative activity and shift the Community aversion ratios in the direction of those associated with national domains.

Figure 12.1   Industry aversion ratios, 1983–92

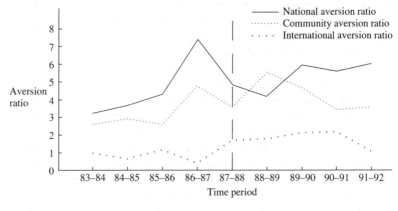

$$\text{Aversion ratio} = \frac{\text{No of mergers}}{\text{No of joint ventures}}$$

Sources: Annual reports on competition policy

To update the analysis, data on industrial merger and joint venture activity provided by the 22nd Report on Competition Policy was used to calculate aversion ratios for all three domains for the four years subsequent to the earlier study (the period to the right of the vertical dotted line). The relationship between aversion ratios is still broadly the same as for the earlier period, with the ratios as follows (1983–88 figures in parentheses): national 5.3 (4.5), Community 4.3 (3.3), international 1.8 (1.0). The stability of the relative positions of the respective aversion ratios suggests that barriers to mergers and acquisitions are still higher in the Community than at the national level, although they are lower at the international level. Barriers to mergers at all levels seem to have decreased, as shown, by a clear increase of 0.8 to 1.0 in aversion ratios in the four-year period compared to the earlier one.

Figure 12.1 also indicates that Community-level aversion did appear to increase in the late 1980s before slumping in the 1990–92 period. There appeared to a corresponding dip in national-level aversion in the late 1980s, which would be consistent with Community firms shifting around that period from national- to Community-level mergers. While too much emphasis should not be placed on figures for a particular year, it is worth considering whether there are any obvious reasons for these patterns of behaviour.

The 22nd Competition Policy Report notes a peak in mergers and acquisitions in 1990–92 (see Annex iv in that report). The report attributes this peak to firms preparing for the opening up of the European market on 1 January, 1993. This explanation does not account for the subsequent slump (from June 1990 to June 1992) in mergers, especially at the Community level. While the incidence of Community-level mergers more than doubled in 1989–90 compared to the previous two years, it fell back to its 1987–88 levels two years later.

The report considers the possibility that

> the entry into force of the Merger Regulation in September 1990 could have had an influence on the peak figure attained in 1989–90, as one could argue that firms might have been prompted to consummate the operations before the date of entry into force of the Regulation so as to avoid being caught by it.
>
> (CEC 1993: 493)

The behaviour of aversion ratios over the 1988–92 period fits this explanation extremely well. The 1990 Merger Regulation was expressly designed to screen mergers with a Community dimension, and while some international mergers might be subject to it, it is Community domain mergers that are particularly targeted by it. It is conceivable that in some cases national domain mergers might also be deemed to have a Community dimension, but this is highly unlikely to be the case in normal circumstances. Thus, the patterns of aversion ratios observed 1988–92 are consistent with a temporary switch in emphasis from national- to Community-level mergers, and the subsequent (also presumed temporary) dip in Community merger activity 1990–92.

However, after raising the possibility of the Merger Regulation affecting activity, the report continues:

> the data that we have for the two years since the Merger Regulation entered into force do not seem to confirm that hypothesis. The number of large mergers, acquisitions and joint ventures falling under the scope of the Regulation (i.e. those involving firms with a turnover greater than ECU 5000 million) has decreased by less than the number of smaller operations.
>
> (CEC 1993: 493)

While that is certainly the case for merger activity aggregated over all domains, for the critical *Community* domain the decline 1990–92 in larger and smaller merger activity was about the same in both cases (activity each year averaging 63 per cent of the 1989–90 peak value). For industrial collaborative activity, the decline in large firm merger activity from the 1989–90 peak was actually more than the decline in smaller firm merger activity (activity each year averaging 57 per cent and 59 per cent of 1989–90 value). However, these are not major differences and are not sufficient in themselves to conflict with the report's general conclusion.

What is questionable is the report's assumption that the introduction of the Merger Regulation is likely to have had an impact only on merger activity that retrospectively can be judged to fall within its remit. There are reasons for believing that smaller firm merger activity could also have been affected by the imminence of the Merger Regulation. As Bishop (1993) points out:

> The member states have agreed to reassess the 5 billion Ecus turnover threshold within four years, with a view to reducing the threshold to 2 billion Ecus. This lower threshold was discussed extensively during the negotiations of the new regulations. However, it was opposed by, among others, the UK, and because of the need for a unanimous vote, a higher threshold satisfying the UK had to be agreed. When the threshold is reassessed, only a qualified majority will be necessary to bring about a change; thus, a lower threshold stands a greater chance of being adopted.
>
> (1993: 305)

The uncertainty *ex ante* concerning the level of the threshold, and the likelihood that it will be lowered shortly in any case, are both likely to have had a stimulating effect on smaller firm merger activity in the Community. For our purposes it is sufficient to point out that it is quite plausible that the Merger Regulation did have spillover effects on smaller firm Community-level merger activity since many firms believed these could be caught up in the legislation. That the Merger Regulation did provide a short-term boost to Community level merger activity appears to be borne out by the trends in aversion ratios in Figure 12.1, contrary to the arguments in the 22nd Competition Policy Report.

12.2 TRENDS IN CO-OPERATIVE ACTIVITY IN HIGH-TECHNOLOGY INDUSTRY

Since the White Paper, there has been particular emphasis by the Commission on the role of co-operative activity in the high-technology sectors as the EU moves towards market completion (see Kay 1991b). Here we briefly comment on trends in these sectors, extending the analysis in Kay (1991b).

As Kay (1991b) pointed out (and Figure 12.2 shows) the analysis for the high-technology sectors (electrical, mechanical, chemical and computers) showed a surprising tendency for aversion ratios for the Community domain to beat even those for national-level domains 1983–88. The Community aversion ratio for the whole period 1983–88 was 4.4, while the national-level aversion ratio was 3.5. While this obviously invited further analysis, it suggested that whereas in these sectors the reduction in the segmentation of Community markets pursued by the Commission had made major advances, Commission programmes designed to stimulate joint ventures were likely to encounter resistance. Further investigation revealed that chemical-industry mergers dominated these figures over the 1983–88 period with 41 per cent of mergers in this category. Many parts of the European chemical industry had been making losses and exhibited overcapacity over this period, and the industry as

Figure 12.2 Aversion ratios for high-technology industry, 1983–92

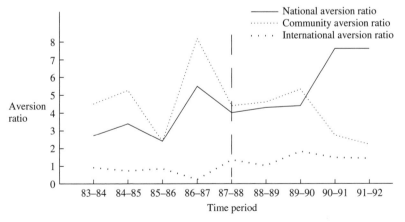

Sources: As for Figure 12.1

a whole was undergoing a major process of reorganisation and rationalisation which may have had an impact on aversion ratios for the
Community domain.

As Figure 12.2 shows, aversion ratios for Community-level high-
technology industry have tended to decline from a peak in 1986–87.
The Community aversion ratio for the whole of the new 1988–92
period (3.8) now lies between national (7.6) and international (1.4)
extremes. This pattern now more closely reflects both prior expectations and the behaviour of aversion ratios for industry as a whole than
was the case for the earlier period, 1983–88. The introduction of the
Merger Regulation in 1990 is again likely to have boosted Community
aversion ratios in 1988–90 and dampened them in 1990–92, since the
change in aversion ratios over both two-year periods were entirely
accounted for by variation in merger activity; the total number of
Community joint ventures 1990–92 was exactly the same as for
1988–90, at 40, while Community merger activity declined from 196
over 1988–90, to 104 over 1990–92.

Because of the potentially distorting effect of chemical industry
rationalisation, Kay (1991b) also calculated aversion ratios for high-
technology industry excluding chemicals. Figure 12.3 illustrates these
for the earlier 1983–88 period and updates them for 1988–92. Because
of the small number of operations involved in some cases, caution is
warranted in interpreting the figures, especially for single years.

Figure 12.3 Aversion ratios for high-technology industry (excluding chemicals),
1983–92

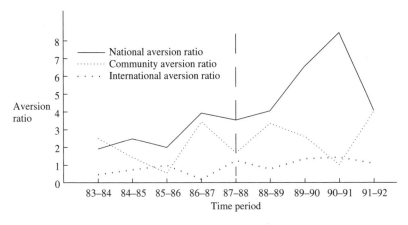

Sources: As for Figure 12.1

However, some clear trends are visible, with Community-level aversion ratios continuing to display values intermediate between national and international domains in all years as expected, except for 1990–91 when the Community aversion ratio dips below international. The composite Community aversion ratio for the two-year period preceding the Merger Regulation was 3.0, while for the next two years it had fallen to 1.6. Again, this is consistent with a Merger Regulation-inspired boom-and-bust effect on Community-level merger activity.

Note also that the aversion ratios in all domains nearly doubled in this second period compared to the earlier period (earlier period in brackets), with national at 5.4 (2.9), Community at 3.2 (1.7), and international at 1.2 (0.6). The increased aversion to co-operative activity observed in all domains, including Community level, does not encourage optimism as to the prospects of fostering co-operative activity as the EU moves towards market completion.

12.3 CONCLUSIONS AND POSSIBILITIES FOR FUTURE RESEARCH

There are a number of provisional conclusions which we make on the basis of this update. Firstly, the aversion ratio measure introduced in Kay (1991b) continues to behave as predicted, with aversion to co-operative activity generally increasing with degree of market completion. This is consistent with our expectations but contrary to those expressed in Emerson *et al.* (1988) and Cecchini (1988).

Secondly, aversion to co-operative activity appears to have increased for national, Community and international domains in the later period, 1988–92, covered here, compared to the earlier 1983–88 period in Kay (1991b). This holds for industrial co-operative activity in general and the high-technology sub-sectors in particular.

Thirdly, aversion ratios provide evidence that the Merger Regulation introduced in 1990 was responsible for a short-term boost and subsequent slump for Community-level merger activity.

Fourthly, given that aversion ratios have proved fairly reliable indicators of the effect of market completion on industrial collaborative activity, they could help resolve the contradictions in Commission policy on industrial collaboration within the Internal Market of the EU pointed out in Kay (1991b). If Community aversion ratios move towards those associated with national domains over time, this would be an indicator that the Internal Market was indeed moving towards increased integration – but it would tend to contradict Commission arguments that market completion would stimulate cross-frontier collaborative activity. On the other hand, if the Community aversion ratio moved in the opposite direction towards the lower values associated with the international domain, this would tend to support the Commission's arguments that European firms will become less averse to cross-frontier collaboration in the future – but the robustness of aversion ratios as indicators of degree of market completion means that this would tend to conflict with claims that the Internal Market was moving towards increased integration. Monitoring the trends indicated by the DGIV series would help highlight and potentially resolve the inherent conflicts in Commission policy in these areas.

Unfortunately, changes to the databases used by DGIV are likely to preclude this. As the 23rd Competition Policy Report (CEC 1993) outlines, from 1992 the collection of data on mergers and joint ventures directly by the Commission (the DOME database) was terminated and substituted by two different databases supplied by outside consultants, one database covering mergers (source Amdata), and the other covering joint ventures (source KPMG). The changes followed a comparative study of DOME and the Amdata databases conducted by DGII (see CEC 1993: 519). The coverage of the respective databases do not correspond directly to DOME's coverage in the respective cases. Also, unlike the DOME database whose coverage was for the largest 1000 Community firms for all domains, the new databases' coverage is not expressly designed to be comparable, and they are constructed separately using different sources, populations and criteria. There appears to be a broken series in the case of joint ventures, with values for 1990–91 only available for January 1991 to May 1991 (CEC 1993: 525), unlike the normal values which are collected from June to May. While the database on mergers still collects national domain data, the database on joint ventures does not. It is therefore not possible to construct aversion ratios for national domains using the new series. Comparability of the new series with the DOME database is at best highly problematic even where there is a potential overlap of coverage.

The termination of the DOME database makes it more difficult to evaluate the Commission's own policies in the areas of industrial collaborative activity in the context of market completion. The radical changes in the series in 1992 impede comparison of trends before and after this critical period. They certainly make comparison of aversion ratios along the lines suggested in Kay (1991b) impossible since the yardstick of completed markets represented by national aversion ratios is now missing. Changes in the databases do not remove, however, the potential contradictions at the heart of Commission policy as far as collaborative activity and market integration is concerned. We feel there is a strong argument for additional research in this area to compensate for the loss of the DOME database. Not only would this perform a valuable academic exercise, it might help show (contrary to the arguments of the Economics Directorate), that the efforts of the technology-orientated Directorates to foster collaborative activity at Community level will be made more difficult by European market integration – not less. Recognition of this fact would assist in a more realistic appraisal of what can reasonably expected of policy initiatives to assist European collaborative activity in the post-1992 environment.

NOTES

1.   This article was co-authored with Jean-Francois Hennart and Harvie Ramsay and was originally published in the *Journal of Common Market Studies*, 34 (1996), pp. 465–75. It is reprinted here by kind permission of the publishers, Blackwell.

Bibliography

Adams-Webber, J. R. (1979) *Personal Construct Theory, Concepts and Applications*, Chichester: Wiley.

Adelman, M. A. (1961) The Anti-merger Act 1950–60, *American Economic Review*, 51, 236–44.

Akerlof, G. A. (1970) The market for lemons: qualitative uncertainty and the market mechanism, *Quarterly Journal of Economics*, 84, 488–500.

Alchian, A. A. (1950) Uncertainty, evolution and economic theory, *Journal of Political Economy*, 58, 221–2.

Alchian, A. A. (1977) *Economic Forces at Work*, Indianapolis: Liberty Press.

Alchian, A. A. and Demsetz, H. (1972) Production, information costs and economic organization, *American Economic Review*, 62–1, 777–95.

Aliber, R. Z. (1970) A theory of foreign direct investment, in C. P. Kindleberger (ed.) *The International Corporation*, Cambridge, MA: MIT Press, 17–34.

Amey, R. R. (1964) Diversified manufacturing business, *Journal of the Royal Statistical Society*, 127, 251–90.

Angelmar, R. (1985) Market structure and research intensity in high-technological-opportunity industries, *Journal of Industrial Economics*, 36, 69–79.

Ansoff, H. I. (1965) *Corporate Strategy*, London: Penguin.

Ansoff, H. I. (1979) *Strategic Management*, London: Macmillan.

Argyle, M. (1991) *Cooperation: The Basis of Sociability*, London: Routledge.

Arrow, K. (1962) Economic welfare and the allocation of resources for invention, in *The Rate and Direction of Inventive Activity*, Princeton, NJ: NBER, 609–25.

Arthur, W. B. (1989) Competing technologies, increasing returns and lock-in by historical events, *Economic Journal*, 99, 116–31.

Baldwin, W. L. (1967) *The Structure of the Defense Market, 1955–64*, Durham, NC: Duke University Press.

Baumol, W. J. (1959) *Business Behaviour, Value and Growth*, New York: Macmillan.

Baumol, W. J. (1977) On the proper cost test for natural monopoly in a multi-product industry, *American Economic Review*, 67, 809–22.

Baumol, W. J. (1986) Williamson's the Economic Institutions of Capitalism, *Rand Journal of Economics*, 17, 279–86.

Baumol, W. J., Bailey, E. E. and Willig, R. D. (1977) Weak invisible hand theorems on the sustainability of multiproduct natural monopoly, *American Economic Review*, 67, 350–65.

Baumol, W. J. and Braunstein, Y. M. (1977) Empirical study of scale economies and production complementary, the case of journal publication, *Journal of Political Economy*, 85, 1937–1948.

Baumol W. J. and Fischer, D. (1978) Cost minimising number of firms and determination of industry structure, *Quarterly Journal of Economics*, 20, 439–67.

Baumol, W. J., Panzar, J. C. and Willig, R. D. (1982) *Contestable Markets and the Theory of Industry Structure*, New York: Harcourt Brace Jovanovich.

Beamish, P. W. and Banks, J. C. (1987) Equity joint ventures and the multinational enterprise, *Journal of International Business Studies* (Summer), 1–16.

Benoit, J-P. (1985) Innovation and imitation in a duopoly, *Review of Economic Studies*, 52, 99–106.

Berg, S. and Friedman, P. (1977) Joint ventures, competition and technological complementarities: evidence from chemicals, *Southern Economic Journal*, 43, 1330–7.

Berg, S. V. and Friedman, P. (1978) Joint ventures in American industry: an overview, *Mergers and Acquisitions* (Summer), 28–41.

Berg, S. V. and Friedman, P. (1979a) Joint ventures in American industry: managerial policy, *Mergers and Acquisitions* (Autumn), 9–17.

Berg, S. V. and Friedman, P. (1979b) Joint ventures in American industry: public policy issues, *Mergers and Acquisitions* (Winter), 18–30.

Berg, S. V. and Friedman, P. (1980) Causes and effects of joint venture activity: knowledge acquisition vs. parent horizontality, *Antitrust Bulletin*, XXV, 141–68.

Berkowtitz, M. (1970) *The Conversion of Military-oriented Research and Development to Civilian Uses*, New York: Praeger.

Biggadike, E. R. (1981) The contributions of marketing to strategic management, in *Academy of Management Review*, 6, 621–32.

Birkett, C. (1985) Boeing's airliner launch criteria, *Flight International*, 9 March, 30–2.

Bishop, M. (1993) European or national? The Community's new merger Regulation, in M. Bishop and J. Kay (eds) *European Mergers and Merger Policy*, Oxford: Oxford University Press, 294–317.

Blaug, M. (1980) *The Methodology of Economics: or How Economists Explain*, Cambridge: Cambridge University Press.

Blois, K. (1972) Vertical quasi-integration, *Journal of Industrial Economics*, 20, 253–72.

Bluestone, B., Jordan, P. and Sullivan, M. (1981) *Aircraft Industry Dynamics*, Boston: Auburn House.

Boulding, K. (1968) *Beyond Economics*, Ann Arbor: University of Michigan Press.

Bourgeois, L. J., III (1980) Strategy and environment: a conceptual integration, *Academy of Management Review*, 5, 25–39.

Bower, J. L. (1982) Business policy in the 1980s, *Academy of Management Review*, 7, 630–8.

Boyle, S. E. (1968) An estimate of the number and size distribution of domestic joint subsidiaries, *Antitrust Law and Economic Review* (Spring), 81–92.

Bozeman, B., Link, A. and Zardkooh, A. (1988) An economic analysis of R&D joint ventures, *Managerial and Decision Economics*, 7, 263–6.

Brander, J. A. and Spencer, B. J. (1983) Strategic commitment with R & D: the symmetric case, *Bell Journal of Economics*, 14, 225–35.

Bresnahan, T. F. and Salop, B. R. (1986) Quantifying the competitive effects of production joint ventures, *International Journal of Industrial Organisation* 4, 155–75.

Bright, C. D. (1979) *The Jet Makers*, Lawrence: Mass.: Regents University Press.

Buckley, P. J (1988) Organizational forms and multinational companies, in S. Thompson and M. Wright (eds) *International Organization, Efficiency and Profit*, Oxford: Philip Allan, 127–68.

Buckley, P. J. and Casson, M. (1976) *The Future of the Multinational Enterprise*, London: Longman.

Burgelman, R. A. (1983) A process model of internal corporate venturing in the diversified major firm, *Administrative Science Quarterly*, 28, 223–44.

Burns, T. and Stalker, G. M. (1961) *The Management of Innovation*, London: Tavistock.

Calabresi, G. (1968) Transaction costs, resource allocation, and liability rules – a comment, *Journal of Law and Economics*, 11, 67–73.

Casson, M. (1979) *Alternatives to the Multinational Enterprise*, London: Macmillan.

Casson, M. (1987) Contractual arrangements for technology transfer: new evidence from business history, in *The Firm and the Market*, Oxford: Blackwell, 121–52.

Casson, M. (1995a) *Entrepreneurship and Business Culture: Studies in the Economics of Trust*, vol. 1, Aldershot: Edward Elgar.

Casson, M. (1995b) *The Organization of International Business: Studies in the Economics of Trust*, vol. 2, Aldershot: Edward Elgar.

Caves, R. E. (1974) The causes of direct investment, foreign firms' shares in Canadian and UK manufacturing industry, *Review of Economics and Statistics*, 56, 279–93.

Caves, R. E. (1980) Industrial organisation, corporate strategy and structure, *Journal of Economic Literature*, 18, 64–92.

Caves, R. E. (1982) *Multinational Enterprise and Economic Analysis*, Cambridge: Cambridge University Press.

Cecchini, P., Catinet, M., and Jacquemin, A. (1988) *The European Challenge: 1992*, Aldershot: Wildwood House.

Chandler, A. (1962) *Strategy and Structure*, Cambridge, MA: MIT Press.

Channon, D. F. (1973) *The Strategy and Structure of British Enterprise*, Cambridge, MA: Harvard University Press.

Child, J. (1977) *Organization*, London: Harper & Row.

Child, J. (1984) *Organisation*, 2nd edn, London: Harper & Row.

Coase, R. H. (1937) The nature of the firm, *Economica*, 4, 386–405.

Coase, R. H. (1960) The problem of social cost, *Journal of Law and Economics*, 3, 1–44.

Coddington, A. (1975) Creating semaphore and beyond (review of G. L. S. Shackle: *Epistemics and Economics*) *British Journal for the Philosophy of Science*, 26, 151–63.

Coddington A. (1983) *Keynesian Economics: the Search for First Principles*, London: George Allen & Unwin.

Cohen, W. M. and Levin, R. C. (1989) Empirical studies of innovation and market structure, in R. Schmalensee and R. D. Willig (eds) *Handbook of Industrial Organization*, Amsterdam: North Holland, 1059–107.

Coley, S. and Reinton, S. (1980) The hunt for value, *The McKinsey Quarterly* (Spring).

Colman, A. (1982) *Game Theory and Experimental Games: the Study of Strategic Interaction*, Oxford: Pergamon.

Comanor, W. S. (1965) Research and technical change in the pharmaceutical industry, *Review of Economics and Statistics*, 47, 182–90.

Commission of the European Communities (CEC) (1984) *Thirteenth Report on Competition Policy*, Brussels/Luxembourg: CEC.

Commission of the European Communities (1985) *Completing the Internal Market*, White Paper from the Commission to the European Council Luxembourg: CEC.

Commission of the European Communities (1987a) *The Cost of Non-Europe*, vol. 7, Luxembourg: CEC.

Commission of the European Communities (1987b) *The Cost of Non-Europe*, vol. 3, Brussels/Luxembourg: CEC.

Commission of the European Communities (1988) Economics of 1992, *European Economy*, 35.

Commission of the European Communities (1989a) Horizontal mergers and competition policy in the European community, *European Economy*, 40.

Commission of the European Communities (1989b) *Eighteenth Report on Competition Policy*, Luxembourg: CEC.

Commission of the European Communities (1992) *Twenty-second Report on Competition Policy*, Luxembourg: CEC.

Commission of the European Communities (1993) *Twenty-third Report on Competition Policy*, Luxembourg: CEC.

Commons, J. R. (1986) *Legal Foundations of Capitalism*, Maddison, WI: University of Wisconsin Press.

Contractor, F. (1981) The role of licensing in international strategy, *Columbia Journal of World Business*, 16, 73–83.

Contractor, F. J. (1983) Technology licensing practice in US companies: corporate and public policy implications, *Columbia Journal of World Business* (Fall), 80–8.

Coombs, R., Saviotti, P. and Walsh, V. (1987) *Economics and Technological Change*, London: Macmillan.

Cooper, A. and Schendel, D. E. (1976) Strategic responses to technological threats, *Business Horizons*, 19, 61–9.

Cowling, K., Stoneman, P., Cubbin, J., Cable, J., Hall, G., Donberger, S., and Dutton, P. (1980) *Mergers and Economic Performance*, Cambridge: Cambridge University Press.

Crockett, W. H. and Meisel, P. (1974) Construct connectedness, strength of disconfirmation and impression change, *Journal of Personality*, 42, 290–9.

Cross, R. (1982) *Economic Theory and Policy in the UK*, Oxford: Martin Robertson.

Culbertson, J. D. (1985) Econometric tests of the market structural determinants of R & D investment: consistency of absolute and relative firm size models, *Journal of Industrial Economics*, 34, 101–8.

Cyert, R. M. and March, J. G. (1963) *A Behavioral Theory of the Firm*, Englewood, NJ: Prentice-Hall.

Dahlman, C. J. (1979) The problem of externality, *Journal of Law and Economics*, 22, 141–62.

Dasgupta, P. (1988a) Trust as a commodity, in D. Gambetta (ed.) *Trust: Making and Breaking Cooperative Relations*, Oxford: Blackwell, 49–72.

Dasgupta, P. (1988b) The welfare economics of knowledge production, *Oxford Review of Economic Policy* 4, 1–12.

Dasgupta, P., Gilbert, R. J. and Stiglitz, J. E. (1982) Invention and innovation under alternative market structures: the case of natural resources, *Review of Economic Studies*, 49, 567–82.

David, P. A. (1985) Clio and the economics of QWERTY, *American Economic Review*, Papers and Proceedings, 75, 332–7.

Davidson, W. H. and McFetridge, D. G. (1984) International technology transactions and the theory of the firm, *Journal of Industrial Economics*, 32, 253–64.

De Brock, L. M. (1985) Market structure, innovation and optimal patent life, *Journal of Law and Economics*, 28, 223–44.

Demsetz, M. (1968) Why regulate utilities? *Journal of Law and Economics*, 11, 55–65.

Demsetz, M. (1969) Information and efficiency: another viewpoint, *Journal of Law and Economics*, 11, 1–22.

Dietrich, M. (1991) Firms, markets and transaction cost economics, *Scottish Journal of Political Economy*, 38, 41–57.

Dosi, G. (1982) Technological paradigms and technological trajectories, *Research Policy*, 11, 147–62.

Dosi, G. (1984) *Technical Change and Industrial Transformation: the Theory and an Application to the Semiconductor Industry*, London: Macmillan.

Dosi, G. and Orsenigo, L. (1985) Order and change: an exploration on markets, institutions and technology in industrial dynamics, Mimeo, Sussex, Science Policy Research Unit.

Dow, G. K. (1987) The function of authority in transaction cost economics, *Journal of Economic Behavior and Organisation*, 8, 13–38.

Dow, S. C. and Earl, P. E. (1982) *Money Matters: a Keynesian Approach to Monetary Economics*, Oxford: Martin Robertson.

Dow, S. C. and Earl, P. E. (1984) Methodology and orthodox monetary policy, *Economie Appliqué*, 37, 143–63.

Dunning, J. H. (1958) *American Investment in British Manufacturing Industry*, London: Allen & Unwin.

Dunning, J. H. (1981) *International Production and the Multinational Enterprise*, London: Allen & Unwin.

Dyas, G. R. and H. T. Thanheiser, (1976) *The Emerging European Enterprise*, London: Allen & Unwin.

Earl, P. E. (1983a) The consumer in his/her social setting: a subjectivist view, in J. Wiseman (ed.) *Beyond Positive Economics?* London: Macmillan 176–91.

Earl, P. E. (1983b) *The Economic Imagination: Towards a Behavioural Analysis of Choice*, Brighton: Wheatsheaf.

Earl, P. E. (1984a) *The Corporate Imagination: How Big Companies Make Mistakes*, Brighton: Wheatsheaf.

Earl, P. E. (1984b) A behavioural analysis of choice, Unpublished doctoral dissertation, University of Cambridge.

Earl, P. E. and Kay, N. M. (1985) How economists can accept Shackle's critique of economic doctrines without arguing themselves out of their jobs, *Journal of Economic Studies*, 12, 34–48.

Economist, The (1984) Cooperative capitalist plots (11 February), p. 69.

Elster, J. (1983) *Explaining Technical Change*, Cambridge: Cambridge University Press.

Emerson, M., Aujean, M., Catinet, M., Goybet, P. and Jacquemin, A. (1988) *The Economics of 1992*, Oxford: Oxford University Press.

Englander, E. J. (1988) Technology and Oliver Williamson's transaction cost economics, *Journal of Economic Behavior and Organisation*, 10, 339–53.

Ergas, H. (1984) Corporate strategy in transition, in A. Jacquemin (ed.) *European Industry: Public Policy and Corporate Strategy*, Oxford: Clarendon Press, 327–42.

Fama, E. (1970) Efficient capital markets: a review of theory and empirical work, *Journal of Finance, Papers and Proceedings*, 25, 383–423.

Fethke, G. C. and Birch, J. J. (1982) Rivalry and the timing of innovation, *Bell Journal of Economics*, 13, 272–9.

Fisher, F. M. and Temin, P. (1973) Returns to scale in research and development: what does the Schumpeterian hypothesis imply? *Journal of Political Economy*, 81, 56–70.

Fisher, F. M., and Temin, P. (1979) The Schumpeterian hypothesis: reply, *Journal of Political Economy*, 87, 386–9.

Fixler, D. J. (1983) Uncertainty, market structure and the incentive to invent, *Economica*, 50, 407–23.

Freeman, C. F. (1982) *The Economics of Industrial Innovation*, 2nd. edn, London: Francis Pinter.

Fukuyama, F. (1995) *Trust: the Social Virtues and the Creation of Prosperity*, London: Hamish Hamilton.

Galbraith, J. K. (1972) *The New Industrial State*, 2nd edn, London: Penguin.

Galbraith, C. and Kay, N. M. (1986) Towards a theory of multinational enterprise, *Journal of Economic Behavior and Organisation*, 7, 1–19.

Gansler, J. S. (1980) *The Defense Industry*, Cambridge, MA: MIT Press.

Geroski, P. (1987) *Competition and Innovation*, Report prepared for the CEC (Brussels).

Gilbert, R. J. and Newbery, D. M. G. (1982) Preemptive patenting and the persistence of monopoly, *American Economic Review*, 72, 514–26.

Gilman, M. (1981) *The Financing of Foreign Direct Investment*, London: Francis Pinter.

Gomes-Cassieres, B. (1987) Joint venture instability: is it a problem? *Columbia Journal of World Business* (Summer), 97–102.

Gorecki, A. K. (1975) An inter-industry analysis of diversification in the UK manufacturing sector, *Journal of Industrial Economics*, 26, 131–43.

Gort, M. (1962) *Diversification and integration in American industry*, Princeton, NJ: Princeton University Press.

Gould, S. J. (1982) *The Panda's Thumb: More Reflections in Natural History*, New York: Norton.

Goyder, D. G. (1988) *EEC Competition Law*, Oxford: Clarendon Press.

Grabowski, H. G. (1968) Determinants of industrial research and development, *Journal of Political Economy*, 76, 292–306.

Grabowski, H. G. and Baxter, N. D. (1973) Rivalry in industrial research and development: an empirical study, *Journal of Industrial Economics*, 21, 209–35.

Gregory, W. H. (1982) editorial, *Aviation Week and Space Technology* (25 January), 13.

Hamel, G., Doz, Y. L. and Prahalad, C. K. (1989) Collaborate with your competitors – and win, *Harvard Business Review* (January–February), 133–9.

Hassid, J. (1975) Recent evidence on conglomerate diversification in UK manufacturing industry, *Manchester School*, 43, 372–95.

Hayes, R. H. and Abernathy, W. J. (1980) Managing our way to economic decline, *Harvard Business Review* (July–August), 67–77.

Heiner, R. A. (1983) The origin of predictable behaviour, *American Economic Review*, 73, 560–95.

Hennart, J-F. (1988) A transaction costs theory of equity joint ventures, *Strategic Management Journal*, 9, 361–76.

Hennart, J-F. (1991) The transaction cost theory of the multinational enterprise, in C. N. Pitelis and R. Sugden (eds) *The Nature of the Transnational Firm*, London: Routledge, 81–116

Hinkle, D. N. (1965) 'The change of personal constructs from the standpoint of a theory of implications', Unpublished doctoral dissertation, Ohio State University.

Hitt, M. A. and Ireland, R. D. (1985) Corporate distinctive competence, strategy, industry and performance, *Strategic Management Journal*, 6, 273–93.

Hofer, C. W., Murray, E. A., Charon, R. and Pitts, R. A. (1980) *Strategic Management*, St Paul, MN: West Publishing.

Hofstadter, D. (1979) *Gödel, Escher, Bach: an Eternal Golden Braid*, Hassocks, Sussex: Harvester.

Hofstede, D. (1984) *Culture's Consequences*, Beverly Hills: Sage.

Holz, R. (1962) Expanding space technology spurs aerospace market growth, *Aviation Week and Space Technology* 12 March, 62–3.

Horst, T. (1972) Firm and industry determinants of the decision to invest abroad, an empirical study, *Review of Economics and Statistics*, 54, 258–356.

Houthakker, H. S. and Taylor, L. D. (1970) *Consumer Demand in the United States: Analyses and Projections*, 2nd edn, Cambridge, MA: Harvard University Press.

Hughes, A. (1989) The impact of merger: a survey of empirical evidence for the UK, in J. A. Fairburn and J. A. Kay (eds), *Mergers and Mergers Policy*, Oxford: Oxford University Press, 30–98.

Hymer, S. H. (1960) 'The international operations of national firms, a study of direct investment', Cambridge, MA: MIT doctoral dissertation.

Ingells, D. J. (1970) *747 – Story of the Boeing Super Jet*, Falbrook: Aero Publishers.

Interavia (1967) The Boeing company today, 2, 202.

Iwai, K. (1984a) Schumpeterian dynamics: part 1: an evolutionary model of innovation and imitation, *Journal of Economic Behaviour and Organization*, 5, 159–90.

Iwai, K. (1984b) Schumpeterian dynamics, part II: technological progress, Firm growth and 'economic selection', *Journal of Economic Behaviour and Organisation*, 5, 321–51.

Jacquemin, A. (1988) Cooperative agreements in R&D and European anti-trust policy, *European Economic Review*, 32, 551–60.

Jacquemin, A. and Spinoit, B. (1985) Economic and legal aspects of coopera-tive research; a European view, Centre for European Policy Studies, Working Paper, Brussels.

Jefferson, M. (1983) Economic uncertainty and business decision making, in J. Wiseman (ed.) *Beyond Positive Economics?* London: Macmillan.

Jemison, D. B. (1981) The importance of an integrative approach to strategic management research, *Academy of Management Review*, 6, 601–8.

Kamien, M. L. and Schwartz, N. (1982) *Market Structure and Innovation*, Cambridge: Cambridge University Press.

Kaplinsky, R. (1983) Firm size and technical change in a dynamic context, *Journal of Industrial Economics*, 32, 39–59.

Katz, M. L. (1986) An analysis of cooperative research and development, *Rand Journal of Economics*, 17, 527–43.

Kay, N. M. (1979) *The Innovating Firm, a Behavioural Theory of Corporate R & D*, London: Macmillan.

Kay, N. M. (1982) *The Evolving Firm: Strategy and Structure in Industrial Organisation*, London: Macmillan.

Kay, N. M. (1983) Multinational enterprise; a review article, *Scottish Journal of Political Economy*, 30, 304–9.

Kay, N. M. (1984) *The Emergent Firm: Knowledge, Ignorance and Surprise in Economic Organisation*, London: Macmillan.

Kay, N. M. (1987) Markets and false hierarchies: some problems in transac-tion cost economics, European University Institute Working Paper, Florence.

Kay, N. M. Robe J.-P. Zagnoli P. (1987) An approach to the analysis of joint ventures, European University Institute Working Paper, Florence.

Kay, N. M. (1988) The R&D function: corporate strategy and structure, in G. Dosi, C. Freeman, R. L. Nelson, G. Silverberg and L. Soete (eds) *Technical Change and Economic Theory*, London: Frances Pinter, 282–94.

Kay, N. M. (1991a) Multinational enterprise as strategic choice: some transac-tion cost perspectives, in, C. N. Pitelis and R. Sugden *The Nature of the Transnational Firm*, London: Routledge, 137–54.

Kay, N. M. (1991b) Industrial collaborative activity and the completion of the internal market, *Journal of Common Market Studies*, 29, 347–62.

Kay N. M (1992a) Markets, false hierarchies and the evolution of the modern corporation, *Journal of Economic Behavior and Organization*, 17, 315–33.

Kay, N. M. (1992b) Collaborative strategies of firms: theory and evidence, in A. Del Monte (ed.) *Recent Developments in the Theory of Industrial organisa-tion*, London: Macmillan, 201–31.

Kay, N. M. (1993) Mergers, acquisitions and the completion of the internal market, in, K. S. Hughes (ed.) *European Competitiveness*, Cambridge, Cambridge University Press, 161–80.

Kay, N. M. (1996a) The economics of trust, *International Journal of the Economics of Business*, 3, 249–60.

Kay, N. M. (1996b) Industrial structure, rivalry and innovation: theory and evidence, in P. Earl (ed.) *Management, Marketing and the Competitive Process*, Cheltenham: Edward Elgar, 47–77.

Kay, N. M. (1997) *Pattern in Corporate Evolution*, Oxford: Oxford University Press.

Kay, N. M., Hennart, J-F. and Ramsay, H. (1996) Industrial collaborative activity and the European internal market, *Journal of Common Market Studies*, 34, 465–75.

Kelly, G. A. (1955) *The Psychology of Personal Constructs*, New York: Norton.

Keynes, J. M. (1936) *The General Theory of Employment, Interest and Money*, London: Macmillan.

Keynes, J. M. (1937) The general theory of employment, *Quarterly Journal of Economics*, 51, 209–23.

Killing, J. P. (1982) How to make a global joint venture work, *Harvard Business Review*, 61, 120–7.

Kindleberger, C. P. (1969) *American Business Abroad, Six Lectures on Direct Investment*, New Haven, CT: Yale University Press.

Kitching, H. (1967) Why do mergers miscarry? *Harvard Business Review*, 45, 84–101.

Kjelgaard, C. (1984) Air transport pulls out of the dive, in M. J. H. Taylor (ed.) *Janes 1983–4 Aviation Review*, London: Janes, 166–75.

Klein, B. (1977) *Dynamic Economics*, Cambridge, MA: Harvard University Press.

Knight, F. M. (1921) *Risk, Uncertainty and Profit*, Boston: Houghton Mifflin.

Koestler, A. and Smithies, J. R. (eds) (1969) *Beyond Reductionism*, London: Hutchinson/Radius Books.

Kohn, M. and Scott, J. T. (1982) Scale economies in research and development, *Journal of Industrial Economics*, 30, 239–50.

Kohn, M. and Scott, J. T. (1985) Scale economies in research and development: a reply, *Journal of Industrial Economics*, 33, 363.

Kraar, L. (1978) Boeing takes a bold plunge to keep flying high, *Fortune* (25 September), 43–50.

Kuhn, T. S. (1970) *The Structure of Scientific Revolutions*, 2nd edn, Chicago: Chicago University Press.

Kuran, T. (1988) The tenacious past: theories of personal and collective conservatism, *Journal of Economic Behavior and Organisation*, 10, 143–71.

Lakatos, I. (1970) Falsification and the methodology of scientific research programmes, in I. Lakatos and A. Musgrave (eds) *Criticism and the Growth of Knowledge*, London: Cambridge University Press, 91–196.

Learmount, D. (1985) Who needs advanced technology airliners? *Flight International* (1 June), 77–80.

Leibenstein, H. (1966) Allocative efficiency Vs 'X-efficiency', *American Economic Review*, 56, 392–415.

Leijonhufvud, A. (1973) Effective demand failures, *Swedish Journal of Economics*, 75, 27–48.

Leontiades, M. (1982) The confusing words of business policy, *Academy of Management Review*, 7, 45–8.

Loasby, B. J. (1967) Long range formal planning in perspective, *Journal of Management Studies*, 4, 300–8.

Lunn, J. (1982) Research and development and the Schumpeterian hypothesis: alternate approach, *Southern Economic Journal*, 49, 209–17.

Lyles, M. A. (1987) Common mistakes of joint venture experienced firms, *Columbia Journal of World Business* (Summer), 79–84.

McKelvie B. and Aldrich, H. (1983) Populations, natural selection and applied organisational science, *Administrative Science Quarterly*, 28, 101–28.

McMaster, R. and Sawkins, J. W. (1995) The contract state, trust distortion and efficiency, Unpublished paper, Aberdeen: Aberdeen University.

Mansfield, E. (1968) *The Economics of Technological Change*, London: Longman.

Mansfield, E. (1985) How rapidly does new technology leak out? *Journal of Industrial Economics*, 34, 217–23.

Mansfield, E. and Romeo, A. (1980) Technology transfer to overseas subsidiaries by US based firms, *Quarterly Journal of Economics*, 95, 737–50.

Mansfield, E., Romeo, A. and Wagner, S. (1979) Foreign trade and US research and development, *Review of Economics and Statistics*, 61, 49–57.

March, J. G. and Shapira, Z. (1982) Behavioural decision theory and organisational decision theory, in G. R. Ungson and D. R. Braunstein (eds) *Decision-making: an Interdisciplinary Perspective*, Boston: Kent Publishing, 92–115.

Mariti, P. and Smiley, R. M. (1983) Cooperative agreements and the organisation of industry, *Journal of Industrial Economics*, 31, 437–51.

Markowitz, H. (1952) Portfolio selection, *Journal of Finance*, 7, 77–91.

Markowitz, H. (1959) *Portfolio Diversification, Efficient Diversification of Investments*, New York: Wiley.

Marris, R. (1964) *The Economic Theory of Managerial Capitalism*, London: Macmillan.

Martin, S. (1988) Joint ventures and market performance in oligopoly, Working Paper, European University Institute, Florence.

Meeks, G. (1977) *Disappointing Marriage: a Study of the Gains from Merger*, Cambridge: Cambridge University Press.

Minsky, H. P. (1975) *John Maynard Keynes*, New York: Columbia University Press.

Morris, D. and Hergert, M. (1987) Trends in international collaborative agreements, *Columbia Journal of World Business* (Summer), 15–21.

Mowery, D. and N. Rosenberg (1979) The influence of market demand upon innovation: a critical review of some recent empirical studies, *Research Policy*, 8, 102–53.

Mowery, D. C. and Rosenberg, N. (1982) The commercial aircraft industry, in R. R. Nelson (ed.) *Government and Technical Progress: a Cross-industrial Comparison*, New York: Pergamon, 101–61.

Mowery, D. and Rosenberg, N. (1985) Commercial aircraft: cooperation and competition between the US and Japan, *California Management Review*, 27, 70–92.

Moxon, R. W., Roehl, T. W., Truitt, J. F. and Geringer, J. M. (1984) *Emerging Sources of Foreign Competition in the Commercial Aircraft Manufacturing Industry*, Interim Report, Washington, DC, Department of Transportation.

Mueller, D. (1980) *The Determinants and Effects of Mergers: an International Comparison*, Cambridge, MA: Oelgeschlager, Gum and Marin.

Mueller, D. (1988) The corporate life cycle, in S. Thompson and M. Wright (eds) *Internal Organisation, Efficiency and Profit*, Oxford: Philip Allan, 38–64.

Mytelka, L. K. and Delapierre, M. (1987) The alliance strategy of European firms in the information technology industry and the Role of ESPRIT, *Journal of Common Market Studies*, 26, 231–53.

Nelson, R. R. (1959) The simple economics of basic scientific research, *Journal of Political Economy*, 67, 297–306.

Nelson, R. R. (1984) *High Technology Policies: a Five Nation Comparison*, Washington, D.C., American Enterprise Institute.

Nelson, R. R. and Winter, S. (1974) Neoclassical vs evolutionary theories of economic growth: critique and prospectus, *Economic Journal*, 84, 886–905.

Nelson, R. R. and Winter, S. (1982) *An Evolutionary Theory of Economic Change*, Cambridge, MA: Harvard University Press.

Newhouse, J. (1972) *The Sporty Game*, New York: M. Knopf.

Odagiri, H. (1983) R & D expenditures, royalty payments and sales growth in Japanese manufacturing corporations, *Journal of Industrial Economics*, 32, 61–71.

O'Lone, R. G. (1966) Flexibility in manufacturing permits with 737 options, *Aviation Week and Space Technology* (6 June), 54–7.

O'Lone, R. G. (1970) Boeing considers wide-body 727 version, *Aviation Week and Space Technology* (20 July), 36–7.

O'Lone, R. G. (1979a) Boeing 757 entering new phase, *Aviation Week and Space Technology* (6 August), 22–4.

O'Lone, R. G. (1979b) Boeing facing new set of challenges, *Aviation Week and Space Technology* (12 November), 43–55.

Ordover, J. A. and Baumol, W. (1988) Antitrust policy and high technology industries, *Oxford Review of Economic Policy*, 4, 13–34.

Ordover, J. A. and Willig, R. D. (1985) Anti-trust for high technology industries: assessing research joint ventures and mergers, *Journal of Law and Economics*, 28, 311–33.

Ouchi, W. (1980) Markets, bureaucracies and clans, *Administrative Science Quarterly*, 25, 129–41.

Ouchi, W. and Boulton, M. K. (1988) The logic of joint research and development, *California Management Review* (Spring), 9–33.

Patrick, H. T. and Rosovsky, H. (1976) *Asia's New Giant: How the Japanese Economy Works*, Washington, DC: The Brookings Institution.

Peck, M. J. (1986) Joint R&D: the case of Microelectronics and Computer Technology Corporation, *Research Policy*, 15, 219–31.

Penrose, E. T. (1959) *The Theory of the Growth of the Firm*, Oxford: Blackwell.

Perlmutter, H. V. and Keenan, D. A. (1986) Thinking ahead: cooperate to compete globally, *Harvard Business Review*, 64, 136–52.

Pfeffer, J. and Nowak, P. (1976) Patterns of joint activity: implications for anti-trust policy, *Antitrust Bulletin*, XXI, 315–39.

Phillips, A. (1971) *Technology and Market Structure*, Lexington, MA: Heath Lexington Books.

Porter, M. E. (1980) *Competitive Strategy*, New York: Free Press.

Porter, M. E. (1981) The contributions of industrial organisation to strategic management, *Academy of Management Review*, 6, 609–20.

Porter, M. E. (1985) *Competitive Advantage*, New York: Free Press.

Pratten, C. (1988) A survey of the economies of scale, *Research on the Cost of Non-Europe*, vol. II, Brussels, EC Commission.

Putnam, R. D. (1995) Bowling alone: America's declining social capital, *Journal of Democracy*, 6, 65–78.

Ramsay, H. (1995) Le Defi Européen: multinational restructuring, labour and EU policy, in A. Amin and J. Tomaney (eds) *Behind the Myth of European Union*, London: Routledge.

Rapaport, A. and Chammah, A. M. (1965) *Prisoner's Dilemma: a Study in Conflict and Cooperation*, Ann Arbor: University of Michigan Press.

Redding, R. and Yenne, B. (1983) *Boeing*, London: Arms and Armour Press.

Regelin, K. (1980) Boeing rides high, *Interavia*, 8, 675–7.

Reich, R. B. and Mankin, E. D. (1986) Joint ventures with Japan are giving away our future, *Harvard Business Review* (March–April), 78–86.

Reinganum, J. F. (1982) A dynamic game of R & D: patent protection and competitive behaviour, *Econometrica*, 50, 671–88.

Reinganum, J. F. (1984) Practical implications of game theoretic models of R & D, *American Economic Review, Papers and Proceedings*, 74, 61–6.

Reinganum, J. F. (1985) Innovation and industry evolution, *Quarterly Journal of Economics*, 100, 81–99.

Renard, P. (1985) Joint ventures – the keys to success and some cautions, *European Management Journal*, 3, 39–47.

Reynolds, R. J. and Snapp, B. R. (1986) The competitive effects of partial equity interests and joint ventures, *International Journal of Industrial Organization*, 4, 141–53.

Rodriguez, C. A. (1979) A comment on Fisher and Temin on the Schumpeterian hypothesis, *Journal of Political Economy*, 87, 383–5.

Roehl, T. W. and Truitt, J. F. (1987) Stormy open marriages are better: evidence from US, Japanese and French cooperative ventures in commercial aircraft, *Columbia Journal of World Business* (Summer), 87–95.

Rothwell, R. and Zegveld, W. (1982) *Industrial Innovation and Public Policy*, London: Francis Pinter.

Rugman, A. M. (1980a) A new theory of multinational enterprise, internationalization versus internalization, *Columbia Review of World Business*, 15, 23–9.

Rugman, A. M. (1980b) Internationalization as a general theory of foreign direct investment, a reappraisal of the literature, *Weltwirtschaftliches Archiv*, 116, 365–79.

Rugman, A. M. (1981) *Inside the Multinationals*, London: Croom Helm.

Rugman, A. M. (ed.) (1982) *New Theories of the Multinational Enterprise*, London: Croom Helm.

Rumelt, R. P. (1974) *Strategy, Structure and Economic Performance*, Cambridge, MA: Harvard University Press.

Rumelt, R. P. (1984) Towards a strategic theory of the firm, in R. B. Lamb *Competitive Strategic Management*, Englewood, NJ: Prentice-Hall, 556–70.

Rydberg, C. R. (1970) Conversion of the marketing function, in S. Melman (ed.) *The Defense Economy*, New York: Praeger.

Sahal, D. (1985) Technological guideposts and innovation avenues, *Research Policy*, 14, 61–82.

Saviotti, P. P. and Metcalfe, J. S. (1984) A theoretical approach to the construction of technological output indicators, *Research Policy*, 13, 141–51.

Schann, J-L. (1988) How to control a joint venture even as a minority partner, *Journal of General Management*, 14, 4–16.

Schendel, D. E. and Hofer, C. W. (1979) *Strategic management, a new view of business policy and planning*, Boston, MA: Little, Brown.

Scherer, F. M. (1965) Firm size, market structure, opportunity and the output of potential inventions, *American Economic Review*, 55, 1096–125.

Scherer, F. M. (1980a) *Industrial Market Structure and Economic Performance*, 2nd edn, Chicago: Rand McNally.

Scherer, F. M. (1980b) Demand pull and technological invention: Schmookler revisited, *Journal of Industrial Economics*, 30, 225–37.

Schiff, B. J. (1967) *The Boeing 707*, Falbrook, Aero Publishers.

Schmookler, J. (1966) *Invention and Economic Growth*, Cambridge, MA: Harvard University Press.

Schumpeter, J. A. (1950) *Capitalism, Socialism and Democracy*, London: Allen & Unwin.

Scott, J. T. (1988) Diversification versus cooperation in R&D investment, *Managerial and Decision Economics*, 9, 173–86.

Selznick, P. (1957) *Leadership in Administration*, Evanston, IL: Harper & Row.

Shackle, G. L. S. (1967) *The Years of High Theory: Invention and Tradition in Economic Thought, 1926–1939*, Cambridge: Cambridge University Press.

Shackle, G. L. S (1972) *Epistemics and Economics: a Critique of Economic Doctrines*, Cambridge: Cambridge University Press.

Shackle, G. L. S. (1973) Keynes and today's establishment in economic theory: a view, *Journal of Economic Literature*, 11, 516–19.

Shackle, G. L. S. (1974) *Keynesian Kaleidics*, Edinburgh: Edinburgh University Press.

Shackle, G. L. S. (1979) *Imagination and the Nature of Choice*, Edinburgh: Edinburgh University Press.

Shackle, G. L. S. (1982) Sir John Hicks 'IS-LM: an explanation': a comment, *Journal of Post Keynesian Economics*, 4, 435–8.

Silk, L. (1968) Outer space: the impact on the American economy, in G. R. Simonson (ed.) *The History of the American Aircraft Industry*, Cambridge, MA: MIT Press, 244–59.

Simon, H. A. (1957) *Models of Man*, New York: Wiley.

Simon, H. A. (1965) *Administrative Behavior*, 2nd edn, New York: Macmillan.

Simon, H. A. (1969) *The Sciences of the Artificial*, Cambridge, MA: MIT Press.

Simon, H. A. (1976) *Administrative Behaviour*, 3rd edn, New York: Macmillan.

Simon, H. A. (1979) Rational decision making in business organizations, *American Economic Review*, 69, 493–513.

Simonson, G. R. (1964) Missiles and creative destruction in the American aircraft industry, 1955–61, *Business History Review*, 38, 302–14.

Smith, K. V. and Shreiner, J. C. (1969), A portfolio analysis of conglomerate diversification, *Journal of Finance*, 24, 413–29.

Smith, L. (1980) 3M – the lures and limits of innovation, *Fortune* (20 October), 84–94.

Spence, M. (1984) Cost reduction, competition and industry performance, *Econometrica*, 52, 101–21.

Spencer, B. J. and Brander, J. A. (1983) International R & D rivalry and industrial strategy, *Review of Economic Studies*, 50, 707–22.

Steinbruner, J. D. (1974) *The Cybernetic Theory of Decision*, Princeton, NJ: Princeton University Press.

Steiner, J. E. (1979) Jet aviation development; a company persecutive, in W. J. Boyle and D. S. Lopez *The Jet Age*, Washington, DC: National Air and Space Museum, 141–83.

Stekler, H. O. (1965) *The Structure and Performance of the Aerospace Industry*, Berkeley: University of California Press.

Stoneman, P. and Vickers, J. (1988) The assessment: the economics of technology policy, *Oxford Review of Economic Policy*, 4, i–xvi.

Stuart, A. (1982) Boeing's new beauties are a tough sell, *Fortune* (18 October), 114–20.

Tandon, P. (1982) Optimal patents with compulsory licensing, *Journal of Political Economy*, 90, 470–86.

Tandon, P. (1983) Rivalry and the excessive allocation of resources to research, *Bell Journal of Economics*, 14, 152–65.

Tandon, P. (1984) Innovation, market structure and welfare, *American Economic Review*, 74, 394–403.

Teece, D. J. (1980) Economies of scope and the scope of the enterprise, *Journal of Economic Behaviour and Organization*, 1, 223–47.

Teece, D. J. (1982) Towards an economic theory of the multiproduct firm, *Journal of Economic Behavior and Organization*, 3, 39–64.

Teece, D. J. (1984) Economic analysis and strategic management, *California Management Review*, 26, 87–110.

Teece, D. J. (1986) Profiting from technological innovation: implications for integration, collaboration, licensing and public policy, *Research Policy*, 15, 286–305.

Teece, D. J. and Pisano, G. (1987) Collaborative arrangements and technology strategy, *School of Business Administration*, Berkeley: University of California.

Teece, D. J. (1989) Competition and cooperation in technology strategy, Berkeley: University of California Working Paper.

Telesio, P. (1979) *Technology Licensing and Multinational Enterprise*, New York: Praeger.

Telser, L. G. (1982) A theory of innovation and its effects, *Bell Journal of Economics*, 13, 69–92.

Thompson, S. (1989) Agency costs of internal organization, in S. Thompson and M. Wright (eds) *Internal Organisation, Efficiency and Profit*, Oxford: Philip Allan, 65–85.

Tirole, J. (1988) *The Theory of Industrial Organization*, Cambridge, MA: MIT Press.

Ullman, J. E. (1965) Occupational problems in conversion, in J.E. Ullman (ed.) *Conversion Prospects of the Defense Electronics Industry*, New York: Hofstra University Press, ch. 8.

Vernon, R. (1971) *Sovereignty at Bay, the Multinational Spread of US Enterprise*, New York: Basic Books.

Vickers, J. (1985) Pre-emptive patenting joint ventures and the persistence of oligopoly, *International Journal of Industrial Organization*, 3, 261–73.

Waddington, C. H. (1977) Stabilisation in systems, *Futures*, 9, 139–46.

Watkins, M. D. (1963) California firms study contract warnings, *Aviation Week and Space Technology* (29 July), 76–7.

Weston, J. F. (1970) The nature and significance of conglomerate firms, *St John's Law Review*, 44, 66–80.

Williamson, O. E. (1964) *The Economics of Discretionary Behaviour: Managerial Objectives in a Theory of the Firm*, Englewood Cliffs, NJ: Prentice-Hall.

Williamson, O. E. (1968) Economies as an antitrust defence: the welfare trade-offs, *American Economic Review*, 58, 18–36.

Williamson, O. E. (1971) Managerial discretion, organisation form, and the multi-division hypothesis, in R. Marris and A. Woods (eds) *The Corporate Economy*, Cambridge, MA: Harvard University Press, 343–86.

Williamson, O. E. (1975) *Markets and Hierarchies, Analysis and Antitrust Implications*, New York: Free Press.

Williamson, O. E. (1979) Transaction cost economics, the governance of contractual relations, *Journal of Law and Economics*, 22, 233–61.

Williamson, O. E. (1985) *The Economic Institutions of Capitalism: Firms, Markets, Relational Contracting*, New York: Free Press.

Williamson, O. E. (1986) *Economic Organisation: Firms, Markets and Policy Control*, Brighton: Wheatsheaf.

Williamson, O. E. (1992) Markets, hierarchies and the modern corporation: an unfolding perspective, *Journal of Economic Behavior and Organization*, 17, 335–52.

Willig, R. D. (1979) Multiproduct technology and market structure, *American Economic Review, Papers and Proceedings*, 69, 346–50.

Wilson, R. W. (1977) The effect of technological environment and product rivalry on R & D effort and licensing of innovations, *Review of Economics and Statistics*, 59, 171–8.

Winter, S. G. (1984) Schumpeterian competition in alternative technological regimes, *Journal of Economic Behavior and Organization*, 5, 287–320.

Wiseman J. (ed.) *Beyond Positive Economics?* London: Macmillan.

Wolf, B. M. (1977) Industrial diversification and internalization, some empirical evidence, *Journal of Industrial Economics*, 26, 177–91.

Wright, B. D. (1983) The economics of invention incentives: patents, prices and research contracts, *American Economic Review*, 73, 641–707.

Yavitz, B. and Newman, W. H. (1981) *Strategy in Action*, New York: Free Press.

Index